Andreas Schyra

Indices as Benchmarks in the Portfolio Management

With Special Consideration of the European Monetary Union

Foreword by Prof. Dr. habil. Eric Frère
and Prof. Dr. Joachim Rojahn, CFA

Springer Gabler

RESEARCH

Andreas Schyra
Essen, Germany

Dissertation Comenius University, Bratislava, Slovakia, 2012

ISBN 978-3-658-00695-2 ISBN 978-3-658-00696-9 (eBook)
DOI 10.1007/978-3-658-00696-9

The Deutsche Nationalbibliothek lists this publication in the Deutsche Nationalbibliografie; detailed bibliographic data are available in the Internet at http://dnb.d-nb.de.

Library of Congress Control Number: 2012955138

Springer Gabler

Printed on acid-free paper

Springer Gabler is a brand of Springer DE. Springer DE is part of Springer Science+Business Media.
www.springer-gabler.de

Indices as Benchmarks in the Portfolio Management

Foreword

Since the financial market crisis the modern portfolio theory (MPT) has been criticized substantially. In these phases of financial turmoil record-high correlations posed challenges for the portfolio selection theory, so that statements like "Markowitz' model is dead" gained popularity in the public. However, investment professionals have to understand the models' shortcomings and simplifications and to deal with it.

Hence, the topic of the PhD-dissertation of Mr. Andreas Schyra is of particular scientific and practical interest: Whereas prominent index concepts mainly focus on single asset classes so that they are static in nature, a dynamic multi asset management approach should capture financial market distortions and rising correlations between risky asset classes solving many of the problems when implementing the MPT.

After explaining the general principles of portfolio management and the practical relevance of indices the PhD-dissertation proves in a first step that correlations between European equities and commodity prices increase in bearish markets, but they diminish in bullish markets. At a first glance, these results even verify the popular skepticism concerning the MPT.

However, in a second research step the shortcomings of popular index concepts are investigated. An empirical analysis of the Eurozone industry and county indices reveals the importance of the industry diversification when the exchange rate as a source of diversification is eliminated: Even a naïvely diversified EMU equity portfolio which is allocated by the elementary consideration of industry indices outperforms a pure EMU country diversification.

The third step of the analysis focuses on index effects when stocks are included into or deleted from an index. In the long run, no permanent index effects can be detected. This analysis for the Dow Jones Euro STOXX 50 illustrates that pure and passive indexing is more feasible than active stock picking.

Based on the results gathered from the previous research steps an alternative equity index – the EMU Correlation Index (ECI) is created. The ECI's index members are weighted inversely according to their correlations towards commodities in order to increase diversification benefits by means of the MPT.

These empirical perceptions build the basis for the implementation of two engineered multi asset portfolios: An EMU Multi Asset Portfolio (EMA) and an enhanced version (EEMA). In both portfolios the equity component is captured by the newly developed ECI. These multi asset portfolios comprise cash, German government bonds, stocks and commodities. The reallocation algorithm is based on a maximum Sharpe-Ratio to take investors' desires and risk aversion into consideration. The enhanced version of these multi asset portfolios additionally includes a stop loss barrier as automatic risk reduction. The performance of both multi asset portfolios allow the conclusion that the criticism of the Markowitz approach is not justified when overcoming the models' limitations.

Consequently, this PhD-dissertation is comprised of several new ideas and results which add to the growing body of literature dealing with portfolio optimization. Because of changing market conditions, capital market requirements, rising correlations and volatilities, demographical changes etc. the insights of this PhD-dissertation are of high current and future relevance for scientists, portfolio managers and investors. The subscribers of this foreword who supported Mr. Andreas Schyra during his earlier studies at the FOM University of Applied Sciences wish that this PhD-dissertation reaches the positive resonance in academic research and practice it deserves. Practically investors and portfolio managers may use this thesis to call to question their own benchmarking procedures.

Prof. Dr. habil. Eric Frère
Dean for internatinonal studies
FOM Hochschule für Oekonomie & Management
University of Applied Sciences

Prof. Dr. Joachim Rojahn, CFA
FOM Hochschule für Oekonomie & Management
University of Applied Sciences

Preface

The scientific, practical and regulatory requirements of benchmarking approaches for investment portfolios have changed conspicuously particularly since the exhalation of the global subprime turmoil and the consequent financial and economic crisis of the years 2007-09. At least these drastic events – which still proceed by means of the Euro crisis – have illustrated that diversified security portfolios should not be compared to indices representing single asset classes as measure of conclusion according to risk and return attributes of the conducted investments. But let us face it, Markowitz identified it in the 1950s and everybody always knew these facts but frequently achieved to ignore them.

Unfortunately this static, single asset benchmarking procedure has not lost its practical predominance in the asset management business. For this reason, the instant elaboration which nearly perfectly complies with my PhD-dissertation is on the one hand addressed to investors, who are interested in practical deductions as error avoidance of frequently conducted allocation imperfections by misinterpretations of market developments and financial theories. On the other hand financial scientists will be concerned with the economical refurbishment of the index functionality as standard of comparison for considerable portfolios and especially the executed empirical evaluations. In this process *inter alia* a dynamic multi asset conception is allocated and back tested over the first decade of this century to balance the aforementioned drawbacks in dependence of a convenient amplification of the Portfolio Selection Theory, developed by Harry M. Markowitz.

The present dissertation is composed in an extra-occupational conferral of a doctorate at the Comenius University Bratislava, Slovakia. I want to use the following lines to thank the persons who have principally supported and accompanied me most, especially during my PhD-study since September 2009 but also the time beyond. Without them and especially their assistance as well as their patience I would not have passed the entire effort and this book would be inexistent.

First of all I want to express my gratitude to my PhD. supervisor, Doz. RNDr. Ján Pekár, PhD., who was always available very helpfully and enabled my external PhD-study at its best. In addition I want to thank my three assessors, Ing. Marta Rošteková, PhD., Doz. Ing. Peter Markovič, PhD. and Prof. RNDr. Jozef Komorník, DrSc. for their detailed opinions.

Furthermore I am very grateful for the support during the conferral of a doctorate and the time of my earlier academic studies at the FOM University of Applied Sciences by Prof. Dr. habil. Eric Frère as well as Prof. Dr. Joachim Rojahn, CFA. Besides their professional considerations and proposals my thanks also compass the motivating discussions which have exceeded the dimension of this work distinctly.

I also want to thank Mr. Svend Reuse, PhD. who provided me with the opportunity to participate in the experience of his own PhD-study and backed me with his proposals also while preparing the manuscript of this book.

I thank my circle of friends for their patience and their understanding for rejecting several invitations to private activities during the last three years, which would have been much more fun than the interminable completion of this thesis.

My special thanks go to my parents and my girlfriend who have granted me a unique and indescribable personal support. I appreciate and regret that my interaction was not the easiest during times of being stressed out, especially while preparing the dissertation examination. Hence, I want to thank them for every single backing they accorded to me and I apologize for the circumstances they had to undergo with me. They have definitely got a major share of managing this elaboration and I want to dedicate this book to them.

Andreas Schyra

List of Contents

List of Figures

List of Tables

List of Abbreviations

AEX	Amsterdam Exchange Index
ASE	Athens Stock Exchange General Index
ATX	Austrian Traded Index
BEL 20	Belgium 20 Index
bps	basis points
CAC	Cotation Asistée en Continu
cap	capitalisation
CML	Capital Market Line
CRB	Thomson Reuters/Jefferies Commodity Research Bureau
DAX	Deutscher Aktienindex
DJ	Dow Jones
EB	Executive Board
EBF	European Banking Federation
EC	European Community
ECB	European Central Bank
ECI	EMU Correlation Index
ECOFIN	Economic and Financial Affairs Council
EEMA	Enhanced EMU Multi Asset Portfolio
EFSF	European Financial Stability Facility
EFSM	European Financial Stabilisation Mechanism
EMA	EMU Multi Asset Portfolio
EMI	European Monetary Institute
EMU	European Economic and Monetary Union
EONIA	Euro OverNight Index Average
ERM I	Exchange Rate Mechanism I
ERM II	Exchange Rate Mechanism II
ESCB	European System of Central Banks
ETF	Exchange Traded Fund
EU	European Union
FTSE	Financial Times Stock Exchange
GC	Governing Council
GCC	Gulf Cooperation Council
GDP	gross domestic product
GICS	Global Industry Classification System
HEX	OMX Helsinki Index
HICP	Harmonised Index of Consumer Prices

Hn	Hypothesis n
IAH	investor's awareness hypothesis
IBEX	Iberia Index
ibid.	ibidem
ICB	Industry Classification Benchmark
IH	information hypothesis
IMF	International Monetary Fund
ISEQ	Irish Stock Exchange Overall Index
LH	liquidity hypothesis
LUXXX	Luxembourg Stock Exchange LuxX Index
M	market portfolio
Max DD	maximum drawdown
MIB	Milano Italia Borsa
MLN	million
MSCI	Morgan Stanley Capital International
MVP	minimum variance portfolio
NYSE	New York Stock Exchange
PAT	Principal-agent theory
PPH	price pressure hypothesis
PSI	Portugal Stock Index
REXP	REX Performance Index
RUBIX	Russell Indexes
S&P	Standard & Poor's
SEC	Securities and Exchange Commission
SGP	Stability and Growth Pact
SMI	Swiss Market Index
SML	Security Market Line
SX5E	DJ Euro STOXX 50 (price index in Euro)
S&P	Standard & Poor's
TBSCT	DJ Euro STOXX TMI Basic Materials (performance index in Euro)
TER	Total Expense Ratio
TFINT	DJ Euro STOXX TMI Financials (performance index in Euro)
TIDUT	DJ Euro STOXX TMI Industrials (performance index in Euro)
TMI	total market index
TSE	Toronto Stock Exchange
T3000T	DJ Euro STOXX TMI Consumer Goods (performance index in Euro)
T5000T	DJ Euro STOXX TMI Consumer Services (performance index in Euro)
yr.	year

List of Symbols

μ	expectancy of returns
μ_{PA}	active return
$1/c$	quality factor
B	benchmark
B_0	base value
d	interim collected capital gains
dd_p	downside deviation of the portfolio
e	Euler number
$E[Ri]$	expected return of asset i
g	maturity in years
i	asset i
$I(t)$	index level at time t
I_0	index level at time 0
I_0	investigation at time 0
I_1	investigation at time 1
I^{Ge}	geometrical price average
I_L	index level by Laspeyres
I_P	index level by Paasche
I_V	value index level
JB	Jarque-Bera
k	kurtosis
ln	natural logarithm
M	market portfolio
max	maximum
$Maxdd_p$	maximum drawdown of the portfolio
min	minimum
n	number of observations
NAV_t	net asset value at time t
NAV_{t+1}	net asset value at time t+1
P	portfolio
p_{i0}	price of asset i at time 0
p_{ij}	correlation of assets i and j
p_{iM}	correlation of asset i and the market portfolio
p_{it}	asset price i at time t
q	weighting factor
$\bar{r}$	average return

R	return
R_B	benchmark return
r^C	constant return
r^D	discrete return
r^{EX}	excess return
r_f	risk-free rate of return
r_i	return of asset i
r_i	return of asset i
R_m	return of the market portfolio
R_p	portfolio return
R_{PA}	active excess return
r_t	return of asset t
s	skewness
SortR	Sortino ratio
SR	Sharpe ratio
t	time
t_0	initial time 0
V[RP]	value of the portfolio
α_p	portfolio alpha
β_B	benchmark beta
β_i	beta factor of asset i
β_P	portfolio beta
ε	confounding variable
σ^2_p	variance of the portfolio return
σ_i	volatility of asset i
σ_{ij}	covariance of assets i and j
σ_j	volatility of asset j
σ_M	volatility of the market portfolio
ω	deviation from the arithmetic mean of expectation
ω_i	deviation from the arithmetic mean of expected returns by asset i
ω_j	deviation from the arithmetic mean of expected returns by asset j
$+\infty$	plus infinite
$-\infty$	minus infinte
$(\beta_{PA}*\mu_B)$	benchmark timing

1 Introduction

1.1 Initial Situation and Definition of the Problem

The superordinated problem of this thesis scrutinizes the latest criticism of the Portfolio Selection Theory[1]. During the financial market crisis[2] even eminently respectable trusts such as the US universities Yale and Harvard – that still prevail as distinct advocates of the Markowitz approach – suffered losses of approximately a quarter of their assets.[3] Several investors[4] advance the opinion that any original assumption of the theory does not resist modern capital market circumstances.[5] Hence, they do not question their allocation conversion by a misconception but constitute any formerly complimented theoretical foundation as misleading or inoperable.[6] Though, their pertinent problem was missing to proceed disciplined by eligible benchmarks[7] or basic investment approaches.[8]

These reviews and the challenging economical environment of the European Economic and Monetary Union (EMU)[9] expand the provocation of the Markowitz theory by a further stage of regional limitation opponent to the primary globally allocated market portfolio[10]. The exclusive consideration of the EMU and Euro dominated securities is deduced from investor's requirements within an area eliminating exchange rate risks and attributing an eternal monetary policy[11]. Furthermore as components of the systematically calculated portfolios maximally four asset classes[12] are adducted as standard of practically convertible population: (1) EMU[13] equities constituted with the help of a generally new composition approach implying indices as members again; (2) commodities[14] traded in Euro due to the conditions of a Euro dominated domestic investor; (3) German governmental bonds[15] and (4) cash[16]. The last two are regarded as quasi riskless in contrast to equities and commodities. Every asset class is comprised by a specific index due to the marketability and diversification[17] benefits of each

---

1 Cp. Markowitz (1952), p. 77ff.
2 Cp. Khademian (2011), p. 841ff.
3 Cp. Swensen (2010), p. 29.
4 Cp. Zheng (2010), p. 22.
5 Cp. Rojahn, Röhl, Frère (2010), p.1.
6 Cp. Patchett, Horgan (2011), p. 37.
7 Cp. Schoenfelder (2004), p. 59f.; Wüthrich (2010), p. 63f.
8 Cp. Ehmer (2009), p. 1.
9 Cp. Bearce (2009), p. 582.
10 Cp. Hwang, Satchell (2002), p. 775.
11 Cp. Ozkan, Sibert, Sutherland (2004), p. 638ff.
12 Cp. Bergmann, Howard (2003), p. 12.
13 Subsequently the items EMU and Eurozone are used synonymously.
14 Cp. Brooks, Langerup (2011), p. 32ff.
15 Cp. Deutsche Börse AG [ed.] (2004), p. 2f.
16 Cp. da Fonseca (2010), p. 728.
17 Cp. Willenbrock (2011), p. 191.

one compassing several single securities. These difficulties are committed as reference to the special economical and monetary framework of the EMU[18] and the defiance if the Markowitz approach is even performing well in constricted allocation requirements.

An exclusive consideration of Euro biased equity investments leads inevitably to the Dow Jones Euro STOXX 50 (SX5E) as practically regarded most important index for the territorial asset class evaluation[19]. This recognition is questionable due to the determinants of the EMU impacting general portfolio management practices. Researchers are dissonant about preferring country or industry based allocation[20] techniques which will be historically recessed and consequently discharged for the allocation of an alternative equity barometer as pendant to the SX5E.

Further the SX5E serves to explain and verify index effects[21] which are anticipated by active investors[22] trying to achieve excess returns[23] in comparison to the index[24]. These changes of the index composition are frequently analysed for the US market[25] but nearly neglected for the EMU. It will be considered if passive index investing[26] or stock picking[27] driven by index effects is more promising in the long-run.

Indices are regularly adducted as benchmarks[28] for specific asset classes[29] or comprehensive portfolios. Also managed accounts or investment funds regularly refer to special proportions[30] selecting their population by risk attributes of the combined asset classes to limit the entire capacity of portfolio risk[31]. Typical security portfolios do not exclusively comprise the asset class of equities. For instance they are also allocated by commodities and (governmental) bonds. Even within professional asset management in the EMU these kinds of multi asset portfolios are frequently benchmarked with a single equity index like the SX5E.[32] This approach fails its intrinsic ambition of performance evaluation considerably because neither a risk adjustment[33] is conducted nor an assimilable asset class is opposed.[34] Multi asset man-

18 Cp. Altavilla (2004), p. 894.
19 Cp. STOXX Ltd. [ed.] (2011t).
20 Cp. Berbena, Jansen (2009), p. 3067.
21 Cp. Elton, Gruber, Busse (2004), p. 270; Wetzel (2000), p. 6; Goetzmann, Massa (1999), p. 2.
22 Cp. Clarke, de Silva, Thorley (2002), p. 48ff.
23 Cp. Schopf (2009), p. 11.
24 Cp. Bechmann (2004), p. 3f.
25 Cp. Collins, Wansley, Robinson (1995), p. 329ff.; Beneish, Whaley (1996), p. 1909ff.
26 Cp. Chen, Huang (2010), p. 1155ff.
27 Cp. Ferruz, Munoz, Vargas (2010), p. 408.
28 Cp. Rohweder (1992), p. 23; Melas, Kang (2010), p. 10; Klement (2011), p. 50f.
29 Cp. Jaggi, Jeanneret, Scholz (2011), p. 134.
30 Cp. Pfau (2010), p. 60.
31 Cp. Dolvin, Templeton, Riebe (2010), p. 60.
32 Cp. STOXX Ltd. (2011b).
33 Cp. Rompolis, Tzavalis (2010), p. 129ff.
34 Cp. Elton, Gruber, Busse (2004), p. 272; Madhavan, Ming (2003), p. 35.

agement should be dynamic in nature but common benchmarks appear as static. Especially during financial market distortions, rising correlations[35] of asset classes can be observed whereby the importance and demand of an appropriate multi asset benchmark is emphasised.[36]

In dependence of variable capital market conditions the constricted weightings of assets compulsorily determines a misconduct of investor's objectives[37]. If equity markets increase investors like to feature portfolios participating maximally of this bull markets[38] by overweighting risky assets.[39] During decreasing markets and within time risks become obvious investors intend to maintain safe assets or at least loss constraints. Conditioned by the respective market performance risk bearing may be detrimental if it is not compensated by adjusted returns[40].

Hence, a general rule of predefined static portfolio proportions[41] of risky and riskless assets, independently of market constitutions, does not coincide with these requirements[42]. Investment reliability has to be assembled by a more profound and dynamic[43] allocation procedure incorporating even alterations of market movements during investment periods[44]. The identified management approach serves as mean-variance[45] optimised multi asset benchmark or investment alternative which has to consider these aspects.

The elaboration does not comprise any corporate bond index even if this asset class has become famous amongst EMU investors. Firstly the corporate bond market is still inefficient[46] as regarded by extensive price movements of primary issued bonds during the financial market crisis[47] and indexing is exclusively reasonable in at least semi-strong[48] efficient markets.[49] Secondly the pricing coherence[50] between listed company's shares and respective corporate bonds is very distinct.[51]

---

35 Cp. Buraschi, Porchia, Trojani (2010), p. 395.
36 Cp. Briand, Owyong (2009), p. 11; Arshanapalli, Nelson (2010), p. 35ff.
37 Cp. Mitra, Mitra, Di Bartolomeo (2009), p. 887.
38 Cp. Wong, Shum (2010), p. 1615.
39 Cp. Jacobsen (2010), p. 53.
40 Cp. Estrada (2008), p. 93.
41 Cp. Lewis (2009), p. 51f.
42 Cp. Curtillet, Dieudonné (2007), p. 410.
43 Cp. Gerber, Hens, Woehrmann (2010), p. 370.
44 Cp. Amenc, Marellini, Milhau, Zimann (2010), p. 100.
45 Cp. Alexander (2009), p. 452.
46 Cp. Downing, Underwood, Xing (2009), p. 1101.
47 Cp. Khademian (2011), p. 841ff.
48 Cp. Fama (1970), p. 383.
49 Cp. Hsu (2006), p. 10; Arnott (2005), p. 12ff.; Rojahn, Schyra (2010), p. 123ff.
50 Cp. Kobelt, Steinhausen (2000), p. 122.
51 Cp. Schyra, Rojahn (2010), p. 11f.; Frère, Rojahn, Schyra (2010), p. 7ff.

Likewise short selling[52] is suspended because practically it is only marginally accessible[53] for investors and remains ethically[54] objectionable. The appraisal exclusively deals with profoundly liquid[55] assets wherefore even alternative investments[56] are excluded.

1.2 Objective and Verifiable Hypotheses

The main objective of the present elaboration is the verification of the Portfolio Selection Theory[57] as still resisting the current EMU capital market requirements.[58] The complexity of problems questions, if mislead and static indexing or benchmarking[59] approaches can be mentioned as justification of challenging the Markowitz theory. This assumption is discussed by an update of the respective state of research together with the empirical consideration of an expanded stock picking approach by active anticipations of index effects[60] in contrast to pure long-term equity index investing.

Finally a systematically, risk constricted and dynamic multi asset benchmark for the Eurozone[61] will be adopted as conclusion of the theoretical and practical expectations as well as investor's requirements for utility maximisation. The benchmark will subsist without predefined asset weights as a capable and variable comparison for comprehensive portfolios[62]. As equity portion the EMU Correlation Index (ECI) is arranged and analysed under the assumptions of enhancing portfolio diversification[63] by reducing asset price correlations[64] designated to Markowitz. The entirely new allocation approach of the ECI should serve to replace the SX5E by an amplification of several so far established and frequently published index weighting procedures. The reallocation technique is developed by the empirical findings of inconstant, statistical asset price dependencies between equities and commodities.

52 Cp. Gastineau (2008), p. 39.
53 Cp. Jagannathan, Ma (2003), p. 1651.
54 Cp. Woolf (2008), p. 16; Angel, McCabe (2009), p. 239ff.
55 Cp. Wohlenberg, Brockmann, Grass (2006), p. 731.
56 Cp. Fischer, Glawischnig (2007), p. 180; Briand, Owyong (2009), p.14.
57 Cp. Sharpe (1966), p. 573ff.; Sharpe (1975), p. 29ff.
58 Equally to the former assumptions of the Portfolio Selection Theory, the implications of the later investigated behavioural finance are comprised only incidentally but without profound importance for the hypotheses; cp. Roßbach (2001), p. 3ff.
59 Cp. Grauer (2008), p. 43.
60 Cp. Bechmann (2004), p. 3f.
61 Cp. STOXX Ltd. (2011b).
62 Cp. Lei, Li (2009), p. 49.
63 Cp. Willenbrock (2011), p. 191.
64 Cp. Eling (2006), p. 32.

Four hypotheses *(Hn)* will be tested compassing the superordinated purpose by appreciating a distinct stringency as improvement of the investigation. The indications are detected in the interim conclusions and practical references by falsifying the respective null hypotheses that assume each hypothesis as invalid which should be rejected to verify the alternative hypotheses *(H1)* to *(H4)*:

(H1): ***Correlations between financial assets rise during times of falling markets.***

The diversification[65] of security portfolios and the designated decreasing portfolio risk depend on the degree of their interrelation which is measured and categorised by the respective correlation coefficients.[66] Since asset price volatilities and correlations[67] are inconstant[68], portfolio managers have to respect the financial market conditions within their asset allocation.[69] During times of falling markets[70] investors depend most on low correlations to compensate security's losses by further portfolio members achieving gains. Based on research statements the investigation in section 2.2.4 will demonstrate that correlations between EMU equities and commodities rise during times of bearish[71] markets and diminish within bullish[72] market trends.

After analysing the interdependence of two specific asset classes, *(H2)* is addicted to the exclusive allocation approaches of equity portfolios in the Eurozone:

(H2): ***Within the Eurozone the industry allocation is more feasible to diversify an equity portfolio in contrast to the country allocation.***

Within the asset management[73] and especially the allocation process[74] for equity portfolios investment practitioners apply different approaches[75] to select and weight assets. The currently available status of research is indifferent if country or industry allocations cause superior investment outcomes.

---

65 Cp. Fernholz (2000), p. 9.
66 Cp. Kobelt, Steinhausen (2000), p. 122.
67 Cp. Buraschi, Porchia, Trojani (2010), p. 394.
68 Cp. Yiu, Ho, Choi (2010), p. 353.
69 Cp. Ball, Torous (2000), p. 373ff.
70 Cp. Knight, Lizieri, Satchell (2005), p. 312.
71 Cp. Dridi, Germain (2004), p. 875.
72 Cp. Wong, Shum (2010), p. 1615.
73 Cp. Snigaroff, Wroblewski (2009), p. 126ff.
74 Cp. Dichtl, Drobetz (2009), p. 236.
75 Cp. Evensky, Clark, Boscaljon (2010), p. 33.

The entire investigation depends on the range of asset classes limited by equities[76], commodities[77], governmental bonds[78] and cash[79]. Currency and regional impacts are constricted by the EMU[80] and a single title selection is replaced by indices representing the implicated asset classes[81].

Hence, as base of this operation for the subsequent multi asset allocation, initially the efficient allocation strategy for an EMU equity index has to be identified. The objective of section 3.5 should define the predominance of an industry based stock selection compared to a country allocation.[82]

Since EMU equity investing is frequently not conducted by systematic industry or country allocation approaches but by stock picking the strategy of actively anticipating index effects is compared to simple indexing:

(H3): ***The SX5E is subject to index effects. Anticipating stock additions or deletions causes short-term excess returns compared to the market, but in the long-run EMU indexing proves superior attributes.***

Globally researchers have demonstrated the positive (negative) return attributes for changes of index members[83] due to stocks being added to (deleted from) indices, especially for the US market.[84] Several types of capital market hypotheses are mentioned as explanatory statements for these index effects[85]. The conducted analysis expands the previously applied research in the context of meanings and functions of indices within the broader framework of the portfolio management[86] in the EMU. The investigation focuses on stock price developments during short- and long-term periods compared to respective Eurozone index returns. Active portfolio managers[87] try to achieve excess returns[88] by selling (buying) deleted (added) stocks at the announcement of index composition changes to outperform the simple index return[89].

---

76 Subsequently different indices located in the EMU are adopted to exhibit this asset class.
77 Commodities are represented by the Reuters/Jefferries CRB Index [in EUR].
78 The German REXP is classified as quasi riskless bond index.
79 The EONIA is adopted as proxy for cash; cp. da Fonseca (2010), p. 728.
80 The Eurozone corresponds to the STOXX EMU investment region; cp. Liedtke (1999), p. 7.
81 Cp. Bergmann, Howard (2003), p. 12.
82 Cp. Cavaglia, Moroz (2001), p. 78.
83 Cp. Frino, Gallagher, Neubert, Oetomo (2004), p. 89.
84 Cp. Chen (2006), p. 409f.
85 Cp. Gygax, Otchere (2010), p. 2500ff.
86 Cp. Gülpinar, Katata, Pachamanova (2011), p. 68.
87 Cp. Xiong, Ibbotson, Idzorek (2010), p. 1.
88 Assumed as excess return unconsidering risk adjustments; cp. Herold, Maurer, (2008), p. 150.
89 Cp. Wallick, Bhatia, Clarke, Stern (2011), p. 29.

The intention of section 4.2 is to constitute the fact that the SX5E is subject to index effects but in the long-run thereby conducted stock picking[90] procedures are assumed as inferior to pure index investments.

After the consideration of active stock picking vs. passive EMU equity indexing by means of the SX5E, the final and superordinated determination of the enduring validity according to the Portfolio Selection Theory has to be examined:

(H4): ***The implications of the Portfolio Selection Theory, founded by Harry M. Markowitz, hold even today for limited multi asset allocations managed in Euro if specific practical requirements are implemented.***

In the year 1952 the later Nobelist[91] Harry M. Markowitz founded the Portfolio Selection Theory.[92] The principal significance was demonstrating the feasibility to combine assets in dependence of their intercorrelation[93] to an efficient portfolio[94] that features marginal risk than the elementary summation of the single security's risks by a mean-variance[95] optimised[96] diversification[97]. Finally a portfolio comprising the previously calculated and correlation weighted ECI, combined to commodities[98], German governmental bonds[99] and the EONIA[100] is allocated. With the help of this multi asset[101] portfolio, as constricted market portfolio[102] of the Markowitz approach – which was criticised by practitioners during the global financial crisis[103] because risk premiums of several asset classes increased[104] isochronal – will be inspected and verified.[105] The essential purpose of sections 4.3 and 4.4 is to identify and apply practical requirements of an exemplary portfolio allocation approach to accord the timeliness and validation[106] of the Portfolio Selection Theory[107].

---

90 Cp. Duan, Hu, McLean (2009), p. 1.
91 In the year 1990 Markowitz, Sharpe and Miller received the Nobel Prize in Economics for their findings; cp. Horasanli, Fidan (2007), p. 2; Rubinstein (2002), p. 1041.
92 Cp. Markowitz (1952), p. 77ff.
93 Cp. Eling (2006), p. 32.
94 Cp. Hu, Kercheval (2010), p. 91.
95 Cp. Mitra, Mitra, Di Bartolomeo (2009), p. 887.
96 Cp. McFall Lamm (2000), p. 26.
97 Cp. Willenbrock (2011), p. 191.
98 Cp. Brooks, Langerup (2011), p. 32ff.
99 Cp. Afonso, Furceri, Gomes (2011), p. 10ff.
100 Cp. da Fonseca (2010), p. 728.
101 Cp. McCormick (2011), p. 20f.
102 Cp. Hwang, Satchell (2002), p. 775.
103 During the years 2007 to 2009; cp. Khademian (2011), p. 841ff.
104 Cp. Patchett, Horgan (2011), p. 37.
105 Cp. Rockel (2010), p. 66ff.
106 Cp. Resnik (2010), p. 11.
107 Cp. Curtis (2004), p. 16.

1.3 Structure and Methodology of the Investigation

Within the introduction of chapter 1 the constitutional background of the entire thesis is expounded. This compasses an explanation of the briefly existent situation and a definition of the problem whereupon the verifiable hypotheses *(H1)* to *(H4)* are assembled as derivation of the consequent elaboration's objective. Any conducted empirical analysis is based on calculations by MS Excel and reffered to data, extracted from Bloomberg.

Chapter 2 demonstrates the essential and inductive framework explaining the theoretical foundations for the subsequent deduction. The status quo of major indexing approaches are illustrated and extended to the requirements of portfolio management approaches as well as the respective important economical theories, like the Portfolio Selection Theory and the Capital Asset Pricing Model (CAPM). *(H1)* is tested in section 2.2.4 as practical denotation of the previous theoretical explanations according to correlation attributes.

Proximately chapter 3 expands the allocation principles by the verifications of individual capital market conditions and circumstances incorporated by a compendium of the specific conditions of the EMU. Concluding an elementary deduction of specific portfolio management procedures for this region is discussed and investigated questioning *(H2)* in section 3.5.

Based on this constitution within chapter 4 different asset classes are exemplified by respective indices. According to challenge *(H3)* in section 4.2 the SX5E is examined concerning index effects. In succession of the received exigencies for the entirely investigated multi asset allocation, a new composition schedule for an index clarifying EMU equity developments is conducted. The final development of a multi asset portfolio serves as practical acknowledgement for the perpetual validity of the Portfolio Selection Theory according to test *(H4)* in sections 4.3 and 4.4. The conducted reverse projections of the computed equity index and the superordinated portfolios are adducted to refute the latest criticism of the Markowitz approach. Generally each investigation is introduced by the respective current state of research and executed over the time frame from January 01st 2001 to December 31st 2010.

Chapter 5 concentrates the empirical perceptions and interim conclusions. References to the previously assembled and verified hypotheses are integrated into a conclusion in accord to chapter 1. Finally outlooks of prospective research investigations are established as completion of the thesis.

Within the entire thesis secondary research is adopted by books and especially professional articles to substantiate each subsequently reinvestigated subject by a profound review of literature. Chapter 2 compasses the most capacious literature examination combined with an application to practical denotations of correlation in section 2.2.4 and the consideration of risky versus quasi riskless assets according to their historical volatilities in section 2.3.2.2. The theoretical foundations are even enlarged in chapter 3.

Further independent primary research is integrated in section 3.5 and chapter 4 as extension of the current status of research. The consideration of country or industry indexing approaches, the confrontation of index effects and pure EMU equity indexing as well as the development of the ECI, the EMA and the EEMA serve as new and expended economical perceptions according to the meaning of index investing, benchmarking and the timeliness of the Portfolio Selection Theory.

2 Principles of Portfolio Management Conditions

2.1 Economical Denotation of Indices

The quantity of stock indices depends on different indexing approaches[108], which escalates analogous to the increasing number of listed companies.[109] Diverse index providers[110] calculate their indices by different rules. The composition and the exchange of index members have to be distinguished as well as their weightings and the treatment of issued rights, dividends and nonstandard payouts[111]. The range is extended by issuers of securities that use their probability to create idiosyncratic indices[112]. In this process an exact, transparent and traceable definition of the composition parameters has to be published for every investor.[113] These own creations are – in contrast to market barometers of pure index providers – only infrequently licensed or resold and feature fewer acceptances by market participants.[114]

Stock indices represent the focus of the economical and especially the exchange business[115] displaying security market developments.[116] Market fragments like industries or sectors[117] can be separated and examined with the help of sub indices.[118]

The global environment of indices changes as fast as the economies, regulatory conditions[119], analyst forecasts, appearances of capital market crunches[120] and technological circumstances do.[121] For this reason governmental influences have modified the universal stock index trading during the last years several times and this continuous process will pursue in the future.[122] Since investors have appreciated that they are exposed by an additional portion of risk because of future uncertainty, they attach greater importance to their asset, risk and liability management.[123] Hence, indexing is and will remain a meaningful subject within the management process of security portfolios.[124]

108 Cp. Ganser (2008), p. 15.
109 Cp. Rühle (1991), p. 1.
110 Cp. Sultan, Hasan (2008), p. 469.
111 Cp. Schmitz-Esser (2000), p. 147ff.
112 Cp. HSBC Trinkaus [ed.] (2008), p. 1ff.; Commerzbank [ed.] (2008), p. 33.
113 Cp. Curtillet, Dieudonné (2007), p. 404.
114 Cp. Wohlenberg, Brockmann, Grass (2006), p. 731.
115 Cp. Sebastião (2010), p. 612.
116 Cp. Andreou, Pierides (2008), p. 212.
117 Cp. Zwick, Collins (2002), p. 66.
118 Cp. Patra, Poshakwale (2008), p. 1401.
119 Cp. Tropeano (2011), p. 46.
120 Cp. Linsmeier (2011), p. 411ff.
121 Cp. Birkner (2010), p. 24ff.; McFarlin (2011), p. 24.
122 Cp. Yang, Gondzio (2010), p. 74.
123 Cp. Yang, Lai (2009), p. 1059; Lin, Yeh (2009), p. 1965.
124 Cp. Branch, Cai (2011), p. 64.

2.1.1 Functions of Indices in the Portfolio Management

Functions of indices prevail for every index provider and clarify the denotation of indices in the context of entire portfolios.[125] The ordinary asset management is subject to diverse assumptions that are analysed[126] and interpreted by indices.[127]

Due to individual marketing strategies and competition a different acquaintance of these functions prevails amongst index providers[128]. During the last years several companies eliminated the gratuitous and public excess to their data. For this reason a replication of indices is just possible with constrictions. Since April 01st 2010 the STOXX Ltd. exclusively releases the index members without their respective weightings. Institutions intending to achieve admission to entire data have to sign a sumptuous license agreement.[129]

2.1.1.1 Benchmark Function

The benchmark function or levelling rule describes the index as dimension of comparison for actively managed portfolios.[130] The active portfolio strategy aims for an outperformance[131] according to its benchmark.[132] For the evaluation of the management success the portfolio is compared to a representative cross selection of the market whereat the basic populations of both portfolios have to exhibit the identical level of risk.[133] Otherwise risk adjustments[134] have to be conducted.[135]

The choice of an appropriate benchmark executes an eminent influence to the investor's behaviour because it arranges the general investment framework.[136] In consideration of the benchmark function, the index ministers to monitor the market segment, the performance evaluation, the determination of a suitable asset allocation as well as the implementation of any investment decisions and risk adjustments.[137]

---

125 Cp. Amenc, Goltz, Martellini (2011), p. 11; Saritas, Aygoren (2005), p. 1299.
126 Cp. Kugler, Henn-Overbeck, Zimmermann (2010), p. 356.
127 Cp. Wüthrich (2010), p. 21.
128 Cp. Barney (2010), p. 1ff.
129 Cp. STOXX Ltd. [ed.] (2011a).
130 Cp. Amenc, Goltz, Martellini (2011), p. 11; Bogle (2005), p. 114f.
131 Cp. Achleitner, Kaserer, Moldenhauer (2005), p. 121.
132 Cp. Rohweder (1992), p. 23; Melas, Kang (2010), p. 10; Klement (2011), p. 50f.
133 Cp. Krein (2010), p. 20; Costa, Jakob (2010), p. 95.
134 Cp. Rompolis, Tzavalis (2010), p. 129ff.
135 Cp. Elton, Gruber, Busse (2004), p. 272; Madhavan, Ming (2003), p. 35.
136 Cp. Schoenfelder (2004), p. 59f.; Wüthrich (2010), p. 63f.
137 Cp. Cloyd, Siegel, Schoenfelder (2004), p. 63ff.

The mediation has to be distinguished ex ante into the asset allocation and ex post into the relative performance evaluation[138]. To fulfil this function an index has to feature preferably humble transaction costs[139], exist enduringly, offer a broad diversification and consequently only fractions of systematic risk as well as assimilable restrictions like the investor's portfolio.[140] These kinds of allocation principles have to be acquainted by the investor before determining the appropriate benchmark index.[141] If these specifications are not met, the objectivity and the acquirement of the portfolio manager could be challenged.[142]

Investment funds and investment management portfolios are even subject to regulative covenants declaring an eligible benchmark[143]. Thereby standardised or individually constructed indices can be adducted, though the second may doubt the requirements of transparency and replication abilities as well as regulative parameters.[144]

2.1.1.2 Information Function

Indices aggregate a multitude of members with homogeneous characteristics in a single, average measure[145] and document the alteration of the asset values during a variation in time.[146] Co-instantaneously this changeableness describes an essential function of indices, in fact the documentation of information in the shape of fluctuating conditions.[147] Individual information of the index members is cumulated in the progressionally[148] calculated price of the index[149].

In the specification of the information function indices serve as the aggregated informational mediums for a cost-efficient[150] preparation of disclosure.[151] In addition to the value of the index further information like the average dividend yields, price earnings ratios[152] and economical measures can be obtained by the use of statistical parameters.[153]

138 Cp. Guojin, Li, Shin (2011), p. 1012.
139 Cp. Martins-da-Rocha, Vailakis (2010), p. 66.
140 Cp. Etterer, Beer, Fleischer (2003), p. 116ff.; Stucki (1996), p. 182; Sharpe (1992), p. 16.
141 Cp. Curtillet, Dieudonné (2007), p. 404.
142 Cp. Roll (1977), p. 129; Christopherson (1998), p. 93; Maguire, Karaban, S&P [ed.] (2009), p. 4.
143 Cp. Rose (2005), p. 21.
144 Cp. Fong, Gallagher, Lee (2008), p. 762.
145 Cp. Amenc, Goltz, Martellini (2011), p. 11.
146 Cp. Bleymüller, Gehlert, Gülicher (2008), p. 181; Ganser (2008), p. 15.
147 Cp. Demchuk, Gibson (2006), p. 867.
148 Cp. Schmitz-Esser (2001), p. 19.
149 Cp. Bleymüller (1966), p. 15.
150 Cp. Kaserer, Achleitner, Moldenhauer, Ampenberger (2006), p. 12.
151 Cp. Vespro (2006), p. 126; Lee, Chien, Liao (2009), p. 828.
152 Cp. Bhargava, Malhotra (2006), p. 87ff.
153 Cp. Marquering, Verbeek (2004), p 407.

This kind of accumulation is *inter alia* influenced by factors like investor's hope and fear as well as wars and prospective economical developments.[154] Indices equal statistical measures[155] exhibiting investor's expectance of future trends, whereupon the celerity of market reactions has been enhanced due to the mobile data transfers.[156]

The central audience tracking individual intentions assembled by the information function is arranged by media, publicity, analysts and investors. Technical[157] signals can be discharged by consolidated information representing the foundation of prospective forecasts[158] and trading decisions.[159]

The entire stock market and the results of the specified information occupied from the ex post index analysis, serving as sufficient resource for several ex ante estimations[160] and the consequent allocations of funds by financial advisors and investors[161].

2.1.1.3 Underlying Function

In the context of the Portfolio Selection Theory and especially the efficient market hypothesis a stock index displays the risk-adjusted and diversified market portfolio within a special framework of composition standards.[162] The original admission into an index equals a fictitious investment into the consolidated underlying securities at the effective date t_0.[163] By an accommodation of about 20 to 25 stocks, a fundamental decrease of the diversifiable unsystematic risks has been accomplished as far as possible. The greater the number of index members, the more realistic is the approach to display the essential total market by the index portfolio.[164] The efficiency of the market return's variance and unbiased estimator is enhanced by diversification.[165] With a completely utilised diversification level of the benchmark an active portfolio manager is unable to achieve an outperformance by widening the portfolio risks in contrast to the reference index.[166] A potential improvement[167] is exclusively possible by the stock selection, weighting and timing aspects.[168]

154 For further information of investor's behaviour; cp. Muga, Santamaria (2007), p. 637ff.
155 Cp. Cloyd, Siegel, Schoenfelder (2004), p. 65f.; Barbosa (2009), p. 37.
156 Cp. Sosvilla-Rivero, Rodriguez (2010), p. 2081f.
157 Cp. Kurz (2010), p. 1184.
158 Cp. Dueker, Assenmacher-Wesche (2010), p. 2910ff,
159 Cp. Wohlenberg, Brockmann, Grass (2006), p. 730f.; Bodie, Kane, Marcus (2005), p. 258ff.
160 Cp. Pilinkus (2010), p. 291f.
161 Cp. Winchester, Huston, Finke (2011), p. 43.
162 Cp. Vespro (2006), p. 126.
163 Cp. Ganser (2008), p. 16.
164 Cp. Schmitz-Esser (2001), p. 103; Bleymüller (1966), p. 21.
165 Cp. Kim, Cho, Mandziuk, Jaruszewicz (2011), p. 95ff.
166 Cp. Griese, Kempf (2003), p. 210ff.; Duan, Hu, McLean (2009), p. 56ff.
167 Cp. Poddig, Brinkmann, Seiler (2009), p. 305.
168 Cp. Brealey, Myers, Marcus (2007), p. 284f.; Bamberg, Baur (1996), p. 148.

Because of the relatively distinct information efficiency of modern capital markets, the contingency of an outperformance by active management is just conditionally feasible.[169] With the help of indexing merely an optimisation of investor's costs and accompanied declining trading activities are conducted.[170] In this characteristic indices officiate for testing market efficiency and predicting future returns.[171]

Within the underlying function the index composes the base value for (derivative) financial products[172] such as index futures[173], options, certificates, warrants or funds and respectively Exchange Traded Funds (ETFs).[174] The index is thereby tradable in one single security.[175]

The establishment of index funds and ETFs[176] caused a further enhancement of transparency and cost-efficiency for investors and desired a more valid contest for actively managed portfolios.[177] Comparing the total expense ratios (TER) of actively managed funds and ETFs illustrates this advantage. An average active fund's TER is at about 1,4% and most ETF's expenses are not half as exalted.[178] The growing importance of ETFs according to equity index benchmarks has increased during the last years accompanied by an expansion of general stock market trading activities.[179] The inserted liquidity and increased market efficiency[180] makes it more comfortable for investors to act in regulated markets with conspicuously constricted possibilities of manipulation.[181]

The index and its members build a guideline displaying a passive investment strategy.[182] In contrast to active allocation decisions it is not attempted to create an outperformance towards the benchmark.[183] Index tracking[184] tends to avoid mean returns compared to the market.[185] The first index investments were documented during the 1970s in the USA. In Europe indexing faces an important role since the end of the 20th century.[186]

169 Cp. Blitz, van Vliet (2008), p. 23ff.
170 Cp. Kat (2002), p. 1.
171 Cp. Patra, Poshakwale (2008), p. 1409.
172 Cp. Booth, So (2003), p. 488.
173 Cp. Gwilym, Buckle (2001), p. 385ff.
174 Cp. Amenc, Goltz, Martellini (2011), p. 11.
175 Cp. Kaserer, Achleitner, Moldenhauer, Ampenberger (2006), p. 12.
176 Cp. Korn (2007), p. 72.
177 Cp. Cloyd, Siegel, Schoenfelder (2004), p. 72f.; Hseu, Chung, Sun (2007), p. 216.
178 Cp. Landis (2008), p. 50.
179 Cp. Milonas, Rompotis (2010), p. 97.
180 Cp. Lim (2009), p. 1129.
181 Cp. Kim, Park (2010), p. 296f.
182 Cp. Bruns, Meyer-Bullerdiek (2001), p. 104ff.
183 Cp. Rompotis (2009), p. 263.
184 Cp. Frino, Gallagher, Neubert, Oetomo (2004), p. 89.
185 Cp. DeFusco, Ivanov, Karels (2011), p. 182.
186 Cp. Black, Scholes (1974), p. 637ff.; Wagner, Diller, Brück (2005), p. 56.

The replication of an index is never perfectly possible due to accruing costs, but tracking can be simplified by declaring special allocation criteria.[187] While arranging the tracking strategy[188] it has to be determined if a full replication[189] or an optimisation strategy is preceded. The replication assumes investments into the identically weighted assets. Opponently the optimisation strategy is an approximate reproduction of the index by securities or derivatives[190] that feature assimilable returns as the index members. This amplifies the hazard of increasing tracking errors.[191]

Tracking products connect the advantages of risk diffusion by different assets with comparable transaction costs[192]. Hence, a replication is possible, if the index calculation and reporting is transparent and the securities are liquidly tradable.[193]

The arising costs are subject to the respective index construction. The higher the degree of index diversification is, the superior are the transaction costs of the tracking process, whereby a trade off arises.[194] Regularly transaction costs are not constant because they depend on the scale of trading activities[195]. Every decision to reallocate[196] the portfolio should therefore create an excess value that exceeds the arising costs to keep the tracking error as marginal as possible[197]. Amongst others these costs combine the management fees, premiums, bid ask spreads and the market impact[198]. The latter composes the most conspicuous effect to the total costs.[199]

2.1.2 Differentiation of Indexing Concepts

A general principle of stock index calculation does not exist. Rather varying approaches can be distinguished.[200] Each index formula defines the measurement of the index level combining the member's prices and their weightings.[201] A further impact depends on the acquaintance of market extrinsic price changes like for example payouts.[202]

187 Cp. Grobys (2009), p. 11f.
188 Cp. Frino, Gallagher, Oetomo (2005), p. 24.
189 Cp. Melas, Suryanarayanan, Cavaglia (2010), p. 39.
190 Cp. Trivellato (2009), p. 5.
191 The tracking error describes the statistical deviation of the (passive) indexing strategy from the underlying index; cp. Barbosa (2009), p. 39.
192 Cp. Jang, Koo, Liu, Loewenstein (2007), p. 2329ff.
193 Cp. Wohlenberg, Brockmann, Grass (2006), p. 731.
194 Cp. Yu, Yang, Wong (2007), p. 135; Griese, Kempf (2003), p. 203; Lovell, Arnott (1989), p. 2.
195 Cp. Hasebrouck (2009), p. 1475.
196 Cp. Atkinson, Storey (2010), p. 323.
197 Cp. Haslem (2009), p. 58.
198 Cp. Bikker, Spierdijk, van der Sluis (2010), p. 369ff.
199 Cp. Jones, Stine (2010), p. 416.
200 Cp. Ganser (2008), p. 15.
201 Cp. Budinsky (2002), p. 216.
202 Cp. Schmitz-Esser (2000), p. 147ff.

The technical requirement of reliability considers the quality of data, the continuity, the consistency and the latitude of manipulation. These elementary factors describe the crucial coefficients that have to be maintained by index providers to be accepted by potential customers and investors.[203] Globally numerous index investments are calculated and traded continuously.[204] Prospectively their importance will rise and further concepts will be developed.[205]

2.1.2.1 Price Index

Price indices are calculated by a fixed number of stocks and display the index level by their quantified developments.[206] In contrast to investments in the underlying stocks, price indices do not take dividend payouts[207] or executed corporate actions of member companies into consideration.[208] At the payout date the index level will *ceteris paribus* decline by the exact amount that is distributed to the shareholders, adjusted by the respective weighting impact.[209] Hence, price index levels are exclusively influenced by changes in the demand and supply chains of the member stocks without regarding the respective interim pay-outs.[210]

Exemplary price indices are the STOXX index family, the Standard & Poor's (S&P) 500 and the Swiss Market Index (SMI).[211]

2.1.2.2 Performance Index

In contrast to price indices, the calculation of a performance index[212] incorporates all kinds of payouts and corporate actions.[213] Dividends, premiums and special payments are instantly reinvested in the concerning stock and implied into the index calculation.[214] This reinvestment takes place analogous to the index weighting of the respective company. The induction occurs either by the gross[215] or the cash dividend[216] whereat the gross amount equals the cash payment adjusted by the corporate tax rate[217].

203 Cp. Schmitz-Esser (2001), p. 107ff.; FTSE [ed.] (1996), p. 6; FTSE [ed.] (1999), p. 2.
204 Cp. Murguia, Umemoto (2006), p. 73.
205 Cp. Etterer, Beer, Fleischer (2003), p. 121.
206 Cp. Rühle (1991), p. 86; Deutsche Börse AG [ed.] (2008), p. 29.
207 Cp. Ganser (2008), p. 26.
208 Cp. Schlienkamp, Frei (1997), p. 69; Grill, Perczynski (2008), p. 270; Jobst (1997), p. 21.
209 Cp. Commerzbank AG [ed.] (2008), p. 35.
210 Cp. Chen, Noronha, Singal (2004), p. 1928.
211 Cp. Spremann, Gantenbein (2005), p. 180.
212 The items performance and total return index are used synonymously; cp. Herrmann (1997), p. 1.
213 Cp. Jobst (1997), p. 21; Schusteritsch, Niederl (2007), p. 8; Schröder, ZEW [ed.] (2005), p. 6.
214 Cp. Garobbio (1995), p. 21.
215 Cp. Hodgkinson, Holland, Jackson (2006), p. 245.
216 Cp. Yilmaz, Gulay (2006), p. 20.
217 Cp. James, Mohideen (2011), p. 46.

Hence, the investor's individual fiscal aspects remain unconsidered. The index calculation by the inclusion of a cash payout presumes the tax rate of the stock holder as identical to the corporate tax rate of the company.[218]

The German DAX is one of the most common and accepted performance indices.[219]

2.1.3 Consideration of Index Weighting Concepts

The most prevalent comprehension of indexing addresses the weighting by market capitalisation (cap).[220] Further indexing approaches exist, which exemplary deal with enhanced or fundamental and active indexing techniques.[221]

2.1.3.1 Price Weighting

Price weighted stock indices represent an average summation of the single member's prices. They do not represent an index in the common sense but rather a moving average[222]. During the calculation at time t all members prices p_{it} are added and divided by the total number of members n. Formula (1) illustrates the index formula with the quality factor $1/c$.[223] This factor ensures the index continuity and considers stock splits or the disbursement of bonus shares[224]. The fraction of company's shares would decrease without a change in the market value of the company.[225] The calculation on the effective day occurs with the use of the new divisor and the altered stock price. It addicts the same index level as prior to the corporate action:[226]

$$(1) \qquad I(t) = \frac{1}{c} * \frac{\sum_{i=1}^{n} p_{it}}{n}.$$

Corresponding to the previous explanations the calculation of an index presupposes the comparison of the current value with the moment t_0 when the base investment was executed.[227] This reference is missing in formula (1) which has to be conducted per dividing the term by the base level at t_0, addicted with the help of formula (2):[228]

218 Cp. Wetzel (2000), p. 20.
219 Cp. Etterer, Beer, Fleischer (2003), p. 123.
220 Cp. Branch, Cai (2011), p. 65.
221 Cp. Orgland, Leveau (2008), p. 24.
222 Cp. Field (2010), p. 34.
223 Cp. Ganser (2008), p. 20ff.; Bodie, Kane, Marcus (2005), p. 49.
224 Cp. Karamjeet, Balwinder (2010), p. 49.
225 Cp. Wetzel (2000), p 11f..
226 Cp. Rühle (1991), p. 35.
227 Cp. Ganser (2008), p. 16.
228 Cp. Schmitz-Esser (2001), p. 147.

(2) $$I_0 = \sum_{i=1}^{n} p_{i0} \ .$$

The Dow Jones (DJ) Industrial Average and the Nikkei 225 are currently the only existing important price weighted stock indices.[229]

The calculation is subject to the disadvantage of weighting every index member independently from its relative denotation with a disproportionate quantity. Hence, the explanatory power of the index expansion for the total market development is only restrictedly representative.[230] The index movement is dominated by severe members which is objectively not justifiable.[231]

Stock price movements of the members have got a price[232] and a size effect[233]. A surpassingly rising stock price provokes a duplicated effect to the index: On the one hand the stock price rises and on the other the relative weighting of the company's shares ascends in the index. Because of this reason a rising price of small (major) index member is overestimated (underestimated) in proportion to the total market.[234]

The DJ Industrial Average could establish because the absolute price standard of the stocks traded at the New York Stock Exchange (NYSE) mainly resides in the interval between 20 and 100 USD. If a stock price exceeds the upper level, a split is generally conducted and the price is relocated into the primary interval. Hence, the influence of the implicit price weighting is therefore restricted by a downward bias.[235]

2.1.3.2 Equal Weighting

Within equally weighted stock indices[236] every member exhibits the identical effect on the index development.[237] Thereby the arithmetical and the geometrical calculation of an equal weighting[238] have to be distinguished.[239] The calculation of a geometrical price average occurs with the help of formula (3):[240]

---

229 Cp. Elton, Gruber, Brown, Goetzmann (2007), p. 21f.
230 Cp. Spremann, Gantenbein (2005), p.180f.
231 Cp. Bleymüller (1966), p. 59; Deininger (2005), p. 1.
232 Cp. Duchin, Levy (2010), p. 625.
233 Cp. Penman, Richardson, Tuna (2007), p. 435.
234 Cp. Wetzel (2000), p. 12f.
235 Cp. Schmitz-Esser (2001), p. 147f.
236 Cp. Cohen (2003), p. 40.
237 Cp. Velvadapu (2011), p. 23.
238 Cp. Hamza, Kortas, L'Her, Roberge (2007), p. 103.
239 Cp. Jobst (1997), p. 21; Commerzbank AG [ed.] (2008), p. 38f.
240 Cp. Schmitz-Esser (2001), p. 148.

$$(3) \qquad I_{t0}^{Ge} = \frac{\sqrt[N]{\prod_{i=1}^{n} p_{it}}}{\sqrt[N]{\prod_{i=1}^{n} p_{i0}}}.$$

The geometrical calculation is subject to two disadvantages: Firstly every stock perceives the same weight. An index tracker has to absorb enormous costs of reallocation[241] to invest the same amounts into the member securities over time. Successful stocks have to be sold and the disengaged amount is reinvested into the decreased stocks to rebalance their weight.[242] The investor is unavoidably following an anti-cyclical investment strategy.[243] Secondly a further disadvantage develops by the systematic undervaluation of price changes. A geometrical price average is always lower than its arithmetical counterpart. The relative changes of the member stocks have different impacts on the entire index development.[244]

The arithmetical equal weighting occurs by the investment of identical amounts into the index members at the base time. In contrast to the geometrical allocation the equations depart by different price changes. The price weight[245] can not be systematically underestimated. Therefore the disadvantage of the geometrical calculation is not granted.[246]

2.1.3.3 Market Capitalisation Weighting

The indexation by market cap weights the single members by their respective market values in proportion to the total market and constitutes the central origin of index constructions.[247] The calculation of a company's market cap occurs by the multiplication of the current stock price with the number of outstanding shares.[248] Frequently containment according to the free tradable stocks is conducted by the free float[249] referring to the stocks that are not held by controlling shareholders.[250] Expensive rebalancings[251] are unnecessary because of the automatically adjusted weightings of the index members.[252] The intrinsic pro-cyclical characteristic of this indexing approach is conspicuous. By tendency the expensive stocks with increasing market caps are over weighted and the lower priced stocks exhibit a comparatively mean

241 Cp. Eberly, Wang (2009), p. 560ff.
242 Cp. Marks, Stuart (1971), p. 300.
243 Cp. Nelles, Uzik, Holtfort (2007), p. 444.
244 Cp. Cootner (1978), p. 95; Lorie, Hamilton (1978), p. 84f.
245 Cp. Goldberg (2009), p. 31.
246 For examplary contrasting calculations; cp. Schmitz-Esser (2001), p. 149ff.
247 Cp. Orgland, Leveau (2008), p. 24; Platt, Pope, Rakvin (2004), p. 121.
248 Cp. Amenc, Goltz, Martellini (2011), p. 14.
249 Cp. Lam, Lin, Michayluk (2011), p. 55.
250 Cp. Deutsche Börse AG [ed.] (2008), p. 11; Achleitner, Kaserer, Moldenhauer (2005), p. 123.
251 Cp. Willenbrock (2011), p. 43.
252 Cp. Platt, Pope, Rakvin (2004), p. 121.

weight.[253] If a company achieves superior returns over a longer period the market cap and analogous the weighting will rise.[254] Finally the index may be biased by the progression of this single stock.[255]

This effect can be explained by the momentum strategy.[256] A further development of winning and loosing stocks into the previous direction is assumed to occur in the future. The former trend is extrapolated prospectively.[257] Following the market efficiency hypothesis stock prices should change by bearish[258] and bullish[259] markets. This presumption does not hold within practical experience.[260] In consideration of the behavioural finance[261], overreaction effects[262] have to be regarded. These foundations are combined to the social psychology[263] and the decision-making theory[264]. They pursue the assumption of capital market participants as only limitedly rational.[265]

During practical experiences indices are calculated by the Laspeyres or the Paasche formula. Both are very similar because prices are firstly weighted, subsequently referred to the base time and finally multiplied with their base value[266] frequently equated by *100* or *1.000* points.[267]

In contrast to the arithmetical equal weighting of indices both mentioned approaches assess the weighting of index members selectively. Weightings occur according to the (free float) market cap, capital stock[268] or volume of stock transactions. The economical meaning and the size of a company are especially emphasised by the help of the market cap and the capital stock. In contrast to this, the remaining criteria highlight the tradability and the liquidity of the index members.[269]

---

253 Cp. Orgland, Leveau (2008), p. 24.
254 Cp. Woods, Richard (2003), p. 7.
255 Cp. Spremann, Gantenbein (2005), p. 181.
256 Cp. Landis (2006), p. 46; Hur, Pritamani, Sharma (2010), p. 1155.
257 Cp. Nelles, Uzik, Holtfort (2007), p. 444.
258 Cp. Dridi, Germain (2004), p. 875.
259 Cp. Wong, Shum (2010), p. 1615.
260 Cp. Orgland, Leveau (2008), p. 24.
261 Cp. Singh (2010), p. 1ff.
262 Cp. Madura, Richie (2004), p. 91.
263 Cp. Offerman, Sonnemans (2004), p. 535.
264 Cp. Dreman, Lufkin (2000), p. 61.
265 Cp. Guo (2002), p. 32.
266 Cp. Ganser (2008), p. 22.
267 Cp. Blümel (1995), p. 33.
268 Cp. Albala-Bertrand (2010), p. 715ff.
269 Cp. Budinsky (2002), p. 219ff.

Various important stock indices as the DAX, the SX5E and the MSCI-Indices depend on the Laspeyres formula.[270] Indexing formula (4) measures the price changes of fictitious stock investments at the base time without reallocations, referring to the buy and hold[271] strategy:[272]

(4) $$I_L(t) = \frac{\sum_{i=1}^{n}(p_{it} * q_{i0})}{\sum_{i=1}^{n}(p_{i0} * q_{i0})} * B_0 .$$

Where p_i refers to the stock price, q is the weighting, t represents the current time, 0 means the base time, i describes the security in the index and B_0 is the base value.

The calculation by the Laspeyres formula is relatively simple and accepted because only the current price changes of the single members are accounted.[273] The concept is taken from the price theory. Hence, corporate actions remain unconsidered.[274]

The weightings of stocks according to the arithmetical indexing are composed in the Paasche formula. Set phrase (5) describes the development of the index with reference to the respective weighting diagram of the accounting period:[275]

(5) $$I_P(t) = \frac{\sum_{i=I}^{n} p_{it} * q_{it}}{\sum_{i=I}^{n} p_{i0} * q_{it}} * B_0 .$$

In opposition to the calculation by Laspeyres, Paasche invariably assesses the index by the use of current price weightings. A consideration of the past is challenging because historical weightings are often available only limitedly.[276] This problem occurs for example if companies did not exist, have not been listed or the index provider does not publish historical weightings.[277]

270 Cp. Wetzel (2000), p. 13.
271 Cp. Ruggiero (2009), p. 42f.
272 Cp. Lützel, Jung (1984), p. 44; Laspeyres (1871), p. 306.
273 Cp. Currier (2009), p. 222.
274 Cp. Rinne (1994), p. 309ff.; Wetzel (2000), p. 13f.
275 Cp. Paasche (1874), p. 172f.; Schmitz-Esser (2001), p. 152f.
276 Cp. Wetzel (2000), p. 14f.
277 Cp. STOXX Ltd. [ed.] (2011a).

The value index exists besides the two mentioned and most common approaches. Formula (6) measures the alteration of stock capitalisations according to the entire members listed in the index:[278]

$$(6) \qquad I_V(t) = \frac{\sum_{i=1}^{n} p_{it} * q_{it}}{\sum_{i=1}^{n} p_{i0} * q_{i0}} * B_0 .$$

The results of the three formulas are almost identical[279] representing real economical relations with respect to the involved industries, countries or general members and permitting passive investors to receive representative cross market sections.[280]

2.1.3.4 Enhanced Indexing

Orgland and Leveau (2008) describe enhanced indexing as the possibility to replicate an index derivatively and investing the remaining amount interest chargingly. Although the interest-bearing assets have to generate an excess value above the implicit future's returns by gathering additional credit risk[281]. This kind of indexing approach esteems as hybrid style between active and passive management techniques, tending towards an outperformance of 25 to 75 basis points (bps) compared to the original index investment.[282] The individual assortment of assumed credit risks suggests this kind of indexing approach to be classified as active management. The index just serves as underlying[283] combined with the benchmark function.[284]

Secondary to the mentioned derivative procedure, as further style the security-level technique is known by the application of long and short positions[285] in the respective underlying index.[286]

Every fund displaying enhanced indexing methods aims at reducing the tracking error[287] occurring by the index reproduction and trying to create alpha[288] opponent to proper index funds

278 Cp. Bleymüller (1966), p. 43.
279 Cp. Richard (1992), p. 32.
280 Cp. Ganser (2008), p. 25; Blümel (1995), p. 82f.
281 Cp. Fontana, Runggaldier (2010), p. 684.
282 Cp. Orgland, Leveau (2008), p. 24.
283 Cp. Kaserer, Achleitner, Moldenhauer, Ampenberger (2006), p. 12.
284 Cp. Klein (2009), p. 760; Schmies (2001), p. 8; Rohweder (1992), p. 23.
285 Cp. Yu, Rentzler, Wolf (2004), p. 44ff.
286 Cp. Wu, Chou, Yang, Ong (2007), p. 50ff.
287 Cp. Johnson (2009), p. 253f.
288 Alpha expresses the active outperformance in comparison to the index; cp. Israelsen (2010), p. 79.

like ETFs.[289] The costs of both kinds of semi-active management styles are less than the known active type of portfolio management because enhanced indexing just focuses on a respectively small and risk-controlled excess returns compared to the market.[290]

2.1.3.5 Fundamental Indexing

Fundamental indices obtain the weightings of their single members not from the foundation of market cap but from price sensitive fundamental data.[291] Examples for frequently used weighting factors are dividends, earnings, cash flows and the sales volume.[292] This approach tries to draw the derivation of the market portfolio[293] in the sense of the CAPM towards the modern capital market theory[294]. By this procedure the positive theoretical characteristics are retained and the negative attributes like the market cap bias and the static portfolio approaches are enhanced.[295] The buy and hold strategy of the market portfolio is assumed as prejudicial but amendable by overhauling weightings with exalted returns generating a positive alpha.[296]

The weighting is arranged by the economies of scale[297] of each company.[298] A controversial debate has emerged, if fundamental indices succeed an active or passive investment philosophy and if investors are effectively enabled to achieve an outperformance because the approach varies from original cap weighted indexing.[299]

Arnott and West (2006) mention fundamental indexing or value investing not as affected by the price of a stock and thereby avoiding the disadvantages of cap weighting. The economical denotation of the company is embraced proportional to the entire economy. Within their study they define a long-term outperformance of fundamental indexing towards cap weighting at the US stock market. As disadvantage they exclusively schedule the emerging transaction costs[300] because of continuous reallocations.[301] Hsu and Campollo (2006) point out the negative influence of increased costs by augmented transactions during the development of bubbles[302]. These additional costs result by the advanced momentum of the markets and the frequent re-

289 Cp. Jennings, Martin (2007), p. 18.
290 Cp. Miller, Meckel (1999), p. 75ff.
291 Cp. Wiandt (2011), p. 8; Amenc, Goltz, Martellini (2011), p. 11.
292 Cp. Blitzer (2011), p. 50; Branch, Cai (2011), p. 65; Klement (2011), p. 46.
293 Cp. Hwang, Satchell (2002), p. 775.
294 Cp. Reuse (2011a), p. 30ff.
295 Cp. Arnott, Hsu, Moore (2005), p. 83; Orgland, Leveau (2008), p. 24.
296 Cp. Estrada (2008), p. 93.
297 Cp. Chandra, Sandilands (2006), p. 194.
298 Cp. Landis (2006), p. 44.
299 Cp. Arnott, Kelesnik, Moghtader, Scholl (2010), p. 17ff.; Schoenfeld, Ginis (2006), p. 1ff.
300 Cp. Jang, Koo, Liu, Loewenstein (2007), p. 2330.
301 Cp. Arnott, West (2006), p. 111ff.
302 Positive financial market overestimation is entitled as bubble; cp. Li, Xue, (2009), p. 2667f.

balancings based on the continuous changes of the fundamental valuations.[303] According to Woods and Richard (2003) [304] as well as Branch and Cai (2011)[305] they document the superiority of indexing approaches depending on market conditions.[306]

2.2 Portfolio Management Theory and Practice

The item portfolio management[307] describes the aggregation of determinations that have to be considered in the context of executing investments.[308] This interdependence between different challenges clarifies the process which extends from planning and realisation to the monitoring and is visualised by figure 1.[309]

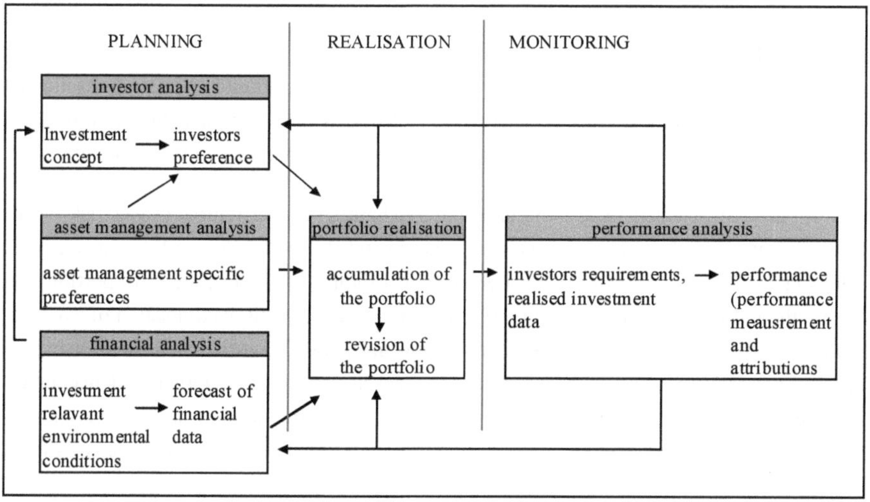

Figure 1: Basic model of the portfolio management process[310]

303 Cp. Bernstein (2006), p. 1f.
304 Cp. Woods, Richard (2003), p. 1ff.
305 Cp. Branch, Cai (2011), p. 74.
306 Cp. Hsu, Campollo (2006), p. 58.
307 Besides the subsequently explained Portfolio Selection Theory e.g. Fischer Black and Robert Litterman (1992) developed a portfolio approach with neutral market equilibrium proportions in contrast to Markowitz's mean-variance optimisation; cp. Black, Litterman (1992), p. 28ff.; Drobetz (2001), p. 59f.
308 Cp. Urwyler, Homberger (2001), p. 1ff.; Lamont, Thaler (2001), p. 17f.
309 For further information concerning the practical portfolio management process; cp. Poddig, Brinkmann, Seiler (2009), p. 15.
310 Self-provided figure in dependenc of: Poddig, Brinkmann, Seiler (2009), p. 15.

Individual parameters are given because of customer's needs, philosophies or cultural circumstances, impacting the overall process of portfolio management. The investment philosophy defines the goal, the conditions and the properties of the capital investment as rudiment of every decision. Thereupon the investment process is conducted, defining the organisational structure and investment culture.[311]

Especially institutional investors[312] occupy professional asset managers to supervise pretentious portfolios.[313] In particular many different approaches concerning graduations between active and passive portfolio management[314] are prevalent.[315]

2.2.1 Portfolio Selection Theory

Harry M. Markowitz developed the Portfolio Selection Theory in the year 1952.[316] According to his publication "Portfolio Selection"[317], investors are able to build efficient portfolios by purchasing low correlated assets.[318] During 1990 Markowitz, Sharpe and Miller were decorated with the Nobel Price in Economics for the protruding importance of their findings.[319]

A portfolio is efficient if there is no alternative exhibiting higher returns (lower risk) at the identical level of risk (return), respectively superior returns with lower risk.[320] As a general rule volatility[321] and returns are comprised as annual figures.[322] In this process of portfolio selection the individual ability to assume risk and the personal profit maximisation of every investor have to be considered.[323] Rationally acting investors[324] constrict their assortments on efficient portfolios because of their distinct and ideal risk/return characteristics. Hence, investors are able to detect their optimum of benefits by an individual allocation of varying assets.[325] The optimal portfolios defined by Markowitz are placed on the "mean-variance boundary"[326].

311 Cp. Bruns, Meyer-Bullerdiek (2008), p. 93ff.
312 Cp. Zheng (2010), p. 22.
313 Cp. Entzian (2008), p. 754ff.; Wallmeier (2000), p. 45.
314 Cp. Rehkugler (2002), p. 3ff.
315 Cp. Schopf (2009), 1f.; Stein (2004), p. 2ff.
316 Cp. Markowitz (1970), p. 3ff.
317 Cp. Markowitz (1952), p. 77ff.
318 Cp. Markowitz (1991), p. 21; Markowitz (2002), p. 154.
319 Cp. Horasanli, Fidan (2007), p. 2; Rubinstein (2002), p. 1041.
320 Cp. Hu, Kercheval (2010), p. 91.
321 Cp. Hatherley, Alcock (2007), p. 450.
322 Cp. Ennis, Sebastian (2005), p. 81.
323 Cp. Wilcox (2003), p. 58.
324 Cp. Guo (2002), p. 32.
325 Cp. Garz, Günther, Moriabadi (2006), p. 42ff.
326 Alexander (2009), p. 452.

Empirically critical Markowitz assumed investors as rational.[327] Though, even in consideration of the almost perfect market efficiency a prospective return is not confidently illustrated by standard deviations.[328] Generally the theory comprehends an ex-ante approach where asset returns, risks and correlations are estimated but historical values serve for analytical reasons.[329] The predicted risk/return combinations in figure 2 allegorise different assets[330] and the connecting line clarifies the efficiency boarder of miscellaneous portfolios.[331] Every item on this curve as well as the minimum-variance portfolio (MVP) demonstrates an efficient investment opportunity.[332] The less the correlation amongst these assets is the more bellied to the left side is the hyperbola.[333] The illustrated Capital Market Line (CML) serves prospectively as reference towards the subsequent explanations of the CAPM.

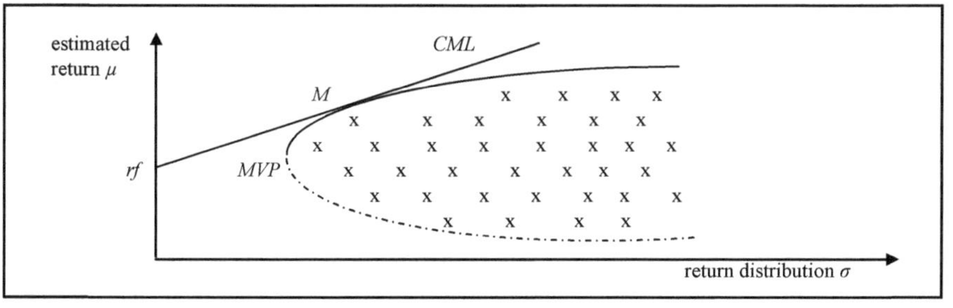

Figure 2: Efficiency curve[334]

Duchin and Levy (2009) labeled the Markowitz model as "diversification theory"[335] due to the fact that diversification depends on correlation of the implicated assets. Although they confirmed the theoretical accurateness of the entire detections, they made up two critical annotations: To their perception Markowitz makes up no declaration about the quantity of assets within any efficient portfolio combination and presumes constant asset returns as well as correlations during an unspecified one-period model.[336] Their conducted challenges insinuated further assumptions by Markowitz of constant[337] correlation over time and undefined maturities of the investment periods.[338]

327 Cp. Wang, Xia (2002), p. 5.
328 Cp. Eling (2007), p. 32.
329 Cp. Horasanli, Fidan (2007), p. 2.
330 Cp. Chhabra (2005), p. 8.
331 Cp. Qi, Hirschberger, Steuer (2009), p. 16.
332 Cp. Kan, Zhou (2007), p. 623.
333 Cp. Spremann, Gantenbein (2005), p. 85ff.
334 Self-provided figure in dependence of: Spremann (2008), p. 18.
335 Duchin, Haim (2009), p. 71.
336 Cp. Bai, Liu, Wong (2009), p. 640.
337 Cp. Yiu, Ho, Choi (2010), p. 353.
338 Cp. Duchin, Haim (2009), p. 71.

Even earlier Steinbach (2001) scrutinized the primary Markowitz theory in an assimilable manner. He made up a multi-period investigation under the assumption of possible total losses[339] that can not be avoided by diversification and expire to the conclusion that real-life asset allocation is impacted by challenges appearing out of individual investor's requirements.[340]

Further Wilcox (2003) suggested that the efficient Markowitz portfolios are unable to achieve long-run excess returns in combination with safety against negative return peaks. Especially risk averse investors are addicted to long-turn sustainable returns with the quantitative elimination of such affecting outliers.[341]

Chhabra (2005) expanded the Markowitz assumptions of combining different securities by the necessary condition of low dependencies within the asset classes. Especially for equities it would be pre-conditioned that the implied stocks are low correlated. Because of the inconstant conditions of correlation, the formerly static one-period allocation process has to be set up dynamically.[342] Even institutional investors do not adequately consider these diversification influencing parameters.[343]

Advocates of the behavioural finance[344] like Horvitz and Wilcox (2007) detected three main prejudices by the Markowitz applications: Firstly most investors are unable to understand his assumptions. Secondly Markowitz extinguishes rational actings, disregarding any investor's behavioural appreciation. And by the third aspect they mention investors as unable to ignore cognitive biases explicable as irrationality. These contracting points are no only intrinsic problem of the Markowitz theory but rather due to a common investor's individual overestimation[345] of their own abilities.[346]

During the financial market crisis[347] hard critics of the Portfolio Selection Theory were announced.[348] New and never mentioned risk factors appeared to investors evoking uncertainty about future developments.[349]

339 Cp. Delquié (2008), p. 6.
340 Cp. Steinbach (2001), p. 31ff.
341 Cp. Wilcox (2003), p. 58.
342 Cp. Chhabra (2005), p. 8.
343 Cp. Goetzmann, Kumar (2008), p. 433.
344 Cp. Singh (2010), p. 1ff.
345 Cp. Guo (2002), p. 32.
346 Cp. Horvitz, Wilcox (2007), p. 43ff.
347 Cp. Ehmer (2009), p. 1.
348 Cp. Sumnicht (2009), p. 16ff.
349 Cp. Patchett, Horgan (2011), p. 37.

Brown and Solow (2009) stated that traditional methods of portfolio management would lose their denotation and new technical aspects have to be evolved considering changing market conditions and especially rising correlation during times of bearish market trends.[350]

Even Markowitz (2010) admitted that further investigations according to top-down analysis, asset allocations and index investments have changed the market circumstances since developing his Portfolio Selection Theory, but these modified determinants do not inevitably have to devaluate his theses.[351] Much more he stated, that asset managers would have to invest along the efficient frontier, to access assets in this process, they rely on and further ignorance of market noise.[352]

Tobin (1958) expanded the Portfolio Selection Theory according to his separation theorem[353] by the aspect of the riskless asset[354] and the riskless return r_f.[355] The combination of risk carrying and riskless investments[356] was established.[357] In figure 2 this constitution is already shown as line beginning in axis intercept r_f on the ordinate, ascending by the market price of risk.[358] The ascending is maximised if the efficiency curve is tangent in the market portfolio (M).[359] In this case the CML is located. Every portfolio on the CML, except the market portfolio, is predominant to the efficient portfolios.[360] On the CML the expected return compensates the respective units of inherent portfolio risk.[361] According to Tobin the market portfolio can be declared as risk carrying fraction of the entire portfolio which is identical for every investor.[362]

2.2.2 Capital Asset Pricing Model

The CAPM[363] conduces as origin of the common modern capital market theory.[364] It was founded in the 1960s by Sharpe (1964), Lintner (1965) and Mossin (1966)[365], and it is still one of the prevailing models to price risky assets under the assumption of risk avoidance and

350 Cp. Holton (2009), p. 22ff.
351 Cp. Buttell (2010), p. 23.
352 Cp. Mitchell (2010), p. 42.
353 Cp. Tobin (1958), p. 65ff.
354 Cp. Perridon, Steiner (2004), p. 270; Brealey, Meyers (2006), p. 194.
355 Cp. Wenzelburger (2010), p. 225f.
356 Subsequently adopted by the EONIA; cp. da Fonseca (2010), p. 728.
357 Cp. Feldman, Reisman (2003), p. 252.
358 Cp. Levy, Levy, Benita (2006), p. 1319.
359 Cp. Arnold, Nail, Nixon (2006), p. 72.
360 Cp. Nielsen, Vassalou (2006), p. 652.
361 Cp. Siegel, Woodgate (2007), p. 1009.
362 Cp. Garz, Günther, Moriabadi (2006), p. 56 ff.; Spremann, Gantenbein (2005), p. 89ff.
363 Cp. Stock (2002), p. 41.
364 Cp. Wang, Xia (2002), p. 145.
365 Cp. Sharpe (1964), p. 425ff.; Lintner (1965), p. 587ff.; Mossin (1966), p. 768ff.

rationality[366]. It is based on two essential assumptions: Firstly capital market participants prevail as portfolio optimisers, respectively to the Portfolio Selection Theory and the endeavour to build efficient portfolios.[367] The proxy of an efficient portfolio is practically adopted by an index as equivalent of the investigated equity market.[368] Secondly the market equilibrium is imputed to exist whereby a consistent market price for risk is addicted and the CML exists as the central proportion of consideration.[369]

The CAPM is subject to the following theoretical assumptions:[370]

- Capital markets prevail as frictionless.
- Neither transaction costs nor taxes are existent.
- Investors are risk-averse and borrow additional risk exclusively if they achieve an adjustment which is incorporated by the beta factor accommodated to the mean-variance optimisation.
- Investors are oriented by the estimated return of their portfolios.
- The market is supposed as informational efficient.
- A positive riskless interest rate of return exists as opportunity to invest or borrow unlimited amounts of capital.
- Ideal competition subsists and every security is discretionary marketable.
- The investment time is one period without further declaration.
- Returns follow the Gaussian distribution or the squared utility function.

Every investor bears a part of his assets in the risk carrying market portfolio[371], depending on his individual risk preference. The excessive proportion is invested at the riskless rate of return. The connection of expected returns of a security and the market portfolio is declared by the systematic risk measure of the beta factor *(β)*. Opponently, the unsystematic risk is not compensated because the market portfolio presumes to be entirely diversified.[372] The expected return of a security is calculated according to formula (7):[373]

$$(7) \qquad E[R_i] = r_f + \beta_i \left(E[R_m] - r_f\right).$$

366 Cp. Hung, Shackleton, Xu (2004), p. 88.
367 Cp. Velvadapu (2011), p. 21.
368 Cp. Dolde, Giaccotto, Mishra, O'Brian (2011), p. 78.
369 Cp. Garz, Günther, Moriabadi (2006), p. 65.
370 Cp. Wang, Xia (2002), p. 146ff.; Stock (2002), p. 42; Fama (2006), p. 2183; Galagedera (2009), p. 341; De Giorgi, Post (2008), p. 527; Lusk, Halperin, Bern (2008), p. 2; Markowitz (2008a), p. 91; Hamada, Valdez (2008), p. 408; Najand, Lin, Fitzgerald (2006), p. 169.
371 Cp. Hwang, Satchell (2002), p. 775.
372 Cp. Garz, Günther, Moriabadi (2006), p. 66.
373 Cp. Hamada, Valdez (2008), p. 388.

Where $E[R_i]$ and βi correspond to the expected return as well as the systematic risk of security i, $E[R_m]$ indicates the return of the market portfolio and variable r_f displays the riskless rate of return.[374]

Figures 3 and equation (7) describe the security market line (SML) as combination of the riskless rate of return and the beta factor as measure of single security's risk in comparison to the market portfolio in the market equilibrium.[375]

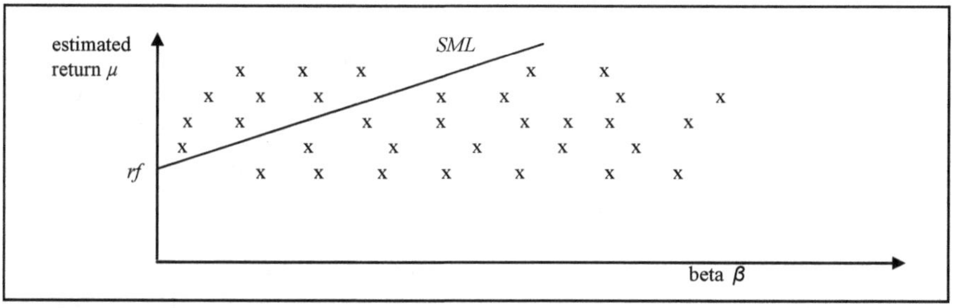

Figure 3: The SML as comparison of systematic risk and return[376]

According to the CAPM-anomalies[377] affecting any of the previously mentioned model assumptions, within several empirical investigations the relevance of the beta factor is not as appropriate as stated because return series[378] are inconstant.[379] Hence, the assumed linear risk premium does not appear in any kind of market condition due to frequent considerations of asset returns, biased by skewness[380] and kurtosis.[381]

Markowitz (2008) revisited the CAPM and the assumption that investors receive a return compensation for bearing additional portions of risk. He does not veto the model but tries to clarify that the market may exist as one of many efficient portfolios and its connection to single securities in the shape of the beta factor may be ascertainable and appear as sloped measure but this does not have to be interpreted as risk that must necessarily be compensated by additional returns.[382]

374 Cp. Wang, Xia (2002), p. 147.
375 Cp. Reilly, Brown (2006), p. 24.
376 Self-provided figure in dependence of: Roll (1978), p. 1053.
377 Cp. Hagtvedt (2009), p. 1593ff.
378 Cp. Hung (2008), p. 998.
379 Cp. Fernandez (2005), p. 1; Yalcin, Ersahin (2011), p. 28.
380 Cp. Harvey, Liechty, Liechty, Müller (2004), p. 4ff.; Jondeau, Rockinger (2003), p. 1699ff.
381 Cp. Hung, Shackleton, Xu (2004), p. 108ff.; Guse, Rudolf (2006), p. 2ff.
382 Cp. Markowitz (2008a), p. 94.

Levy (2010) reinvestigated the CAPM due to announced critics by behavioural[383] researchers who state the investor as irrational[384]. The CAPM was detected as effectual even under the circumstances that investors do not act as rational return optimising individuals and returns are not Gaussian distributed.[385] Levy relegates the criticism to the difficulty in predicting future return series. According to this analysis the CAPM is valid for the use of ex post data or the tentative approximation of forecasted security developments.[386]

2.2.3 Theoretical Denotation of Correlation

In contrast to a discretionary stock picking, theoretical foundations constrain that a diversified portfolio eliminates the unsystematic portion of risk. The investor is exclusively subject to the remaining market risk[387]. Preferably various securities are contained in the asset allocation[388], whereby the entire portfolio is approximated towards the benchmark or respectively the market portfolio, in terms of Markowitz.[389]

Referring to the Portfolio Selection Theory an investor is able to lower the portfolio volatility by diversification.[390] Practical evidence occupies a sufficient degree of diversification exeunt 15 securities[391]. The extent of the unsystematic risk correlates negatively to the degree of diversification as illustrated in figure 4.[392]

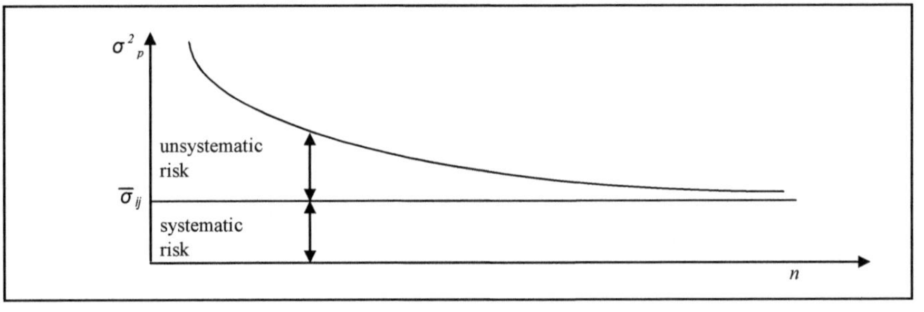

Figure 4: Degree of diversification in dependence of the number of securities[393]

383 Cp. Horvitz, Wilcox (2007), p. 43ff.
384 Cp. Mittal, Vyas (2009), p. 27.
385 Cp. Najand, Lin, Fitzgerald (2006), p. 169.
386 Cp. Levy (2010), p. 67f.
387 Cp. Urwyler, Homberger (2001), p. 1; Herrmann (1997), p. 8; Markowitz (1978), p. 49.
388 Cp. Dolvin, Templeton, Riebe (2010), p. 60.
389 Cp. Schmitz-Esser (2001), p. 105.
390 Cp. Fernholz (2000), p. 9.
391 According to rising correlations due to global eocnomic dependencies the number of needed securities is growing. For a discussion concerning the number of required assets; cp. Jondeau, Rockinger (2008), p. 16.
392 Cp. Garz, Günther, Moriabadi (2006), p. 27ff.
393 Self-provided figure in dependence of: Dorenkamp (2002), p. 29.

The covariance[394] σ_{ij} calculated by formula (8) exemplifies the dependence of two variables *i* and *j* e.g. illustrating the return developments of two asset prices r_i and r_j in comparison to their average.[395]

The correlation coefficient[396] p_{ij} measured by formula (9) divides the covariance by the multiplied volatilities σ_i and σ_j of both assets and limits the covariance in the interval of *-1* to *+1*.[397] Whereat *+1* expresses perfect positive correlation[398], hence prices move identically and diversification is impossible because the single asset volatilities are combined ancillary to the entire portfolio risk.[399] A correlation coefficient[400] of *0* denotes uncorrelated[401] or statistically independent return devolutions and the negative extreme value of *-1* corresponds to perfect negative correlation[402], illustrated by oppositional price deviations.

(8) $$\sigma_{ij} = \frac{\sum_{i=1}^{n}\left(r_i - \overline{r_i}\right)*\left(r_j - \overline{r_j}\right)}{n}.$$

(9) $$p_{ij} = \frac{\sigma_{ij}}{\sigma_i * \sigma_j}.$$

A classification of correlation coefficients and their respective significance of interrelations are illustrated in table 1.

Correlation coefficient	Degree of interrelation
$p_{ij} = -1$	perfect negative interrelation
$-0,7 < p_{ij} < -1,0$	strong negative interrelation
$-0,5 < p_{ij} \leq -0,7$	mean negative interrelation
$-0,5 < p_{ij} \leq 0$	weak negative interrelation
$p_{ij} = 0$	no statistically significant interrelation
$0 < p_{ij} \leq 0,5$	weak positive interrelation
$0,5 < p_{ij} \leq 0,7$	mean positive interrelation
$0,7 < p_{ij} < 1,0$	strong positive interrelation
$p_{ij} = 1$	perfect positive interrelation

Table 1: Correlation coefficients and their significance of interrelation[403]

394 Cp. Spremann (2008), p. 81.
395 Cp. Poddig, Brinkmann, Seiler (2009), p. 52; Fischer (2010), p. 398f.
396 Cp. Williams, Zumbo, Ross, Zimmermann (2003), p. 296ff.
397 Cp. Steiner, Bruns (2007), p. 66f.; Specht, Gohout (2009), p. 17.
398 Cp. Bleymüller, Gehlert, Gülicher (2008), p. 145.
399 Cp. Steiner, Bruns (2007), p. 11f.
400 Cp. Garz, Günther, Moriabadi (2006), p. 27ff.
401 Cp. Schlittgen (2004), p. 14.
402 Cp. Specht, Gohout (2009), p. 19.
403 Self-provided table in dependence of: Kobelt, Steinhausen (2000), p. 122.

To achieve a diversified portfolio the accumulated unsystematic portions of risk according to every comprised asset should constituently be major than the developing portfolio risk due to their varying correlation[404] coefficients. Hence, for the overall portfolio risk σ_P established by the single asset risks σ_1, σ_2 to σ_n the equation $\sigma_P \leq \sigma_1 + \sigma_2 + \ldots + \sigma_n$ is valid.[405]

At the stock market a comparable synchronisation of returns is observable, hence in practical references negative correlations only exist between different asset classes.[406] Returns are highly but not perfectly correlated[407]. As consequence the portfolio risk can be limited but not eliminated by diversification.[408] Item C in figure 5 illustrates the theoretically possible border case of maximal diversification in the context of negative correlation. Normally the dispersion of the asset returns resembles a hyperbola between the securities A and B, delineating the imperfectly correlated interdependence of the single returns.[409]

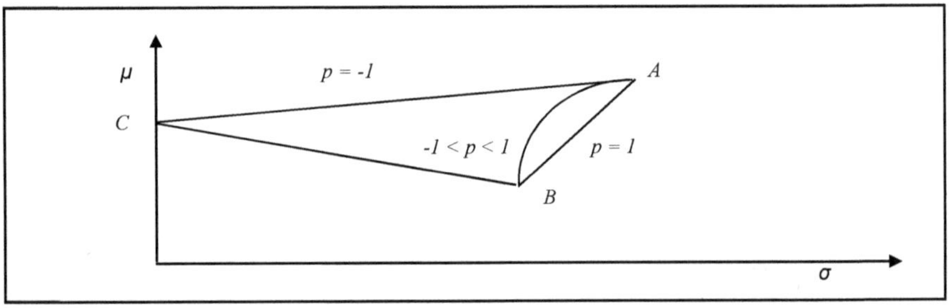

Figure 5: Possibility curves in dependence of the correlation coefficient[410]

A challenging attribute within the portfolio management is the inherent variability of volatility and correlation over time.[411] Amongst others Buraschi, Porchia and Trojani (2010) explicated the rising correlation of single equities and equity indices in the USA during times of negative market trends.[412] As explained by Markowitz in the 1950s, the success of diversification depends on low correlation.[413] Negative attributes of increasing dependencies are especially detrimental during times investors are mostly reliant on low correlations.[414] Yiu, Ho and Choin (2011) expanded their investigation to transnational equity index dependencies

404 Cp. Loy, Jostarndt (2006), p. 488.
405 Cp. Spremann (2008), p. 100; Artzner, Delbaen, Health (1997), p. 68f.
406 Cp. Döhnert, Kunz, Wälchli (2000), p. 8.
407 Cp. Reuse (2011b), p. 272.
408 Cp. Markowitz (1959), p. 5.
409 Cp. Garz, Günther, Moriabadi (2006), p. 36f.
410 Self-provided figure in dependence of: Garz, Günther, Moriabadi (2006), p. 36.
411 Cp. Ball, Torous (2000), p. 373ff.
412 Cp. Buraschi, Porchia, Trojani (2010), p. 395.
413 Cp. Markowitz (1970), p. 3ff.
414 Cp. Ang, Chen (2002), p. 444.

during the global financial crisis between US and Asian equity markets. Both findings are analogous and illustrate that international investments in an equal asset class like equities do not suffice to diversify risk effectually.[415]

D'Antonio and Johnsen (2011) referred the losses of various investors and collapsing risk management techniques during the global financial crisis to the assumption of invariant persistence of the asset correlations.[416] According to scrutinize this misbelieve, Bernhard, Höcht, Neugebauer, Neumann and Zagst (2011) extended their analysis by considering different asset classes like European equities compared to governmental bonds. Correlations within asset classes are mentioned as comparatively equal and increasing in times of market crisis but the portfolio diversification and comprising of different asset classes performs well during market turmoil because their mean dependencies even decrease or remain unchanged.[417]

Reuse (2011) illustrated long-term average correlations between ten asset classes during 1996 and 2010. In the long-run nearly no profound or negative correlated pair of asset exists but in the short view correlations fluctuate.[418] This remains unconsidered within the adoption of estimated single period risk/return characteristics within the Portfolio Selection Theory[419]. Adjaoute and Danthine (2000) even located rising dependencies in the EMU due to the introduction of the Euro.[420]

2.2.4 Deduced Practical Denotations of Correlation

Following the specified results within the subsequent allocations, correlations[421] between different asset classes will be implemented in the collection process to achieve superior performance attributes. The rapid changes within the correlations between different asset classes as mentioned by Reuse (2011)[422] are illustrated in figure 6, applying the SX5E, the CRB index [in EUR] and the REXP for a ten year lasting period from January 01st 2001 to December 31st 2010 by the use of rolling 52 week[423] correlations.

415 Cp. Yiu, Ho, Choin (2011), p. 351ff.
416 Cp. D'Antonio, Johnsen (2011), p. 37.
417 Cp. Bernhard, Höcht, Neugebauer, Neumann, Zagst (2011), p. 20f.
418 Cp. Reuse (2011a), p. 149f.
419 Cp. Markowitz (2008b), p. 150ff.
420 Cp. Adjaoute, Danthine (2000), p. 2.
421 Cp. Piplack, Straetmans (2010), p. 397ff.
422 Cp. Reuse (2011a), p. 149f.
423 Rolling 52 week or annual correlations are used synomymously. Daily returns are combined in a spinning operation during January 01st 2001 and December 31st 2010; hence the first data point in the correlation charts illustrates the end of the initial 52 week period; cp. Reuse (2011b), p. 272f.

The subsequent explanations serve as test of *(H1)* where the null hypothesis of *(H1)* means a rejection of the assumption, that correlations between financial assets rise during times of falling markets. The constraint of financial assets is adducted with reference to the CRB [in EUR] and the SX5E.

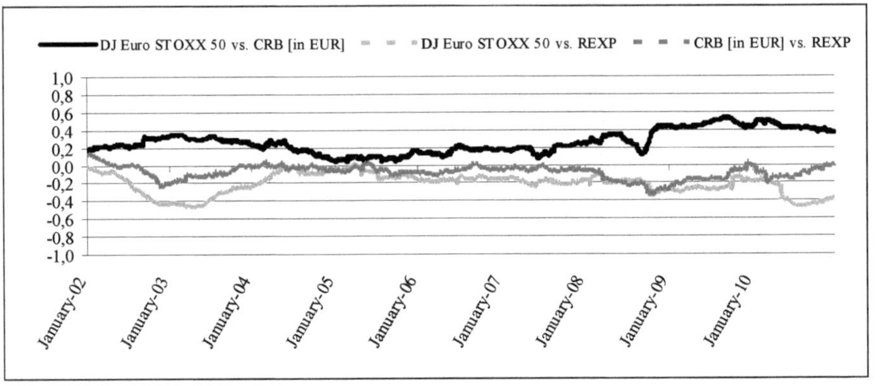

Figure 6: Rolling 52 week asset class correlation[424]

The three correlation structures[425] develop within the interval between -0,49 and 0,54 with the positive extreme of 0,54 between the CRB [in EUR] and the SX5E in September 2009, one year after the US investment bank Lehman Brothers Holdings Inc. (Lehman Brothers) filed bankruptcy[426] and provoked the peak of the global financial crisis[427]. The lowest ratio of -0,49 is located as dependence of the SX5E and the REXP in August 2010 confirming the positive diversification attributes of equities and governmental bonds.[428]

In comparison to table 2, showing the averaged correlation coefficients of the three asset pairs, the rolling annual correlations exhibit the rapid deviations independently from their mean. The correlation matrixes[429] illustrate just one conspicuously positive average coefficient between the SX5E and the CRB [in EUR]. Hence, the subsequent (re)allocation process of the ECI has to take these dependencies into account.

424 Self-provided figure in dependence of: Bloomberg [ed.] (2011b) to ibid. (2011d).
425 Cp. Breuer, Gürtler, Schuhmacher (2004), p. 305.
426 Lehman Brothers filed insolvency by chapter 11 of the US Bankruptcy Code on September 15th 2008; cp. Lehman Brothers [ed.] (2011).
427 Cp. Cortez, Ke (2010), p. 28.
428 Cp. Bernhard, Höcht, Neugebauer, Neumann, Zagst (2011), p. 20f.
429 Cp. Specht, Gohout (2009), p. 18.

Table 2 represents the correlation matrixes over the entire decade, which can be subdivided into temporal groups of financial market turmoil or relief. This serves to revise if correlations actually rise in times of falling markets as stated before.[430]

average correlation	DJ Euro STOXX 50	CRB [in EUR]	REXP
DJ Euro STOXX 50	1	0,30	-0,24
CRB [in EUR]		1	-0,10
REXP			1

maximum / minimum correlation	DJ Euro STOXX 50	CRB [in EUR]	REXP
DJ Euro STOXX 50	1	0,535 0,038	0,002 -0,487
CRB [in EUR]		1	0,125 -0,348
REXP			1

Table 2: Correlation matrixes of the selected asset classes[431]

The entire period is divided into four sections based to market trends of the SX5E: (1) January 01st 2001 to March 12th 2003, (2) March 13th 2003 to June 01st 2007, (3) June 04th 2007 to March 06th 2009 and (4) March 07th 2009 to December 31st 2010, though the fourth time series remains unconsidered because equity markets rose since the beginning of this sub-period but at the ende of 2010 the EMU crisis, due to increasing public deficits and rating downgrades[432] of southern European countries, still provoked uncertainty about future expectations. The analysis is focussed on completed market trends[433] up to their reversal. Since the market turmoil according to fiscal challenges for instance in Greece still persists[434], the fourth space of time is ignored in this consideration.[435]

Period	Market tendency	Correlation coefficient DJ Euro STOXX 50 vs. CRB [in EUR]	Grade
01.01.2001 - 12.03.2003	Baisse	0,26	2
13.03.2003 - 01.06.2007	Hausse	0,15	3
04.06.2007 - 06.03.2009	Baisse	0,43	1
07.03.2009 - 30.12.2010	Hausse	0,37	

Table 3: Trend dependent correlation of EMU equities and commodities[436]

430 Cp. Ang, Chen (2002), p. 444.
431 Self-provided table in dependence of: Bloomberg [ed.] (2011b) to ibid. (2011d).
432 Cp. Howard (2010), p. 48.
433 Cp. Cohen (2011), p. 45f.
434 Date: December 31st 2011.
435 Cp. Antzoulatos (2010), p. 255.
436 Self-provided table in dependence of: Bloomberg [ed.] (2011b); ibid. (2011c).

The classification of the sub-periods identified by the price development of the SX5E and its instant tendencies are illustrated in table 3, where a "baisse"[437] ("hausse"[438]) is related to falling (rising) equity market prices.

The calculated correlation coefficients refer to the dependence of the SX5E towards the CRB [in EUR]. This simplified comparison of two assets is adopted to receive a focussed view of equity market interrelation to commodity prices.

The index development of the SX5E shown in figure 7 illustrates that periods (1) and (3) refer to bearish markets and period (2) constitutes the interim bullish trend. The different tendencies are divided and compared to the rolling annual correlation of the SX5E towards the CRB [in EUR] and its standardised price development.

The charts clarify that correlations amongst equities and commodities depend negatively on equity market up and down slopes. The distinction is even confirmed by table 3, where the correlation coefficients of baisse[439] periods (1) and (3) exhibit values of 0,26 and 0,43 opponent to hausse period (2) with the calculated measure of only 0,15, which is near to statistical independence.[440]

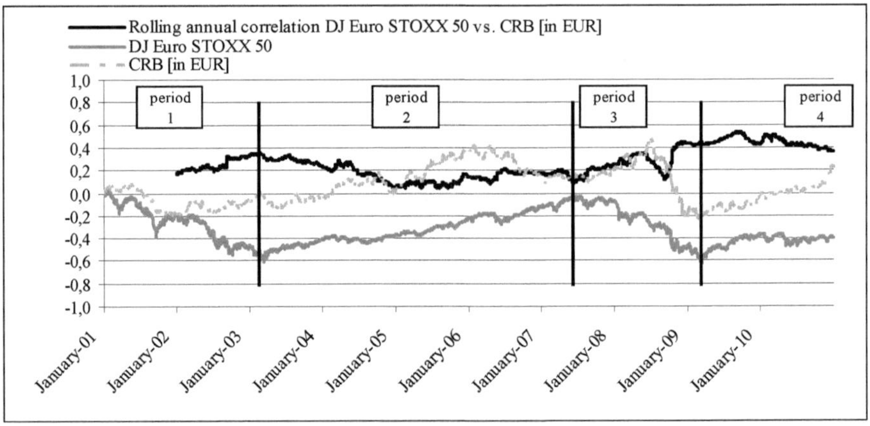

Figure 7: Trend dependency of EMU equities and commodities[441]

437 Cp. Dridi, Germain (2004), p. 875.
438 Cp. Wong, Shum (2010), p. 1615.
439 Cp. Okunev (2010), p. 66.
440 Cp. Kobelt, Steinhausen (2000), p. 122.
441 Self-provided figure in dependence of: Bloomberg [ed.] (2011b); ibid. (2011c).

According to the previous results the null hypothesis of *(H1)* has to be rejected because within the EMU correlations of equities and commodities are negativey addicted to equity market circumstances, they increase (decrease) in times of falling (rising) market prices.[442] This is especially detrimental for investors because during market downturns they depend mostly on diversification benefits, provoked by low correlated[443] asset prices.

2.3 Definition of Selected Performance Attributes

The performance[444] of a portfolio measures the success of the executed transactions for example as positive or negative alpha corresponding to a benchmark[445] and makes the success of the investment comparable.[446] By the help of performance measures[447] investors are able to detect if the historical growth of portfolios have to be returned to luck, an excessive borrowing of risk or the management ability.[448]

In addition to the attributes of risk and return the liquidity is adapted within the performance evaluation[449] and the respective target function.[450] The market exemplifies the inherent correspondence of all three parameters but commonly the performance is specified as ratio of risk and return.[451] This two-dimensionality leaves the liquidity unconsidered because it is difficult to measure.[452]

2.3.1 Return Measurement

The return provides a ratio that compares the investment outcome with the raised capital. Ex post it is possible to estimate if the ex ante forecasted added values are realised by the executed investments. The absolute result in monetary units is declared as relative value in comparison to the originally invested capital.[453] The outcome of a period is commonly considered not isolated, but compared to a benchmark as the critical equation.[454]

---

442 Cp. Ball, Torous (2000), p. 373ff.
443 Cp. Markowitz (1959), p. 5.
444 Cp. Chamberlain (2011), p. 18.
445 Cp. Bruns, Meyer-Bullerdiek (2008), p. 1ff.
446 Cp. Meijun (2011), p. 370.
447 Cp. Barton, Hansen, Pownall (2010), p. 754.
448 Cp. Barras, Scaillet, Wermers (2010), p. 180; Evans (2010), p. 1582ff.; Yong (2011), p. 1074.
449 Cp. Yu (2011), p. 5.
450 Cp. Rakowski (2010), p. 223f.
451 Cp. Scholz, Wilkens (2006), p. 1278.
452 Cp. Poddig, Brinkmann, Seiler (2009), p. 24.
453 Cp. Spremann (2008), p. 71.
454 Cp. Fernholz (2000), p. 13.

The process of portfolio management[455] tends to obtain risk adjusted returns[456]. Investment decisions are administrated under the assumption that every unit of absorbed risk has to be adjusted by appropriate returns because of the assumed risk aversion[457] of rationally acting investors. The attendance to assume risk depends on personally, individual parameters and has to be examined selectively.[458]

The following specifications of returns are due to the basic calculation of formula (10).[459] This phrase assumes the singular investment without in- or outflows of funds. Accrued earnings during the examination period are subsumed in variable I_1:[460]

$$(10) \qquad R = \frac{I_1 - I_0}{I_0} = \frac{I_1}{I_0} - 1 \qquad\qquad R = \frac{I_1 - I_0}{I_0} * 100 = \left(\frac{I_1}{I_0} - 1\right) * 100 .$$

The return of portfolio R_P is calculated by the aggregated and weighted returns of the single assets as illustrated in formula (11):[461]

$$(11) \qquad R_P = \sum_{i=1}^{n} q_i R_i .$$

In the analysis of long-term empirical time series commonly constant monthly or quarterly returns are adducted.[462] Thereby excess or risk adjusted returns are attended as measuring units whereat the security's (trading) liquidity remains unconsidered.[463]

The prediction of future returns is just limitedly possible with the exclusive help of an historical capital market analysis.[464] Hence, the characteristics of prospective returns are appreciated as random[465] variables, which are influenced by their dispersion and the expectancy μ as well as the deviation from the arithmetic mean of expectations ω.[466]

455 Cp. Bruns, Meyer-Bullerdiek (2008), p. 1ff.
456 Cp. Gregoriou, Pascalau (2010), p. 189.
457 Cp. Rubinstein, Stephens (2001), p. 22.
458 Cp. Klos (2003), p. 39ff.; Rubinstein, Stephens (2001), p. 22.
459 Cp. Garz, Günther, Moriabadi (2006), p. 314f.
460 Cp. Fischer (2010), p. 6.
461 Cp. Specht, Gohout (2009), p. 16.
462 Cp. Meric, Meric (1997), p. 138; Ripley (1973), p. 356ff.; Lessard (1976), p. 32ff.
463 Cp. Dash, S&P [ed.] (2005), p. 8ff.
464 Cp. Klos (2003), p. 48.
465 Cp. Smith (2007), p. 587.
466 Cp. Poddig, Brinkmann, Seiler (2009), p. 30.

The operator of the expectancy value devotes the anticipated return of the overall portfolio with the vector $\mu = (\mu_1, \mu_2, \ldots \mu_n)$ that comprises the respective implicit returns analogous to the calculation by formula (12):[467]

$$(12) \qquad \mu_P = E[R_P] = E\left[\sum_{i=1}^{n} \omega_i R_i\right] = \sum_{i=1}^{n} \omega_i E[R_i] = \sum_{i=1}^{n} \omega_i \mu_i = \omega' \mu .$$

2.3.1.1 Discrete Return

The discrete return r_t^D assumes a singular interest payment at the end of the period from $t\text{-}1$ to t and is calculated by formula (13), where p equals the price of the asset at time t and d exhibits the interim collected capital earnings. The reinvestments of potential payouts are neglected and the maturity of the investment distance can vary. The application of discrete returns appears as problematic, if annual returns are obtained by fractions of years.[468] The elementary and unambiguous calculation is advantageous:[469]

$$(13) \qquad r_t^D = \frac{p_{it} - p_{it-1} + d_t}{p_{it-1}} .$$

The chronological assignment of discrete returns takes place via a multiplication as illustrated by formula (14) for the case of $n > 0$.[470]

$$(14) \qquad (1 + r_t^D) = (1 + r_1^D) * (1 + r_2^D) * \ldots * (1 + r_n^D).$$

Due to the linear calculation of discrete returns, they are implemented in the Portfolio Selection Theory and the CAPM.[471]

2.3.1.2 Constant Return

The constant return is rather subject to the normal distribution than the discrete return because it refers to continuous interest calculations[472] of the invested amount of capital; hence it is more suitable for empirical analysis.[473] This attribute clarifies that in contrast to the discrete

467 Cp. Specht, Gohout (2009), p. 16.
468 Cp. Spremann (2008), p. 72.
469 Cp. Poddig, Brinkmann, Seiler (2009), p. 30ff.; Hielscher (1988), p. 22.
470 Cp. Fischer (2010), p. 66.
471 Cp. Dorfleitner (2002), p. 217ff.
472 The following conducted empirical analyses refer to calculations of constant returns; cp. Schmidt-von Rhein (1996), p. 138.
473 Cp. Fischer (2010), p. 69.

method of return measurement[474] there does not appear a mercurial increase of the invested funds but rather a steady growth is assumed.[475]

The calculation of constant returns r_t^C occurs by formula (15).[476] It uses log-returns because of their advantage according to equal, absolute and relative changes in value and their additivity. This characteristic illustrates the applicability of constant returns within the measurement of time course models and the pricing of options:[477]

$$(15) \qquad r_t^C = \ln\left(1 + r_t^D\right).$$

The near allusion to the Gaussian[478] distribution of constantly calculated returns can assume values within the interval of $+\infty$ and $-\infty$, which is only limited by the maximally possible total loss in value, if any additional contributions are neglected.[479] The aspect of normally distributed constant returns applies prevalently according to the appraisal of long-term investment periods.[480]

2.3.1.3 Excess Return

Corresponding to formula (16) the excess return is expected as the difference of the return given by an investment strategy R_P in comparison to the assumed riskless interest rate r_f. It clarifies the risk premium[481] due to the compensated risk by the amount exceeding the return of a quasi riskless investment alternative.[482]

$$(16) \qquad r^{EX} = R_P - r_f.$$

Active excess returns[483] R_{PA} referring to equation (17) denominate the surplus portion of the portfolio return R_P relative to the implied benchmark return R_B. Generally active the portfolio management is targeted on excess returns according to a comparable benchmark. Where applicable, an emerging tracking error expresses the difference of the portfolio risk and the chosen benchmark:[484]

---

474 Cp. Merchant (2010), p. 560.
475 Cp. Sydsaeter, Hammond (2006), p. 412f.
476 Cp. Poddig, Brinkmann, Seiler (2009), p. 35.
477 Cp. Steiner, Bruns (2007), p. 52.
478 Cp. Liow, Chan (2005), p. 164.
479 Cp. Kerling (1998), p. 30ff.
480 Cp. Steiner, Bruns (2007), p. 51; Brealy, Myers (2006), p. 152ff.
481 Cp. Rompolis, Tzavalis (2010), p. 126.
482 Cp. Poddig, Brinkmann, Seiler (2009), p. 35f.
483 Cp. Fieldings (2006), p. 8.
484 Cp. Schopf (2009), p. 11.

$$(17)\qquad R_{PA} = R_P - R_B = \sigma_P + \beta_P * R_B + \varepsilon_{PA}.$$

The alpha of the portfolio α_P is measured by the active return μ_{PA} plus the benchmark timing $(\beta_{PA}*\mu_B)$ and is affiliated by formula (18) where β_{PA} shows the active beta of the portfolio and β_B exhibits the benchmark beta:[485]

$$(18)\qquad \mu_{PA} = \mu_P - \mu_\beta$$

$$\mu_{PA} = (\alpha_P * \beta_{PA} * \mu_B) - (\beta_B * \mu_B)$$

$$\mu_{PA} = \alpha_P + \beta_{PA} * \mu_B$$

$$\text{with}\quad \beta_{PA} = \beta_P - \beta_B \quad \text{and}\quad \beta_B = 1.$$

Referring to practical tasks, active portfolio managers[486] are more commonly able to beat the benchmark and achieve an outperformance in times of falling markets[487]. The acceptance of this generated positive alpha is frequently limited because in the case of extreme losses[488] of the benchmark, active managers only rarely realise positive portfolio returns after transaction costs[489].

2.3.2 Risk Measurement and Return Dispersion

Risk can be sub-divided into uncertainty[490] and ambiguity.[491] The ambiguity displays even the impossibility to estimate future expected returns[492]. In the context of uncertainty at least the probabilities of prospective returns[493] are identifiable.[494]

Asset managers campaign for the interest of investors by promoting their investment opportunities that permit superior return characteristics together with promises of security.[495] It has been described that returns exceeding the riskless interest rate can only be developed, if additional risk is contracted.[496] These kinds of investment risks are commonly measured by vola-

485 Cp. Grinold, Kahn (2000), p. 102.
486 Cp. Mulvey, Kim (2008), p. 127.
487 Cp. Bird, Gallagher (2002), p. 323.
488 Cp. Lescourret, Robert (2006), p. 205.
489 Cp. Kahn (2010), p. 5.
490 Cp. Yeung (2009), p. 273.
491 Further explanations are dedicated to the interpretation of risk in the shape of uncertainty.
492 Cp. Chua, Goh, Zhang (2010), p. 104.
493 Cp. Ang, Boyer (2010), p. 946.
494 Cp. Bruns, Meyer-Bullerdiek (2008), p. 8.
495 Cp. Zimmerer (2008), p. 129.
496 Cp. Poddig, Brinkmann, Seiler (2009), p. 35f.

tility whereat this is an absolute figure of risk in contrast to the relative beta factor.[497] Investors are liable to trade-offs[498] between returns and risks. The minimisation of risks is *ceteris paribus* accompanied by declining returns.[499] Hence, every investor should be aware of his individual risk preference[500] due to squared utility functions as well as emotional influences[501] and additionally base his investments on an efficient cost management.[502]

On average stocks impute higher risks than bonds or money market investments, whereas a general increase of risk can be recorded in the inverted order of the mentioned asset classes.[503] The risk of a company's share frequently[504] depends negatively on the size of the organisation that can *inter alia* be evaluated by market cap.[505] Further determinants are the capital market composition[506] and their respective constitution.[507]

Risk reduction[508] is one of the major goals of portfolio management. The preferential opportunity is the diversification in which portfolios are allocated by the help of individual risk and return attributes according to the prospective assets.[509] To decrease the overall portfolio risk the manager should preferably invest into low- or uncorrelated securities.[510] For instance alternative investments tend to exhibit low correlations towards stock markets but they frequently feature above average attributes of risk.[511]

2.3.2.1 Systematic and Unsystematic Attributes of Risk

The systematic measure of risk[512] is not reducible by diversification due to its fundamental market inherence. In contrast to the unsystematic attributes of risk, systematic parameters are comparatively more elementary to estimate. Influencing coefficients are for instance political decisions or macro economical trends not only referring to single assets but to the global market or entire market segments.[513]

---

497 Cp. Fischer (2010), p. 391.
498 Cp. Tarasi, Bolton, Hutt, Walker (2011), p. 1.
499 Cp. Lovell, Arnott (1989), p. 5f.
500 Cp. Campbell (2006), p. 227.
501 Cp. Shefrin (2000), p. 21; Swedroe (2010), p. 48.
502 Cp. Perold, Sharpe (1995), p. 149; Klein (2009), p. 760.
503 Cp. Jagannathan, McGrattan (1995), p. 2ff.; Stehle, Hartmond (1991), p. 371ff.
504 The negative correlation of company size and respective attributes of risk can even be inverted during Times of strongly increasing equity prices.
505 Cp. Borys, Zemcik (2011), p. 51.
506 Macro economical factors as market trends, economical conditions, the level of interest rates or the liquidity can influence the ordinary risk/return attributes of a company and its share.
507 For further explanations to the size-effect; cp. Bogle, Malkiel (2003), p. 14; Siegel (2006), p. 14.
508 Cp. Fletcher (2009), p. 953ff.
509 Cp. Yu, Yang, Wong (2007), p. 135f.
510 Cp. Curtillet, Dieudonné (2007), p. 408f.; King (2007), p. 302.
511 Cp. Fischer, Glawischnig (2007), p. 180; Briand, Owyong (2009), p.14.
512 The items systematic or market risk are synonyms.
513 Cp. Steiner, Bruns (2007), p. 54f.; Drummen, Lips, Zimmermann (1992), p. 82.

The denotation of systematic risks is attended by the CAPM and the assessment of the not diversifiable portion of risk according to the comprised beta factor. The return contribution of a single stock in the context of the CAPM is investigated by the summation of the endued riskless rate of return e.g. taken form an AAA-rated governmental bond or a SWAP rate[514], added by the asset's individual risk premium. The measurement of this risk premium occurs by multiplying the difference of the market rate of return and the riskless interest rate with the security's beta[515] factor.[516] The latter only prices the systematic risk of a single asset in comparison to the entire market because the market portfolio[517] is expected as perfectly diversified; hence the unsystematic portion of risk is eliminated.[518] The approximation of target returns and their modification should exclusively be defined by the principle of systematic portions of risk according to the CAPM.[519]

The beta factor β_i can be interpreted as relative measure of an asset's risk in comparison to the insinuated market portfolio M or the respective benchmark. Hence, it is denominated as sensitivity identification symbol and is calculated by formula (19), with σ_i and σ_M expressing the particular volatilities of the asset i and the market portfolio M:[520]

$$(19) \qquad \beta_i = \frac{p_{iM} * \sigma_i}{\sigma_M}.$$

The systematic portion of risk is biased by two different components: Initially it reduces possible gains of diversification and auxiliary the risk of extreme losses[521] is increased by leveraged[522] portfolios in times of sudden negative capital market shocks[523] that can provoke total losses or even obligations of subsequent payments. Risk adverse investors should in general not be advised to leverage their portfolios[524] and consider their changing systematic portions of risk.[525] A further negative aspect becomes eminent by a precise observation of the entire lack of any diversification possibilities. Idiosyncratic risks lead to an increase of the costs of capital that dilute positive returns or provoke escalated losses.[526]

514 Cp. Kawaller (2007), p. 15.
515 Cp. Hsia, Fuller, Chen (2000), p. 283.
516 Cp. Timmreck (2002), p. 300.
517 Cp. Hwang, Satchell (2002), p. 775.
518 Cp. Kryzanowski, Rahman (2008), p. 324.
519 Cp. Lovell, Arnott (1989), p. 6; Elton, Gruber, Busse (2002), p. 264.
520 Cp. Poddig, Brinkmann, Seiler (2009), p. 621; Damodaran (2002), p. 668.
521 Cp. De Melo Mendes (2006), p. 594.
522 Cp. Mertens, Raven (2011), p. 413ff.
523 Cp. Devereux, Yetman (2010), p. 103.
524 Cp. Van der Spek, Hoorenman (2011), p. 87.
525 Cp. Das, Uppal (2004), p. 2831f.
526 Cp. Dichtl, Petersmeier, Schlenger (2003), p. 182; Gleißner, Wolfrum (2008), p. 604f.

The unsystematic risk[527] is addicted by the difference of the portfolio risk and the systematic[528] portion of risk. It does not depend on the entire market condition but is individually biased by any single asset. Due to this attribute the elimination of unsystematic portions of portfolio risk is possible by diversification and allocating low correlated assets.[529]

Stocks or other kinds of single security investments can for instance be subject to unsystematic risks in specifications of dangers occurring by their operational business[530] e.g. product deficiency or the loss of key personalities. The reason for such occasions will *ceteris paribus* be downward sloping stock prices independently from the general price movement of the total market or the entire segment.[531]

2.3.2.2 Volatility

Even Markowitz[532] used the statistical dimension of variance or the annualised standard deviation to calculate the risk attributes of efficient portfolios[533]. His developments still serve as the cutting-edge findings of portfolio management.[534] The volatility is regarded as the one-dimensional fluctuation oriented risk measure which expresses the deviation intensity of asset prices.[535] The portfolio risk in specification of the variance is defined by formula (20) with ω_i and ω_j expressing the weights as well as σ_i^2 and σ_j^2 identifying the single variances of each implicated asset:[536]

(20)
$$\sigma_P^2 = V[R_P]$$

$$\sigma_P^2 = V\left[\sum_{i=1}^{n} \omega_i R_i\right]$$

$$\sigma_P^2 = \sum_{i=1}^{n} \omega_i^2 \sigma_i^2 + \sum_{i=1}^{n} \sum_{j=1, i \neq 1}^{n} \omega_i \omega_j \sigma_{ij}$$

$$\sigma_P^2 = \sum_{i=1}^{n} \sum_{j=1}^{n} \omega_i \omega_j \sigma_{ij} = \omega' \sum \omega \quad or \quad \sigma_P^2 = \left(\sum_{i=1}^{n} \omega_i \sigma_i\right)^2.$$

527 The unsystematic risk is frequently mentioned as single asset or title risk.
528 Cp. Drummen, Zimmermann (1992), p. 82; Fischer (2010), p. 390f.
529 Cp. Steiner, Bruns (2007), p. 53f.
530 Cp. Moosa (2007), p. 167.
531 Cp. Fischer (2010), p. 391.
532 Cp. Markowitz (1952), p. 79.
533 Cp. Hatherley, Alcock (2007), p. 450.
534 Cp. Cain, Zurbruegg (2010), p. 358f.
535 Cp. Achleitner, Kaserer, Moldenhauer (2005), p. 119; Kaplanski, Kroll (2002), p. 1ff.
536 Cp. Specht, Gohout (2009), p. 16.

The annualisation is calculated by the square root of the variance.[537] Risk in unison with volatility defines positive and negative aberrations from the average.[538]

Every deviation from the Gaussian curvature[539] to the left (right) side of the mean value constitutes below (above) average returns. The respective confidence interval[540] represents the probability of occurrence for each deviation.[541] The broader these intervals are accommodated the rather the return of an analysed security is situated within this containment. Historical volatilities are measured by formula (21). Here r_i allegorises the return of the asset i during the period of analysis, μ illustrates the average return and n represents the number of monitored instances of time:[542]

(21) $$\sigma = \sqrt{\frac{1}{n} * \sum_{i=1}^{n} (r_i - \mu)^2} \qquad where \qquad \mu = \frac{1}{n} * \sum_{i=1}^{n} R_i \,.$$

Assets are frequently categorised as risky or quasi riskless by their historical attributes of volatility.[543]

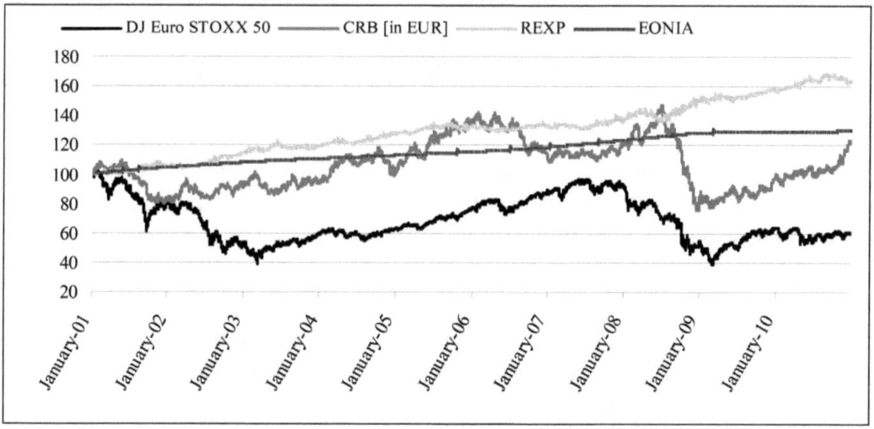

Figure 8: Standardised index comparison of selected asset classes[544]

537 Cp. Heidorn, Hoppe, Kaiser (2006), p. 560.
538 Cp. Mayhew (1995), p. 8ff.
539 Cp. Chazal, Cohen-Steiner, Lieutier, Thibert (2009), p. 1488.
540 Cp. Liau (2009), p. 675.
541 Cp. Wilcox (2006), p. 321.
542 Cp. Fischer (2010), p. 392; Bosch (1992), p. 94; Hakenes, Wilkens (2003), p. 823.
543 Cp. Pang, Warshawsky (2010), p. 28ff.
544 Self-provided figure in dependence of: Bloomberg [ed.] (2011b) to ibid. (2011d); ibid. (2011bd).

Within the subsequent index and portfolio allocations the assets (1) EMU equities, (2) commodities, (3) German governmental bonds and (4) cash will be implemented and explained. Figure 8 illustrates standardised indices[545] of the asset classes during January 01st 2001 to December 31st 2010.

The ordinary inspection of the charts suffices to determine the more risk carrying assets by equities and commodities due to their disproportionate degree of fluctuation in comparison to cash and German governmental bonds[546]. Table 4 amplifies this indentation by the annual and average volatilities calculated on the base of monthly log-returns for the entire period.

	CRB [in EUR]	DJ Euro STOXX 50	REXP	EONIA
2001	12,71%	23,02%	3,22%	0,18%
2002	13,65%	32,48%	3,08%	0,07%
2003	18,10%	20,71%	3,77%	0,10%
2004	15,31%	8,96%	2,28%	0,03%
2005	13,89%	11,33%	2,59%	0,04%
2006	11,27%	8,53%	2,64%	0,12%
2007	11,17%	8,78%	3,07%	0,09%
2008	35,12%	23,80%	4,57%	0,16%
2009	14,13%	25,93%	2,84%	0,14%
2010	11,23%	19,48%	4,43%	0,03%
average	15,66%	18,30%	3,25%	0,10%
max	35,12%	32,48%	4,57%	0,18%
min	11,17%	8,53%	2,28%	0,03%

Table 4: Annual volatilities of selected asset classes [547]

Even the minimum volatilities of the risky assets[548] exceed the maximum ratios of the quasi riskless[549] securities clearly. The CRB [in EUR] never features a single-digit measure of risk. Opponent to these findings the REXP and the EONIA never reach annual binary dimensions of volatility. Comparing the mean values finally clarifies the different degrees of risk according to the elected asset classes. The results constitute the SX5E[550] as more deviating than the CRB [in EUR] during the first three years from 2001 to 2003 and within the last two observed periods of 2009 and 2010. In the meantime asset volatilities are generally lower but the regressive degree of fluctuation displayed by equities is even more conspicuous than the declining volatility cycle[551] of commodities.

545 The indices are calculated with a base value of 100 on January 01st 2001.
546 Cp. Chauvin, Laibson, Mollerstrom (2011), p. 233ff.
547 Self-provided table in dependence of: Bloomberg [ed.] (2011a) to ibid. (2011d).
548 Within the subsequent explanations the item of risky asset is used for equities and commodities.
549 The following accomplishments of riskless assets mention German governmental bonds and cash.
550 Cp. Vo, Daly (2008), p. 569ff.
551 Cp. Kim, Lee (2008), p. 145.

Volatility exclusively conduces to represent an eligible risk measure, if the observed returns follow the standard normal distribution.[552] If the hypothesis of normal distribution has to be refused, the returns are subject to higher moments, indeed the third moment of skewness and/or the fourth moment of kurtosis.[553]

2.3.2.3 Skewness

The resemblance of return frequencies with the Gaussian bell curve depends on their concentration and this in turn requires a narration of the respective distribution in addiction to their arithmetic average.[554] The skewness coefficient s measures if returns are symmetrically allotted around their mean.[555] Within a right-skewed (left-skewed) frequency scale the result of formula (22) is positive (negative). If the returns are standardised normally distributed, the skewness coefficient is zero:[556]

$$(22) \qquad s = \frac{\frac{1}{n}\sum_{i=1}^{n}\left(r_i - \bar{r}\right)^3}{\sigma^3}.$$

Ceteris paribus investors prefer assets or allocations subject to right-skewed return distributions.[557] Due to the higher probability of extreme outrights of negative returns, investors generally avoid returns that are skewed to the left.[558] In order to achieve a return distribution skewed to the right, investors would give up a portion of estimated return premiums if the volatility level is insinuated.[559]

2.3.2.4 Kurtosis

In contrast to skewness, the measure of kurtosis k characterises the concavity of a distribution bell.[560] Hence, the curve can be steeply sloped or rather flat, whereat the latter clarifies large-scale return deviations from the arithmetic mean that can lead to extensive losses or gains.[561]

A normally distributed bell is subject to the kurtosis coefficient of three and the deviated excess zero. Positive (negative) excesses or values of kurtosis exceeding (below) three, exhibit

552 Cp. Duvall, Quinn (2001), p. 250.
553 Cp. Fang, Lai (1997), p. 293; Bao, Ullah (2009), p. 233.
554 Cp. Dufour, Farhat, Gardiol, Khalaf (1998), p. 154ff.
555 Cp. Eckey, Kosfeld, Türck (2008), p. 92ff.
556 Cp. Füss, Rehkugler, Disch (2005), p. 45.
557 Cp. Bergh, van Rensburg (2007), p. 104.
558 Cp. Kaiser, Thießen (2007), p. 426f.
559 Cp. Duvall, Quinn (2001), p. 250.
560 Cp. Fiori (2008), p. 2665ff.
561 Cp. Van de Locht (2009), p. 1ff.

a distribution maximum that is major (minor) than the comparable standardised normally distributed bell shape. The so called fat (thin) ends describe leptokurtic (platykurtic) distributions.[562]

The kurtosis coefficient is calculated with the help of formula (23), where an addition of the term *(-3)* would adjust the kurtosis to the explained excess:[563]

$$(23) \qquad k = \frac{\frac{1}{n}\sum_{i=1}^{n}\left(r_i - \bar{r}\right)^4}{\sigma^4}.$$

Miscellaneous economical studies have explained asset returns as frequently biased towards fat-tailed distributions according to negative kurtosis attributes, influencing the investor.[564] Especially stock returns are subject to such asymmetries.[565] This phenomenon is a negative impact for investors because the probability of extreme negative outliers is disproportionally but has to be known and recognised within the process of portfolio management.[566]

2.3.2.5 Jarque-Bera Test

A feasible test of standardised normal distribution can be conducted by the Jarque-Bera test.[567] If the analysed data set is subject to third and/or fourth moments of skewness and/or kurtosis the test results will undertake large figures demonstrating extreme outliers or unequal dispersions from their respective arithmetic mean.[568]

The Jarque-Bera test *JB* is shown by formula (24), where n illustrates the number of observed parameters, s exemplifies the skewness and k constitutes the kurtosis.[569] The null hypothesis assumes returns as normally distributed. In contrast the alternative hypothesis states that returns do not follow the Gaussian distribution.[570] If the analysed returns are not normally distributed and feature kurtosis and/or skewness results deviating from three, respectively zero, the null hypothesis[571] has to be rejected. The Jarque-Bera test becomes more significant with a growing size of observations:[572]

---

562 Cp. Toutenburg, Heumann (2008), p. 81ff.
563 Cp. Guse, Rudolf (2006), p. 2f.
564 Cp. Fang, Lai (1997), p. 294; Liow, Chan (2005), p. 164; Lau, Martin (1987), p. 1484ff.
565 Cp. Haas (2009), p. 1277; Baixauli, Alvarez (2006), p. 26.
566 Cp. Watanabe (2000), p. 353.
567 Cp. Bera, Jarque (1981), p. 314f. ; Asai, Dashzeveg (2008), p. 461.
568 Cp. Boutahar (2010), p. 196ff.
569 Cp. Thadewald, Büning (2007), p. 91.
570 Cp. Füss, Rehkugler, Disch (2005), p. 46.
571 The hypothesis of normal distribution (null hypothesis) is tested for a confidence level of 5% at a Chi value with two degrees of freedom; cp. Reuse (2010), p. 87; Lawford, (2005), p. 351.
572 Cp. Yazici, Yolacan (2007), p. 180.

$$(24) \qquad JB = \frac{n}{6} * \left(s^2 + \frac{(k-3)^2}{4} \right).$$

2.3.2.6 Downside Deviation

In general terms the volatility can be classified as positive and negative deviation from a mean value.[573] The downside deviation *dd* solely considers negative aberrations from a preassigned trigger point[574] and is assessed by the help of formula (25):[575]

$$(25) \qquad dd_p = \sqrt{\frac{1}{n} * \sum_{t=1}^{n} (\max(0, R_{\min} - R_{Pt}))^2} .$$

In this formula the mentioned barrier is determined by R_{min} and can for instance be assumed as virtual riskless rate of return.[576] Returns below this trigger value illustrate an insufficient pricing of risk because the bered portion of risk is not compensated by adjusted[577] returns. These rates of return are subjectively administered as loss because alternative riskless investment opportunities generate a surplus in value or at least a compensation of applicable predominant inflation rates[578]. Reciprocally investors realise returns above this trigger as gain due to the generation of an excess return in comparison to the riskless investment facility.[579]

The downside deviation dissociates and limits the entire volatility e.g. used by Markowitz[580] exclusively to the downside risk or an inferior performance than the estimated rates of return.[581] This derived meaning can be regarded as more relevant within practical applications because positive predominance in comparison to a specific benchmark or marginal value is frequently not realised as risk. According to the downside deviation risk is not interpreted as general discrepancy from a mean but just as underperformance according to a predetermined value.[582] Hence, the downside deviation can undertake individual specifications in dependence of the assumed target or minimum rate of return[583]. Especially this difficulty makes each calculated and indicated measure of downside deviation individual and inconsistent to inter-

573 Cp. Kochman, Badarinathi (1996), p. 381.
574 Frequently adopted by zero as absolute return measure; cp. De Souza, Gokcan (2004), p. 62ff.
575 Cp. Kaiser, Thießen (2007), p. 426.
576 Cp. Heidorn, Hoppe, Kaiser (2006), p. 566.
577 Cp. Rompolis, Tzavalis (2010), p. 126.
578 Cp. Smith (2004), p. 253.
579 Cp. Füss, Rehkugler, Disch (2005), p. 48f.
580 Cp. Markowitz (1952), p. 77ff.
581 Cp. Kochman, Cenac (1992), p. 1ff.
582 Cp. Miller, Leiblein (1996), p. 92ff.
583 Within the subsequent investigations the trigger value is assumed by an annual return on zero.

pret.[584] The more risk affine an investor is, the higher will be the imputed trigger value and the more probable is the appearance of negative aberrations from the estimated rate of investment return.[585]

2.3.2.7 Maximum Drawdown

The risk measure of a maximum drawdown is especially conventional amongst stock investors and the management of hedge funds.[586] It describes the maximum negative return after achieving an interim high price level.[587] Consequently the difference between the historical high watermark and the incidental lowest level is quantified.[588] The results provide information about the sustainability of the instant return distribution.[589] Investors tend to implicate this identification figure more frequently within their investment decision process to measure potential losses in deduction of the asset's past performance.[590] The use and acceptance of the ratio has become more frequent within times of the financial crisis during the year 2007/09 because even several hedge fund indices were subject to maximum drawdowns of about 25%.[591]

For stock brokers or portfolio managers this kind of drawdown constitutes a hardness test of their management techniques and the risk management systems.[592] The exemplified loss of a security price does not inevitably have to succeed immediately after reaching the interim high but may accelerate within a longer period. During this price movement the degree of cumulated negative returns transcends the positive flows and prices decline over time. The chronological duration of the maximum drawdown remains indefinite to engage the entire price movement but maximum drawdowns can also be declared in dependence of time frames.[593] With respect to its sustainable recognition Acar and James (1997) detected the frequently missing but needed matter of this risk measure in reportings of investment funds but for a constitution of superior attention further research would be imperative.[594] Magdon-Ismail and Atiya (2004) described the maximum drawdown as one of the most important risk measure featuring insufficient relevance due to its analytical complexity.[595]

584 Cp. Trachtenberg (2001), p. 76.
585 Cp. Mukherji (2003) p. 64.
586 Cp. Hayes (2006), p. 26ff.; Pospisil, Vecer (2010), p. 617.
587 Cp. Füss, Rehkugler, Disch (2005), p. 48f.
588 Cp. Bruns, Meyer-Bullerdiek (2008), p. 8.
589 Cp. Kaiser, Thießen (2007), p. 427; Heidorn, Kaiser, Roder (2009), p. 89.
590 Cp. Lang, Gupta, Prestbo (2004), p. 1.
591 Cp. Szado (2009), p. 68.
592 Cp. Pereira, Vaz de Melo Mendes (2005), p. 83.
593 Cp. Fischer (2010), p. 500f.; Wüthrich (2010), p. 83ff.
594 Cp. Acar, James (1997), p. 3ff.
595 Cp. Magdon-Ismail, Atiya (2004), p. 102.

A couple of banks established automatic sell orders following the maximum drawdown *Maxdd* where a so-called trailing stop loss intervenes as soon as a predetermined dynamic loss barrier is affected.[596] For investment funds the measure is calculated by formula (26) where the NAV_t declares the net asset value of the analysed fund at time *t* which can be replaced by monetary values or asset prices:

$$(26) \qquad Maxdd_p = \left[\min\left(\frac{NAV_{t+1}}{NAV_t} \right) - 1 \right] * 100 .$$

2.3.3 Relevance of Liquidity

The aspect of liquidity remains unconsidered within the Portfolio Selection Theory because of the determination and the premises of a perfect capital market.[597] This assumption does not hold in practical experience where liquidity is a decisive parameter that defines the possibility to trade assets. Investors will *ceteris paribus* prefer a liquid, compared to an illiquid portfolio. Commonly the aspect of liquidity is subordinated to the performance parameters of risk and return.[598]

Securities like stocks or bonds generally enact a high degree of liquidity to the core of their fungible exchange trading[599]. In contrast, real estates and artworks are more complex to trade and thus much more illiquid. The requirement of minimum liquidity is an individual assumption which has to be assessed separately by every investor. Frequently the guidance towards cash flows provokes a valuation haircut of illiquid assets.[600] Amihud and Mendelson (1986) observed the coherence of accumulative (decreasing) demands of returns with a decreasing (accumulative) liquidity of a stock in the shape of the liquidity preference hypothesis[601] that causes a recession (boost) of the price or respectively an increase (decrease) of the deducted risk.[602] Aussenegg and Grünbichler (1999) used these findings to constitute the size-effect.[603] From the mean liquidity of small caps[604] they discharged the compensation of liquidity as disadvantage opponent to blue chips during positive market trends.[605]

596 Cp. Heidorn, Kaiser, Roder (2009), p. 5; James, Yang (2010), p. 1ff.
597 Cp. Sharpe, Alexander, Bailey (1999), p. 248ff.
598 Cp. Bruns, Meyer-Bullerdiek (2008), p. 93ff.
599 Cp. Chae, Wang (2009), p. 34.
600 Cp. Steiner, Bruns (2007), p. 77.
601 Cp. Guido, Walsh (2005), p. 31.
602 Cp. Gerke, Arneth, Fleischer (2001), p. 48; Amihud, Mendelson (1986), p. 223ff.
603 Cp. Postert (2007), p. 39ff.
604 Cp. Comerton-Forde, Gallagher, Nahhas, Walter (2010), p. 314.
605 Cp. Aussenegg, Grünbichler (1999), p. 654.

The liquidity of a market or an asset determines the accruing transaction or trading costs[606]. The higher the cost of trading, the minor is the willingness of investors to trade an asset, which again delimitates the liquidity. The stock exchange dealing of securitised assets increases the efficiency fundamentally because the accumulated transaction costs are diminished importantly.[607]

Beside directly imputed liquidisation costs as provisions, commissions or other charges, indirect costs are attributed to a predominant importance.[608] They occur if price premiums or markdowns have to be approved.

A reason for such impacts can be seen in the inadequate market depth. The market is unable to absorb large orders without distortions at the equilibrium price.[609] The arising market impact influences the asset return negatively. As far as block orders[610] are possible to the equilibrium price, perfect liquidity can be insinuated. This is one of the ideal premises of the perfect capital market, assumed by Markowitz.[611]

The following four dimensions of trading liquidity have to be differentiated:[612]

- The market depth describes the impervious averaging of sell (buy) orders directly above (beneath) the lowest (highest) ask (bid) price. An exceeding depth causes absorptions of large orders without veritable price alteration.
- High volumes behind bid and ask prices are entitled as market breadth. This enables the clearing of comprehensive and unlimited orders to the best price.
- The fast adjustment of interim market imbalances by new imputed buy and sell orders delineates the resiliency of a capital market.
- The chronological duration according to the completion of an order by large size and predefined costs describes the time aspect of trading liquidity.

Further indirect costs occur in succession of the bid-ask spread[613] which clarifies the difference between buy and sell prices. [614] The more liquid the market is, the smaller is the resulting difference between these prices. Active portfolio managers[615] contribute more liquidity be-

606 Cp. Jang, Koo, Liu, Loewenstein (2007), p. 2330.
607 Cp. Garz, Günther, Moriabadi (2002), p. 80f.
608 Cp. Poddig, Brinkamm, Seiler (2009), p. 202f.; Lang, Röder (2008), p. 303.
609 Cp. Bruns, Meyer-Bullerdiek (2008), p. 40.
610 Cp. Anderson, Cooper, Prevosi (2006), p. 248.
611 Cp. Schmitz-Esser (2001), p. 119.
612 Cp. Garbade (1982), p. 420ff.; Oesterhelweg, Schiereck (1993), p. 391; Boemle (1998), p. 185; Chen, Wu (2009), p. 73; Qi, Zhao (2008), p. 66.
613 Cp. Riepe, Iachini (2011), p. 32.
614 Cp. Levesque, Libby, Mathieu, Robb (2010), p. 46.
615 Cp. Rompotis (2010), p. 5.

cause they transform new information into capital market orders and provide new supply and demand to the market.[616]

Highly capitalised stocks generally offer exalted liquidity in contrast to small businesses because of their publicity and their contingent index membership.[617] Arnott, Hsu and Moore (2005) as well as Hsu (2006) deduced a clear connectivity between the capitalisation of a stock and its trading liquidity. Cap weighted indices tend to an exalted weighting of liquidly tradable stocks whereby the transaction costs of the index or respectively the replication portfolio decline.[618]

Liquidity is not static but subject to oscillations in dependence of the capital market consistency. Especially during times of crises – in which the sufficient liquidity would be of outstanding importance – it frequently exists only marginally. As liquidity ratios of stocks especially the stock market turnover, the free float, the extent of the bid-ask spread[619], the number of exchanges where the particular security is traded and their availability can be mentioned.[620]

An elementary increase of trading liquidity at the European capital market has been operated by the adoption of the EMU. The transition of cash flows[621] in a homogeneous currency between countries administrated a more efficient allocation of financial resources and a more efficient pricing at the new established, integrated capital market[622] amongst the EMU members.[623]

2.4 Differentiation of Selected Performance Measures

According to the performance measurement even Markowitz (1952)[624] argued, that risk and return have to be opposed, because rational[625] investors just bear additional risk if this is compensated by an adjustment within the offered rate of return.[626] This appreciation has maintained over decades and investors still employ comparative measures like the Sharpe or Sortino ratios within their performance measurement.[627]

616 Cp. Stein (2004), p. 2.
617 Cp. Hsu, Campollo (2006), p. 34.
618 Cp. Arnott, Hsu, Moore (2005), p. 84; Hsu (2006), p. 3.
619 Cp. Riepe, Iachini (2011), p. 32.
620 Cp. Bruns, Meyer-Bullerdiek (2008), p. 40.
621 Cp. Santillan, Bayle, Thygesen (2000), p. 11ff.
622 Cp. Galati, Tsatsaronis (2003), p. 165ff.
623 Cp. Giofré (2008), p. 130.
624 Cp. Markowitz (1952), p. 77ff.
625 Practically investors frequently act irrationally, as detected by the behavioural finance but neglected by the Portfolio Selection Theory; cp. Roßbach (2001), p. 3ff.
626 Cp. Hung, Jan (2005), p. 75; Huang, Liu (2007), p. 2000.
627 Cp. Gemill, Hwang, Salmon (2006), p. 190.

Table 5 illustrates the most frequently regarded performance measures and explains their calculation. It becomes obvious that the exclusive distinctions are constituted in varying measures of risk used in the denominators that may partially even be adjusted to skewness and kurtosis if returns do not follow the Gaussian distribution.

The final allocation will be based on the Sharpe ratio, complemented by the Sortino ratio within the performance evaluation. This consideration is conducted with respect to the reasoning of Heidorn, Hoppe and Kaiser (2006) who mentioned deviating results of several performance measures as marginally and not decisive for the entire investment prosperity.[628]

Especially the use of the Sharpe and approximately the Sortino ratio is performed according to the original mean-variance assumptions of Markowitz, using the excess return of risky assets in comparison to volatility.[629] The consideration of volatility by the Sharpe ratio is even more beneficial for investor's allocation procedures than the limitation by the downside deviation of the Sortino ratio.[630]

No.	Performance measure	Calculation
1	Sharpe ratio	Excess return of an asset compared to a minimum return e.g. equal to the inflation rate or a riskless rate of return, devided by volatility as measure of risk
2	Sortino ratio	Excess return of an asset compared to a minimum return e.g. equal to the inflation rate or a riskless rate of return, devided by the downside deviation as measure of risk
3	Treynor ratio	Excess return of an asset compared to a minimum return e.g. equal to the inflation rate or a riskless rate of return, devided by the beta factor as relative measure of risk
4	Calmar ratio	Excess return of an asset compared to a minimum return e.g. equal to the inflation rate or a riskless rate of return, devided by the maximum drawdown as measure of risk
5	Sterling ratio	Excess return of an asset compared to a minimum return e.g. equal to the inflation rate or a riskless rate of return, devided by the maximum drawdown that is increased by ten percent as disproportionate measure of risk
6	Sharpe ratio for higher third moments	Excess return of an asset compared to a minimum return e.g. equal to the inflation rate or a riskless rate of return, devided by volatility as measure of risk that is adjusted by by the negative skewness
7	Sharpe ratio for higher third and fourth moments	Excess return of an asset compared to a minimum return e.g. equal to the inflation rate or a riskless rate of return, devided by volatility as measure of risk that is adjusted by by the negative skewness and kurtosis

Table 5: Exemplification of selected performance measures[631]

628 Cp. Heidorn, Hoppe, Kaiser (2006), p. 571.
629 Cp. Markowitz (1952), p. 77ff.
630 Cp. Beach (2006), p. 16.
631 Self-provided table in dependence of : Füss, Rehkugler, Disch (2005), p. 45ff.

2.4.1 Declaration of the Sharpe Ratio

One of the most regarded and accepted performance measures is the Sharpe ratio developed in the year 1966 as further deduction of the Portfolio Selection Theory.[632] In later empirical studies it has been documented that maximum Sharpe ratio portfolios are able to advance the investors utility.[633] Hence, portfolio managers are able to categorise assets and asset combinations in dependence of their maximum utility function by measuring the respective Sharpe indices.[634]

In imitation of the Markowitz theory as well as the CAPM Sharpe developed his ratio as a one-period[635] measure without defining the maturity of this investment time.[636] Though investors prefer different intervals to survey the return distribution and rebalancing[637] cycles of their portfolios, the validity of each stated Sharpe result depends on the investment time and the rate of allocation dynamics.[638]

The Sharpe ratio *SR* is also called "reward-to-variability ratio"[639] because in the numerator of formula (27) it becomes obvious that the portfolio's average return is deduced by the risk-free rate of return[640] and the resulting excess return is divided by the portfolio volatility as measure of risk:[641]

$$SR = \frac{\bar{r}_P - r_f}{\sigma_P}. \tag{27}$$

Its simplicity of calculation and interpretation has made the Sharpe ratio become as such as famous because it illustrates the reward per unit of bared risk in a single measure.[642] It is just feasible to compare and rank Sharpe ratios within equal asset classes and not across different categories because returns and volatilities can vary conspicuously.[643]

---

632 Cp. Sharpe (1966), p. 573ff.; Sharpe (1975), p. 29ff.
633 Cp. Christensen, Platen (2007), p. 1340.
634 Cp. Nielsen, Vassalou (2004), p. 103ff.
635 Cp. Lettau, Wachter (2007), p. 55.
636 Cp. Scholz (2006), p. 348; Zhang (2009), p. 1255; Fogler (2008), p. 130.
637 Cp. Willenbrock (2011), p. 43.
638 Cp. Sangbae, In (2005), p. 105f.; Zakamouline, Koekebakker (2009), p. 935.
639 Alexander, Baptista (2003), p. 93.
640 Cp. da Fonseca (2010), p. 728.
641 Cp. Avellaneda, Lee (2010) p. 764; Kelly, Clark (2011), p. 135: Knight, Satchell (2005), p. 87; Sheu, Wei (2011), p. 42.
642 Cp. Israelsen (2004), p. 423; Dempsey (2009), p. 156; Lee, Hsu, Chiang (2010), p. 223.
643 Cp. Israelsen (2001), p. 51.

The Sharpe index can be used ex post by analysing historical security's performance as deviation of decisions for future activities.[644] An ex ante prediction can be conducted by estimating forward risk and return attributes of the underlying assets.[645]

As discussed asset returns frequently are not Gaussian distributed.[646] Several empirical studies have stated the Sharpe ratio as an appropriate performance measure only if the assumption of standardised normally distributed returns holds.[647] Opdyke (2007) analysed return series of investment funds and compared those pair wise. He detected the Sharpe ratio as acceptable classification figure even according to biased return distributions.[648] Following these findings the subsequently evaluated returns of different indices, portfolios and asset classes will be biased by skewness and kurtosis.[649] But regardless the Sharpe ratio[650] will be implemented as decisive performance measure.

2.4.2 Declaration of the Sortino Ratio

The Sortino ratio *Sort* was developed by Sortino and van der Meer (1991)[651] and published again amongst others by Sortino and Price (1994)[652]. Investors frequently do not realise volatility as risk because it comprises positive and negative dispersions from a mean. According to the downside deviation the risk is not interpreted as general discrepancy from a mean or estimated value but as underperformance according to a predetermined trigger.[653]

Within the calculation of the Sortino ratio according to formula (28), the applied volatility, expressing the portfolio risk in the denominator of the Sharpe index, is substituted by the downside deviation *dd*.[654] For this comparative reason Casarin, Lazzarin, Pelizzon and Sartore (2005) described the Sharpe ratio and the index of Sortino as "risk-adjusted measure based on absolute benchmarks"[655].

644 Cp. Pilotte, Sterbenz (2006), p. 149f.
645 Cp. Best, Hodges, Yoder (2007), p. 70; Durand, Jafarpour, Klüppelberg, Maller (2010), p. 91.
646 Cp. Fang, Lai (1997), p. 294; Liow, Chan (2005), p. 164; Lau, Martin (1987), p. 1484ff.
647 Cp. Jobson, Korkie (1981), p. 889ff.; Lo (2002), p. 36; Ziemba (2005), p. 108; Gregoriou (2004), p. 150; Mahdavi (2004), p. 47; Eberlein, Madan (2009), p. 267.
648 Cp. Opdyke (2007), p 308ff.
649 Cp. Van de Locht (2009), p. 1ff.; Eckey, Kosfeld, Türck (2008), p. 92ff.
650 As it becomes visible in table 5, the Sharpe ratio could even be adjusted by higher moments but this doesnot serve for predominant results; cp. Füss, Rehkugler, Disch (2005), p. 45ff.
651 Cp. Sortino, van der Meer (1991), p. 27ff.
652 Cp. Sortino, Price (1994), p. 59ff.
653 Cp. Miller, Leiblein (1996), p. 92ff.
654 Cp. Füss, Rehkugler, Disch (2005), p. 48; Chen, Estes (2010), p. 99.
655 Casarin, Lazzarin, Pelizzon, Sartore (2005), p. 302f.

(28) $$SortR = \frac{\bar{r}_p - r_f}{dd_p}.$$

Assimilable to the meaning of the Sharpe ratio, a high Sortino index is preferable to lower ones; hence assets can be extracted or ranked[656] by the help of this measure.[657] The greater the ratio is, the higher is the return per unit of incurred risk.[658]

Leggio and Lien (2003) explained the different considerations implicated by the Sharpe or Sortino ratio. Based on the behavioural finance[659] they challenged the meaning of volatility according to investor's preferences of excess returns as superior to the average rate of return. Their analysis does not demonstrate a predominance of any ratio, hence financial managers should consider their and their customer's risk linking[660] and agree to one of the mentioned performance measures.[661]

Petersen and Satchell (2002) advocated the use of downside risk and the Sortino ratio as performance measure but have to admit that advocates for each ratio can be found like e.g. the CAPM favours the Sharpe index. Within their analysis of asymmetric returns they initiate further necessary inspections of the downside deviation and related performance measures to maintain an unavoidably indispensable and more profound insight into the particular eligibility.[662]

Chaudhry and Johnson (2008) explained the Sortino measures as slightly lower than any comparable Sharpe ratios if returns are skewed.[663] The following analyses will exhibit skewed return distributions for most analysed asset classes; hence the allocation of a multi asset portfolio will be impaired by the Sharpe ratio.[664] Divergent performance measures remain disregarded because both listed ratios appear as most important and assimilable to the primary calculations by Markowitz using volatility or respectively the variance as indicator of risk[665].

656 Cp. Chaudhry, Johnson (2008), p. 486f.
657 Cp. Moreney, Sweet, Carlson, Wright, Walle (2011), p. 2.
658 Cp. Scherer (2004), p. 6.
659 Cp. Reuse (2011a), p. 51ff.
660 Cp. Campbell (2006), p. 225.
661 Cp. Leggio, Lien (2003), p. 85f.
662 Cp. Pedersen, Satchell (2002), p. 222.
663 Cp. Miller, Leiblein (1996), p. 500.
664 Cp. Fang, Lai (1997), p. 294; Liow, Chan (2005), p. 164; Lau, Martin (1987), p. 1484ff.
665 Cp. Markowtiz (1952), p. 79.

3 Evaluation of the Allocation Framework

The aspect of diversification describes a process that has to be passed as well as a condition that is aspired.[666] During this process, different assets are combined in a portfolio concerning their respective correlations.[667] If the portfolio has passed this instance, the condition of diversification[668] is reached.[669] In general terms the diversification concerns the intention to generate a maximised return by the help of a pretended portion of risk or to achieve a decisive return while minimising risk.[670] The more extensive the volatility is, the higher are the resulting opportunities incorporated by increased risks.[671]

The detection of a diversification strategy is challenging for every investor, affected by informational asymmetries[672] e.g. occurring of agency conflicts[673]. Within the considerations of any portfolio investments a "home bias"[674] is frequently declared because investors suppose to be most conversant with their domestic market.[675] Numerous economical surveys document the superior degree of diversifications for international portfolios.[676] The subsequent investigations are constricted to investments in the EMU respectively allocating selective assets issued within this region or at least calculated in Euro. A further aspect occurs by the distinction of EMU[677] equity index allocations depending on industry or country determinants.[678]

3.1 Information Efficiency

The share deliberates the deviation of property and decision rights of a business. This aspect confers to an ambivalent impression: In dependence of the respective ownership size[679] the shareholder's influence can be irrelevant for actings of the company.[680] The intrinsic decision rights remain exclusively by the management. Especially minority shareholders and their informational rights are subject to the benevolence of managers.[681] This led Hermann Josef Abs

---

666 Subsequently both interpretations are used interchargeably.
667 Cp. Schyra, Rojahn (2010), p. 11f.
668 Cp. Müller-Stewens, Lechner (2001), p. 213ff.; Voigt (1993), p. 114ff.
669 Cp. Wulf (2007), p. 7; Schüle (1992), p. 13f.
670 Cp. Dorenkamp (2002), p. 10ff.; Salter, Weinhold (1978), p. 171.
671 Cp. Döhnert, Kunz, Wälchli (2000), p. 7; Jorion, Goetzmann (2000), p. 22; Wegmann (2001), p. 4.
672 Cp. Liu, Peleg, Subrahmanyam (2010), p. 1222.
673 Cp. Holmes (2007), p. 58; Swedroe (2011), p. 148.
674 Cp. Hau, Rey (2008), p. 333.
675 Cp. Bernhard (2005), p. 1.
676 Cp. Lessard (1974), p. 18ff.; Levis (1999), p. 668ff.; Kang, Stulz (1997), p. 3ff.
677 Cp. Parker (2011), p. 9; STOXX Ltd. [ed.] (2011b).
678 Cp. Furrer, Herger (1999), p. 194ff.; Beckers, Connor, Curds (1996), p. 31ff.; Beckers, Grinold, Rudd; Stefek (1992), p. 75ff.; Heston, Rouwenhorst (1994), p. 3ff.; Rouwenhorst (1999), p. 57ff.
679 Cp. Conyon, Florou (2002), p. 211.
680 Cp. Belkhir (2009), p. 1582ff.
681 Cp. Mura (2007), p. 82.

former spokesman of the Deutsche Bank AG to constitute the shareholder as dumb and cheeky. Dumb because funds are allocated to a company and cheeky due to the demand for a dividend.[682]

This kind of view discharges an incomplete distribution of information between the management and different groups of shareholders. In combination with the resulting stock price movements it is questioned by the market efficiency hypothesis as a central paradigm of the capital market theory.[683] Regularly capital markets are embossed by unequal information and heterogeneous expectations as well as costs of preparation with information.[684] Fama (1970) developed the efficient market hypothesis and created three levels of information efficiency at capital markets whose reciprocal dependency is extractable from figure 9.[685]

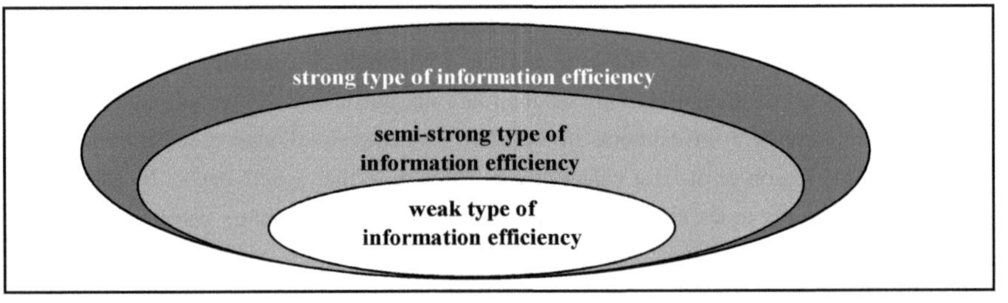

Figure 9: Three stages of information efficiency by Fama[686]

3.1.1 Weak Type of Information Efficiency

All past oriented information is reflected in market prices.[687] The technical security analysis[688], decisive trading strategies or respectively a strategically, quantitative analysis[689] of historical prices is not able to adduce superior returns in comparison to a simple buy and hold[690] strategy. The processing of historically oriented information is not suited to predict future developments and stock prices follow a random walk even biased by calendar anomalies.[691] Investigations of stock exchanges, as sample of complex and profoundly organised markets, have acknowledged this thesis.[692]

682 Cp. Spremann, Gantenbein (2005), p. 161f.; Stein (2004), p. 12.
683 Cp. Malevergne, Sornette (2005), p. 22f.
684 Cp. Jackson (2003), p. 122.
685 Cp. Perridon, Steiner (2004), p. 344ff.; Fama (1970), p. 383; Stock (2002), p. 19ff.
686 Self-provided figure in dependence of: Steiner, Bruns (2007), p. 42.
687 Cp. Witte (2010), p. 1057.
688 Cp. Lai, Chen, Huang (2010), p. 18.
689 Cp. Gregory-Allen, Shawky, Stangl (2009), p. 42.
690 Cp. Ruggiero (2009), p. 42f.
691 Cp. Bohdalová, Greguš (2010), p. 57f.
692 Cp. Garz, Günther, Moriabadi (2006), p. 85; Fama, Blume (1970), p. 55ff.

3.1.2 Semi-Strong Type of Information Efficiency

Besides the information available for investors in shape of the weak characteristic of information efficiency, within the semi-strong type even publicly accessible information[693] is processed in the market prices.[694] A superior return is not procurable by the fundamental analysis[695] of any balance sheets, interim reports, ad hoc disclosures, financial measures or press information. Frequently event studies are used to reveal it.[696]

3.1.3 Strong Type of Information Efficiency

In addition to the information contained in the semi-strong shape of information efficiency, within the supreme level even unpublished news as well as insider[697] information is expected to be converted into security prices.[698] People who receive precocious insight of information that is relevant for the company or the entire market due to their occupational status[699] or their predestined interconnection to economically relevant institutions are constituted as insiders. They have got advanced information[700] that can impact the prospective share price.[701]

Jensen (1978) expanded the strong type of information efficiency by the aspect that investors are unable to achieve systematic excess returns at efficient capital markets. In this specification the theory of information efficiency can be understood as zero profit condition in the equilibrium according to the classical pricing theory at the financial markets.[702] Within informational efficient markets featuring the mentioned criteria, investors would act logically if they apply to the subsequent behaviour:[703]

- New information is analysed immediately and transferred into market orders.
- Every prospective investor shares equal appreciation how information determines the distribution of current and future stock prices.

693 Cp. Mandal, Rao (2010), p. 2.
694 Cp. Fama (1970), p. 383.
695 Cp. Alexakis, Patra, Poshakwale (2010), p. 1321.
696 Cp. Garz, Günther, Moriabadi (2006), p. 84; Alexakis, Patra, Poshakwale (2010), p. 1321.
697 Cp. Brochet (2010), p. 419.
698 Cp. Fama (1970), p. 383; Fama (1991), p. 1576f.; Orgland, Leveau (2008), p. 24.
699 Cp. Cespa (2008), p. 639.
700 Cp. Hodgson, van Praag (2006), 820.
701 Cp. Rühle (1991), p. 198; Schlienkamp, Frei (1997), p. 364.
702 Cp. Bouleau, Thomas (2004), p. 98.
703 Cp. Garbade (1982), p. 238.

At the same time these assumptions imply that market participants are able to abstract any price and dividend relevant information from intuition, noise[704], supposed hints or wrong discretions and react exclusively to appropriate information.[705]

3.1.4 Informational Implications of Capital Markets

The weak level of the information efficiency hypothesis is precisely located within the presumption about rational[706] expectations of market participants. Transactions are frequently subject to noise trading[707]. This explains the foundation of orders, biased by unsecure or speculative specifications. Investors try to achieve an advantage at the expenses of ulterior market actors because irrational[708] information is published.[709]

Within the modern capital markets and considerations of investment decisions a single investor is frequently unable to receive information on his own. Brüggelambert (2004) analysed the institutional information aggregation[710] at the German stock market. He stated that traders are able to achieve gains due to asymmetrically distributed information in the market.[711]

A further critical aspect describes the financial markets as constitutionally inefficient[712] and limitedly able to evaluate the efficiency empirically.[713] The market rather has to be arranged efficiently by active providings of information. Otherwise stock prices would exhibit any information and the incentive of information sourcing[714] loses its value.[715] During the process of expending information, efficiency costs for accessible information appear and have to be paid.[716] If information is symmetrically distributed, risk premiums, price discounts and funding costs can be reduced.[717] Prices never reflect any available information because the sumptuous generation of information enables investors to realise additional gains.[718] The acceptable requirement of gratuitously available information becomes an essential but unrealistic precondition.[719]

---

704 Cp. Cipriani, Guarino (2005), p. 315.
705 Cp. Willman, Fenton-O'Creevy, Nicholson, Soane (2006), p. 1358.
706 Cp. Wang, Xia (2002), p. 5.
707 Cp. Laopodis (2008), p. 273.
708 Cp. Willman, Fenton-O'-Creevy, Nocholson, Soane (2006), p. 1361.
709 Cp. Black (1986), p. 530.
710 Cp. Nöth, Weber (2003), p. 179.
711 Cp. Brüggelambert (2004), p. 767.
712 Cp. Hand (2011), p. 20.
713 Cp. Rayhorn, Hassan, Yu, Janson (2007), p. 22.
714 Cp. Murthy (2010), p. 36.
715 Cp. Zimmermann, Bill, Dubacher (1989), p. 95.
716 Cp. Chun, Xiaujun (2010), p. 402.
717 Cp. Chan, Lo (2011), p. 482.
718 Cp. Martins, Serra (2007), p. 383.
719 Cp. Fama (1991), p. 1575.

Cai, Keasey and Short (2006) demonstrated the impact of corporate governance[720] activities according to the reduction of costs for obtaining information and gaining an increased level of information efficiency in the security market.[721] The Securities and Exchange Commission (SEC) in the USA imposed regulatory guidelines to reduce the information asymmetry between different categories of investors.[722] DeFusco, Mishra and Raghunandan (2010) examined the US stock market during the period from 1999 to 2005 and found out that the SEC regulatory implementations in the year 2000 have actually improved informational efficiency compared to the time before.[723]

Sinha and Watts (2001) described the increased number of financial statements and the regulatory pressure[724] to decrease informational asymmetry but considered that only a minority of published and available information is really forward looking[725] and not historically descriptive. Future outlooks of companies would be positively approved by investors to decrease informational inefficiency.[726]

The formerly mentioned critics according to the information efficiency and the aggregation of autonomous and interactive instances at the market as well as their macro economical behaviour and the respective stimulation of individual profit maximisation directs the consideration towards the Principal-agent theory (PAT).[727]

3.2 Principal-Agent Theory

Asymmetric distributions of returns between two pressure groups based on unequal access to information emboss the contemporary economic life.[728] The PAT is build up on the neoclassical microeconomics[729] and expands it by the aspect, that investors exhibit limited information and constricted scope of action.[730] Varying objective targets of the capital market participants result by these different rights and possibilities as well as the deviant preferences of investors and capital seekers.[731]

720 Cp. Benz, Frey (2007), p. 92ff.
721 Cp. Cai, Keasey, Short (2006), 782.
722 Cp. Hossain, Mitra, Rezaee, Sarath (2011), p. 279ff.
723 Cp. DeFusco, Mishra, Raghunandan (2010), p. 164.
724 Cp. Kozelmann, Wilkinson, Fovargue-Davies, Sankey (2010), p. 929ff.
725 Cp. Dietrich, Kachelmeier, Kleinmuntz, Linsmeier (2001), p. 244.
726 Cp. Sinha, Watts (2001), p. 665ff.
727 Cp. Malevergne, Sornette (2006), p. 23.
728 Cp. Mankiw (2004), p. 517f.
729 Cp. Ekelund, Hébert (2002), p. 197ff.
730 Cp. Camerer (2003), p. 3; Elschen (1991), p. 1002ff.
731 Cp. Itoh (2004), p. 19.

The foundation of the PAT is built up as follows:[732] One party – the principal – delegates a specific mission to a second party – the agent – who should arrange an assignment as defined by the principal.[733] Challenges appear by the individual targets of respective utility maximisation and opportunism[734].

The information asymmetry[735] is subdivided into different aspects frequently appearing chronologically:[736] Initially the unobserved agent's operation is classified as hidden action[737]. Within this shape the agent accomplishes his work not in the principal's interest.[738] Contrariwise hidden characteristics describe any concealed attributes[739]. In this regard the agent features a superior level of knowledge than the principal and misappropriates this advanced information[740].

3.2.1 Principal-Agent Challenges

Before signing a contract the agent is able to peculate selective innate attributes or pretends additional personal features, he does not essentially feature, which are mentioned as hidden characteristics.[741] The principal experiences the real quality of the agent just as recently as the formation of the contract has been executed.[742]

During the validity of the contract the agent is able to transpose the concealed propositions by hidden intentions. Breaking the contract or controlling the agent by the principal is impossible without bearing additional expenditures.[743]

While the contract continues the agent acquires hidden knowledge or information[744] and implements it opportunistically to manipulate his occupation.[745]

Throughout the assignment the agent extracts alternatives to simulate extraordinary expenditures of work, he actually does not accomplish. Addicted to this behavioural pattern, the problematic of moral hazard is affiliated.[746] The agent is able to take advantage of discretionary

732 Cp. Jost (2001), p. 13ff.
733 Cp. Caers, Du Bois, Jegers, De Gieter, Schepers, Pepermans (2006), p. 26.
734 Cp. Gauld (2007), p. 18.
735 Cp. Tsai (2008), p. 242.
736 Cp. Saam (2002), p. 28f.
737 Cp. Cvitanic, Wan, Zhang (2009), p. 100f.
738 Cp. Ding, Jia, Tang (2003), p. 149.
739 Cp. Clark (2009), p. 60.
740 Cp. Iyer, Schwarz, Zenios (2005), p. 108.
741 Cp. Zhang, Stefanos (2008), p. 685ff.
742 Cp. Eisenhardt (1989), p. 57ff.
743 Cp. Goldberg (1976), p. 439ff.; Klein, Crawford, Alchain (1978), p. 3ff.; Spremann (2008), p. 3ff.
744 Cp. Yang, Yeh (2002), p. 17.
745 Cp. Arrow (1985), p. 37ff.
746 Cp. Young, Peng, Ahlstrom, Bruton, Jiang (2008), p. 207.

latitude.[747] This challenge of moral hazard[748] describes the risk of the agent's disproportionate proceedings. It arises if the principal is not capable to supervise the agent sufficiently.[749] The agent performs his task with less effort than preferable for the principal.[750]

3.2.2 Solution Statements of Principal-Agent Challenges

Contractual monitoring[751] can curb the complex of moral hazard[752] problems. The covenant between the contracting parties has to be arranged determining the principal's target and the strategic action of the agent consistently. Finally an eternal risk adjusted motivation[753] of the management has to be mediated.[754] Examples for such monitoring installations exist as specific remuneration frameworks like performance-related donations[755] or the detention of incentives paid subsequently if defined suppositions are achieved.[756]

At the capital market several moral hazard[757] difficulties are revealed if the management pursues deviant goals than the shareholders or investors[758]. Directors operate less venturous than constituted and prefer idiosyncratic concerns as visible in figure 10.[759]

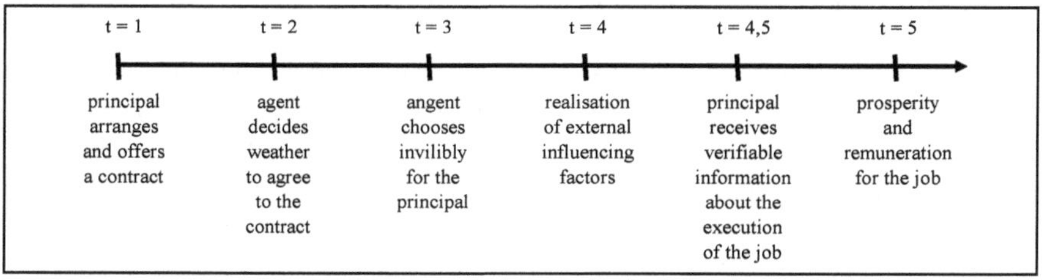

Figure 10: Interaction of principal and agent[760]

747 Cp. Gahn (1994), p. 87.
748 Cp. Parson (2003), p. 451ff.
749 Cp. Nyberg, Fulmer, Carpenter (2010), p. 1030.
750 Cp. Mankiw (2004), p. 517f.
751 Cp. Nygaard, Myrtveit (2000), p. 350.
752 Cp. Robinson, Bingyong (2010), p. 968.
753 Cp. Kocabiyikoglu, Popescu (2007), p. 834ff.
754 Cp. Bruce, Buck, Main (2005), p. 1494.
755 Cp. Murdock (2002), p. 651.
756 Cp. Jost (2001), p. 17f.
757 Cp. McAllister, Hughes, Gallimore (2008), p. 271f.
758 Cp. Conyon (2006), p. 25.
759 Cp. Stein (2001), p. 12ff.
760 Self-provided figure in dependence of: Jost (2001), p. 27.

Agency costs[761] appear by an expanded control of the management.[762] They are composed by the monitoring costs[763] for controlling activities, the bonding costs for accountability and guarantee expenditures in the case of misconducts as well as the residual loss as difference between the best and second-best opportunities.[764]

A preconditioned compatibility of incentives is established via the agency costs.[765] They should impact the operations of the agent to the extent that is anticipated by the principal.[766] This kind of contractual constitution surrenders in the adverse selection[767]. If the agent is merely offered an ordinary treaty, the principal must suspect to receive an agent with just iniquitous attributes.[768] Such an insufficient agent would dissimulate his negative conditions and decorate himself with nonexistent commendations. An applicable agent would dismiss the averaged contracts. Hence, the principal runs the risk of encountering an unqualified agent.[769]

The adverse selection can be resolved by self-selection[770], screening[771] or signalling[772]. Within the self selection the agent is offered diverse contracts[773] by the principal. The diverse risk[774] and profit considerations have to be bared by the agent who in turn signals his readiness to assume risk by choosing a specific contract.[775]

By the cost-intensive screening with assessment centres or expert evidence, the principal can verify the credibility of an agent.[776] Again the agent substantiates his eligibility by presenting references e.g. of previous employments. The success of signalling and screening depends on the charges emerging by the respective procedure.[777]

761 Cp. Ang, Cole, Lin (2000), p. 81.
762 Cp. Cronqvist, Nilsson (2003), p. 696.
763 Cp. Aizenman, Spiegel (2006), p. 690.
764 Cp. Jensen, Meckling (1976), p. 310f.; Meinhövel (1998), p. 42.
765 Cp. Allen, Lueck (1995), p. 448ff.
766 Cp. Boivie, Lange, McDonald, Westphal (2011), p. 552.
767 Cp. Wimmer, Chezum (2006), p. 202.
768 Cp. Abbring, Heckman, Chiappori, Pinquet (2003), p. 513.
769 Cp. Jost (2001), p. 19ff.; Mankiw (2004), p. 519f.
770 Cp. Longhofer, Peters (2005), p. 238.
771 Cp. Banal-Estanol, Heidhues, Nitsche, Seldeslachts (2010), p. 795ff.
772 Cp. Del Brio, de Miguel (2010), p. 482.
773 Cp. Van Long, Sorger (2010), p. 493.
774 Cp. Ollier (2007), p. 2.
775 Cp. Arrow (1989), p. 1183ff.; Hartmann-Wendels (1989), p. 713ff.; Jung, Spremann (1989), p. 94ff.
776 Cp. Jensen, Meckling (1976), p. 1177ff.; Strong, Walker (1987), p. 32; Franke (1987), p. 809ff.
777 Cp. Wolf (1995), p. 64f.

3.2.3 Agency Phenomenons at the Capital Market

The mentioned accomplishments define the division of ownership and depository rights.[778] This measure can be conferred to the relation between the shareholders and the management in a company or the client and his portfolio manager.[779] The respective shareholder or client acts as principal whereas the manager exhibits the agent.[780]

The more influential the principal is, the better are his possibilities of screening the market for suitable agents. Especially institutional investors relish an information advantage opponent to minority shareholders[781] or private clients.[782] Managers frequently notice the concerns of principals but do not perennially act according to their instructions.[783]

Heath (2009) made up a coherency of the agency theory and business ethics[784] due to an irrational and immoral behaviour of profit maximisation. Generally the PAT assumes the denegation of ethical attitudes. Unfortunately real economical life frequently exhibits this conflicted and limited scope of ignoring any moral behaviour.[785]

The entire set of principal-agent problems confers to the conflict of misallocating funds, a principal has delegated to an agent as appearing in the asset management contractual relationship where financial advisors feature different goals than their clients.[786] Ambacher (2005) proposed a diminishment of the management commission to create a positive cash value and increased allocation efficiency between the investor and the respective service provider.[787] A second but infrequently mentioned conflict exists between the advisory company and their hired manager's individual career concerns, determining the degree to assume investment and personal risk.[788]

---

778 Cp. Janakiraman, Radhakrishnan, Tsang (2010), p. 673ff.
779 Cp. Stracca (2006), p. 823.
780 Cp. Seifert, Gonenc (2010), p. 2.
781 Cp. Holmén, Knopf (2004), p. 167f.
782 Cp. Schnatterly, Shaw, Jennings (2008), p. 219ff.
783 Cp. Spremann, Gantenbein (2005), p. 162f.
784 Cp. Festé (2010), p. 534.
785 Cp. Heath (2009), p. 522.
786 Cp. Kuhnen (2009), p. 2185f.
787 Cp. Ambachtsheer (2005), p. 32.
788 Cp. Ferris, Yan (2007), p. 493.

A general requisition of regulatory interference does not concern the entire range of investment vehicles. For example hedge funds are usually nearly unregulated.[789] Hence, internal control mechanisms and due diligence[790] processes have to compensate any appearing mistrust. The complexity of generating external reliability is positively correlated to the degree of financial risk taken by the fund.[791]

The increased importance and rising number of passive investment vehicles tracking a publicly available index can even have resulted from the mentioned uncertainty amongst investors.[792] Economical investigations exhibit that investors do not need to bear the agency-problems occurring by active portfolio management because index investing prevalently outperforms active portfolios and exhibits lower costs.[793] Subsequently different allocation approaches will be explained.

3.3 Consideration of Asset Allocation Approaches

The asset allocation generally combines different types of single assets or superordinated assets classes[794] like equities, real estate, commodities and fixed income securities in a portfolio according to the investor's appraisal[795]. As described by Dolvin, Templeton and Riebe (2010) especially bonds[796] and equities are frequently related to maximum portfolio weights[797], determining the entire risk, investors are willing[798] and able[799] to bear.[800] The proportions[801] of risky and riskless assets as well as money market emphasis[802] are generally determined by investor's requirements[803] e.g. for future cash flows, investment maturity[804] and the expectancy of life.[805]

789 Cp. Cumming, Dai (2010), p. 830.
790 Cp. Cumming, Johan (2008), p. 3.
791 Cp. Cassar, Gerakos (2010), p. 1917f.
792 Cp. Milonas, Rompotis (2010), p. 97.
793 Cp. Holmes (2007), p. 58; Swedroe (2011), p. 148.
794 Cp. Jaggi, Jeanneret, Scholz (2011), p. 134; Kyrychenko (2008), p. 70ff.
795 Cp. Reuse (2011a), p. 14.
796 Cp. Ervin, Faulk, Smolira (2009), p. 315.
797 Cp. Pfau (2010), p. 60.
798 Cp. Jacobsen (2010), p. 52.
799 The accepted comprehension assumes that younger investors can bear higher proportions of risk in comparison to older people but if applicable, risk can be chosen independently from enduring investment maturity; cp. Dow (2009), p. 433.
800 Cp. Dolvin, Templeton, Riebe (2010), p. 60.
801 Cp. Lewis (2009), p. 51f.
802 Cp. Diesinger, Kraft, Seifried (2010), p. 346.
803 Cp. Curtillet, Dieudonné (2007), p. 410.
804 Cp. Gintschel, Scherer (2008), p. 215.
805 Cp. Gerrans, Clark-Murphy, Speelman (2010), p. 302f.

Their implementation into the calculation of an appropriate benchmark[806] can vary between different advisors[807] and investors whereby the common regard of an asset allocation as an individual approach[808] has reached particular attention during the last years.[809]

Amongst others Evensky, Clark and Boscaljon (2010) argued that risk related performance measures, tailed as well as skewed returns and dynamic[810] reallocation processes have to be considered more distinctly. They based their view on several studies that refer to changing paradigms of the asset allocation practice.[811] Amenc, Martellini, Milhau and Ziemann (2010) criticised the general process as inappropriate because the undertaken assumptions of continuous prices and correlation[812] characteristics[813] are practically inexistent.[814] Their review is even expanded by comparing different professional asset management approaches achieving unequal returns.[815] This varying prosperity illustrates the inconsistency and individuality of any existent allocation technique.[816]

Even though capital markets do not follow a constant Gaussian distribution but deviate distinctly form the model assumptions Yu, Yang and Wong (2007) constituted the Sharpe ratio as prospective alternative to (re-)allocate[817] portfolios efficiently.[818] Jacobsen (2010) argued that past performance does not inevitably serve as general rule for predicting future trends but the analysis of historical developments frequently indicates prospective dependencies or return paradigms of asset prices.[819] These findings will be implemented in the later index and portfolio developments.

The general allocation process can be divided into the strategic macro allocation and the tactical micro replenishments which have to be separated mutually.[820]

806 Cp. Grauer (2008), p. 43.
807 E.g. retirement funds reduce the weights of risky assets converging towards the time of going on pension; cp. Pang, Warshawsky (2010), p. 34.
808 Cp. Landsberg (2012), p. 40.
809 Cp. Hsu, Kalesnik, Myers (2010), p. 1.
810 Cp. Gerber, Hens, Woehrmann (2010), p. 370.
811 Cp. Evensky, Clark, Boscaljon (2010), p. 32f.
812 Cp. Basu, Oomen, Stremme (2010), p. 1024.
813 Cp. Sheikh, Qiao (2010), p. 8.
814 Cp. Amenc, Martellini, Milhau, Zimann (2010), p. 100.
815 Cp. Xiong, Ibbotson, Idzorek, Chen (2010), p. 7.
816 Cp. Ibbotson (2010), p. 1.
817 Cp. Brown, Jones (2011), p. 69.
818 Cp. Yu, Yang, Wong (2007), p. 145.
819 Cp. Jacobsen (2010), p. 53.
820 Cp. de Groot, Swinkels (2008), p. 71.

3.3.1 Strategic Asset Allocation

After characterising the customer's individual investment preferences and even fiscal impacts[821] as illustrated in figure 1 the manager has to build an efficient portfolio to create a predefined benchmark[822] that fits the needs best and is allocated by proportions of different asset classes that may be comprised.[823] The strategy is generally monitored continuously but revised after several years, hence the strategic allocation features a long-term maturity.[824] Strategical elements are regularly established by quantitative[825] measures to assess the portfolio proportions based on an historical capital market analysis for the future prevision.[826] As explained by Sharpe (2007) the formerly optimal portfolio relation of risk and return characteristics, according to a specific asset mix, is projected into the future and adjusted by modifying approaches. Hence, this process of "reverse optimisation"[827] assumes the future as assimilable to the past performance.[828]

The allocation strategy of funds is regularly placed as addition in their respective denomination e.g. by items like offensive, balanced or defensive, whereby the risk tolerance and the maximum weighting of risky assets should be outlined. Furthermore the asset class weighting is predefined by the terms as mixed, equity or bond fund and the geographic location[829] of assets is determined by quoting the investment region.[830]

According to Ibbotson and Kaplan (2000) the most important characteristics of a portfolio are imputed by the strategic allocation and the accompanied long-term selection and weighting of asset classes.[831] About 90% of the portfolio performance is related to the strategic orientation.[832] Hence, fundamental portfolio arrangements are much more important than the timing and the choice of single securities.[833]

821 Taxation of assets may be treated unequally; cp. Reichenstein (2007), p. 45.
822 Cp. Amenc, Goltz, Martellini (2011), p. 11; Bogle (2005), p. 114f.
823 Cp. Paolo Natale (2008), p. 374.
824 Cp. Sharpe (1987), p. 27.
825 Cp. Beach (2007), p. 61.
826 Cp. de Groot, Swinkels (2008), p. 71f.
827 Sharpe (2010), p. 45.
828 Cp. Sharpe (2007), p. 18ff.
829 For example every equity index applied in this paper is located in the Eurozone.
830 Cp. Youngjun (2010), p. 347f.
831 Cp. Ibbotson, Kaplan (2000), p. 26ff.
832 Cp. Benson, Gallagher, Teodorowski (2007), p. 571.
833 Cp. Bekkers, Doeswijk, Lam (2009), p. 61.

3.3.2 Tactical Asset Allocation

In terms of Dichtl and Drobetz (2009) the tactical approach of active management is placed beneath the level of a strategic asset allocation and depends on the forecasting abilities of the investment managers[834] and the appearing amount of transaction costs[835], straining the portfolio performance.[836] In addition to the appearing trading cost the portfolio may be predetermined by a maximum (minimum) number (weighting) of comprised assets. Hence, several investment specifications have to be considered.[837] Generally the tactical allocation criteria should serve as perfection of the more comprehensive strategic specifications whereby the success rises (is reduces) by decreasing (increasing) market efficiency because the accessibility of active returns depends on market circumstances.[838]

The active timing[839] of market entry (exit) with buy (sell) orders for single assets is a mayor attitude of the tactical management opportunities.[840] The generally involved problem is that over longer periods most investors are unable to generate an outperformance towards the benchmark because they misjudge future prices and derive wrong investment determinations.[841]

Mallick (2010) combined the strategic allocation as regarded by long-term trends and the tactical short-term management as dynamic[842] reaction to interim capital market shifts. Strategically oriented portfolios can be reallocated systematically to maintain the tactical variability towards uncontinuous[843] return fluctuations.[844] Mallick's interpretation is succeeded by the subsequent (re-)allocation[845] process of a dynamic[846] mean-variance and correlation optimised[847] multi asset[848] portfolio of the EMU, whereby the EMU as investment region is explained in the following sections.

834 Cp. Winchester, Huston, Finke (2011), p. 49.
835 Cp. Martins-da-Rocha, Vailakis (2010), p. 66.
836 Cp. Dichtl, Drobetz (2009), p. 248f.
837 Cp. Gülpinar, Katata, Pachamanova (2011), p. 68.
838 Cp. Blitz, van Vliet (2008), p. 23ff.
839 Cp. Boscaljon, Filbeck, Zhao (2011), p. 37.
840 Cp. Herold, Maurer (2004), p. 39.
841 Cp. Benson, Gallagher, Teodorowski (2007), p. 572.
842 Cp. Switzer, Omelchak (2009), p. 71.
843 Cp. Paolo Natale (2008), p. 375.
844 Cp. Mallick (2010), p. 310.
845 The terms of reallocation and rebalancing are used synonymously; cp. Huang (2010), p. 467.
846 Cp. Basu, Oomen, Stremme (2010), p. 1024.
847 Cp. Boido, Fulci (2010), p. 75.
848 Cp. Lynch, Tan (2010), p. 1016.

3.4 Compendium of EMU Implications

A general summary of financial implications occurring by the EMU, that have to be regarded by Euro based investments, will be explain in the following sections. Due to the rapid changes occurring out of the global financial and economical crisis[849] a few southern European countries suffer from drawbacks of their fiscal deficits and the EMU could potentially be faced by considerable variations of its master conditions.[850] The consequent information will almost exclusively deal with the common initiation of the EMU covenants. The currently fast moving political and selective national challenges[851] originated by growing state indebtedness will be introduced in scattered extracts without fulfilling the claim of integrity and entire timeliness.

3.4.1 Development and Legal Framework of the EMU

In the year 1988 the European Council declared to build an eternal economical, political and monetary union and established a mutual commission – the Delors Committee[852] – of the national central bank presidents of the former European Community (EC), added by further monetary experts to propose an appropriate proceeding to reach this goal.[853] The committee suggested arranging the monetary union within three integrative steps.[854] The legal framework and chronological schedule expired to the Maastricht Treaty leading the EC to the European Union (EU) on February 07th 1992.[855]

The first stage lasted from July 01st 1990 to the end of 1993. In the years 1992/93 the Exchange Rate Mechanism I (ERM I) became evident, abolishing asymmetries between the involved countries moving towards an integrated union.[856] During this time free capital, personal, service and good movements were established.[857] In 1992 the Maastricht Treaty and the Stability and Growth Pact (SGP)[858] as well as the convergence criteria ("Maastricht criteria" [859]) have been developed.[860]

849 Cp. Khademian (2011), p. 841.
850 Cp. Heinen, Böttcher [ed.] (2010), p. 3.
851 Cp. Serfaty (2010), p. 54ff.
852 The Delors Committee was named by the president of the European Commissions and former French Finance Minister Jacques Delors; cp. Verdun (1999), p. 311.
853 Cp. Hodson (2009), p. 508.
854 Cp. Thygesen (1989), p. 638.
855 Cp. Liebscher (2009), p. 377.
856 Cp. Janackova (1998), p. 81.
857 Cp. Altavilla (2004), p. 870.
858 This aspect is described in detail on the following pages according to the ERM II.
859 Greiner, Semmler (2001), p. 271ff.
860 Cp. Hildebrand (1996), p. 50f.

In the second stage of the EMU, during the time from the beginning of 1994 to the end of 1998, the first steps towards a unique currency in combination with budget discipline and a consolidated convergence of fiscal and monetary policies between the EU and the first EMU members were introduced.[861] Nevertheless every member country and its political administration remained responsible for their individual economical policy. These countries abandoned their former individual monetary policy[862] towards collective monetary instruments, directives and goals.[863] The European Monetary Institute (EMI), as precursor of the European Central Bank (ECB), was founded on January 01st 1994 and displaced by the ECB in June 1998.[864]

On January 01st 1999 the EMU has been founded as European currency area with eleven countries that necessarily still remained part of the EU and abdicated their former national currency for the Euro.[865] With Britain, Denmark, Greece and Sweden four EU members did not join the EMU.[866] At the beginning of the year 1999 the third and final stage of the EMU was adopted with the final fixing of any exchange rates between the former member currencies and the integrated Euro[867] which was exclusively imposed as book money[868] at this time.[869]

The entire goal of forming a monetary union was evoking political integration, economical advantages and reducing fiscal costs due to a unique currency within the common market of the member countries.[870] Since the final stage was adopted, the ECB is in charge of the common monetary policy.[871]

The first EMU members were Austria, Belgium, Finland, France, Germany, Ireland, Italy, Luxemburg, the Netherland, Portugal and Spain.[872] With hindsight Greece was the first country joining the EMU at the beginning of 2001 though, meanwhile it has become obvious that Greece[873] did not meet the convergence criteria due to a higher public debt ratio than the maximum permissible 60% according to the gross domestic product (GDP).[874]

861 Cp. Buti, van den Noord (2004), p. 737.
862 Cp. Ozkan, Sibert, Sutherland (2004), p. 638ff.
863 Cp. Bearce (2009), p. 583f.
864 Cp. Pisani-Ferry (2006), p. 825f.
865 Cp. Strobel (2005), p. 1449.
866 Cp. Rodrigues-Fuentes, Dow (2003), p. 970.
867 Cp. Hildebrand (1996), p. 50.
868 Cp. Camaro, Esteve, Tamarit (2000), p. 149f.
869 Cp. Andréani (2001), p. 15.
870 Cp. Jacquet (1998), p. 55f.
871 Cp. Bearce (2009), p. 582.
872 Cp. Van Poeck, Borghijs (2001), p. 1328.
873 As well as Italy and Belgium.
874 Cp. Featherstone (2003), p. 929.

Every country in the EMU and every new state that is willing to accede the EMU and fulfil the third stage of the integration process has to pervade the predefined convergence criteria according to the Maastricht Treaty and a two year lasting admission to the Exchange Rate Mechanism II (ERM II).[875] The ERM II denotes a bonding of the currency development to the Euro without violating a predefined spectrum.[876] Further requirements of the SGP are: (1) a maximum domestic budget deficit of three percent according to the national GDP[877], (2) a debt/GDP ratio of less than 60%, (4) an inflation rate maximally 1,5% above the three member countries with the lowest inflation rates in the EMU, (5) the existence of an independent national central bank and (6) long-term government interest rates exceeding the lowest three member's rates by at least two percent.[878]

These convergence criteria have been converted into European common right by the Amsterdam Treaty signed in October 1997.[879] Hence, it is obvious that since the development of the approaches by the Maastricht Treaty in 1991 about six years elapsed until the legal implementation was accomplished.[880]

The efforts made up by the convergence criteria aimed at consistent economical cycles amongst all EMU members in combination with harmonised budgetary discipline leading to increased economical correlations between the involved industries and countries.[881] Altavilla (2004) acknowledged the rising extent of statistical dependence among the EMU members and a parallel shifted economic cyclic appearing out of the equal monetary policy and fiscal discipline.[882] Containing systematic risks and interdependencies, nor countries, neither the community is liable for any member's debt[883] because of the so called "no-bail-out-clause"[884].

This convention should prevent that countries, executing pressure on partner countries or the ECB bearing any national public debt for instance by the purchase of governmental bonds. [885]

During the years 2002 and subsequently amongst others countries like France and Germany violated the convergence criteria written in the SGP.[886] A simplification of the excessive deficit procedures is visualised in appendix 1. Thereupon the deficit rules had to be readjusted be-

875 Cp. Yeh (2007), p. 81.
876 Cp. Rostowski (2003), p. 994; Egert, Kierzenkowski, Reininger (2005), p. 82.
877 Cp. Trotignon (2005), p. 4.
878 Cp. Rollo, (2006) p. 106; Balassone, Franco, Rizza (2009), p. 231.
879 Cp. Svendrup (2002), p. 121.
880 Cp. Camaro, Esteve, Tamarit (2000), p. 149f.
881 Cp. Hardouvelis, Malliaropulos, Priestley (2006), p. 366.
882 Cp. Altavilla (2004), p. 894.
883 Cp. Article 125 of the Treaty on the Functioning of the European Union.
884 Greeley, Czuczka, Cullen, Frye (2011), p. 11.
885 Cp. Mayer (2011), p. 2
886 Cp. Donnelly (2004), p. 176.

cause otherwise these countries would have been faced by fiscal treatments supervised by the Economic and Financial Affairs Council (ECOFIN)[887], provoking a further enhancement of destabilisation.[888] The sanctions accompany treatments of fiscal deficits and the violation of the SGP with the exaltation of bank deposits, which can be reconverted into retribution payments if the respective country does not keep to the guidelines.[889]

On November 23rd 2003 the ECOFIN agreed to interrupt the excessive deficit procedures against Germany and France and casted the EMU and the convergence criteria into doubt.[890] The original SGP[891] was maintained but adapted by crediting country specific facts, suspending the excessive deficit procedures and accounting for homogeneous combinations of fiscal and monetary policies if countries miss the budget deficit.[892] A comparison of the original and the reconditioned weak measurements of the SGP is visible in appendix 2.[893] Jonung, Larch and Fischer (2008) argued that these macerations of the stability criteria constituted an unmanageable bias towards public debt overload and long-term fiscal instability that can again provoke the risk skip to partner countries.[894] Generally a conflict appears between a severe interpretation of the SGP, effecting economical problems during times of downturns or an informal view, evoking behavioural disadvantages due to exploitations and moral hazard.[895] Within the subsequent explanations, the practical matters of exactly these delineated market aberrations caused by moral hazard[896] will be illustrated.

Slovenia entered the EMU in January 2007[897] as 13th member. One year later Malta, Slovakia and Cyprus replenished the monetary union. So far Estonia was the 17th and last assimilated country at the beginning of the year 2011.[898]

Before introducing the EMU many sceptics argued the union would be instable because of differing single economical developments, countries would miss the convergence criteria and a failure of the entire process could interfere the EU.[899] In contrast to these contradicting views at the beginning of the 21st century, King Abdullah of Saudi Arabia advocated the model made up by the EMU as possible ideal for the Gulf Cooperation Council (GCC) to in-

887 Cp. Nieto, Penalosa (2004), p. 228.
888 Cp. Cini (2001), p. 194.
889 Cp. Hodson, Maher (2004), p. 799ff.
890 Cp. Leblond (2006), p. 969f.
891 According to Fourans and Warin (2007) the added flexibility made up an SGP II that replaced the primary specifications; cp. Fourcans, Warin (2007), p. 52.
892 Cp. Van Aarle, Di Bartolomeo, Engwerda, Plasmans (2004), p. 2.
893 Cp. Becker (2005), p. 1f.
894 Cp. Jonung, Larch, Fischer (2008), p. 541f.
895 Cp. Fingland, Bailey (2008), p. 230.
896 Cp. Young, Peng, Ahlstrom, Bruton, Jiang (2008), p. 1030.
897 Cp. Dunn (2008), p. 86.
898 Cp. European Commission [ed.] (2011), p. 23.
899 Cp. Sutherland (1997), p. 9.

tegrate a unique currency.[900] Following Yeh (2007) these considerations and the building of the EMU are opposed by two harassments like speculative attacks[901] occurring out of an optimum currency areas[902] and destabilising divisions of monetary and fiscal policies.[903] Hence, one solution to the appearing challenges is mentioned as a combined fiscal institution, harmonising the currency and fiscal policy within the union and provoking integral and even external reliability.[904]

3.4.2 Introduction of the Euro

Since January 01st 1999 the Euro[905] exists as joint book money in the EMU.[906] The instrument of cash payments was introduced on January 01st 2002.[907] One entire goal was to establish trade and investment flows in a common currency without exchange rate deviations[908], intended as global counterbalance to the US dollar.[909]

A further aspect concerns the financial and security trading market integration[910] for instance by a collectvve financial industry throughout the consolidated monetary union and the supraregional capital market institutions.[911]

Beetsma and Giuliodori (2010) mentioned the Euro has instrument, evoking financial[912] and product market deregulation of the member countries in the EMU. Consequentially the occurring challenges[913] make reforms of these markets necessary but their enforcement will be very provocative. The financial market distortions[914] are even changing the willingness of countris to join the union and influence the institutional structure of the EMU.[915] Hence, the membership in the union depends on cost (dis-)advantages appearing out of the participation and the consistency of the Euro.[916]

900 Cp. Rutledge (2008), p. 124.
901 Cp. Cornand, Heinemann (2009), p. 73ff.
902 For further information concerning optimum currency areas, like exemplary free mobility of capital and labor; cp. Tavlas (2009), p. 536ff.
903 Cp. Matthes (2009), p. 114.
904 Cp. Yeh (2007), p. 81ff.
905 For further information according to the introduction of the Euro as common medium of exchange in the EMU as well as the establishment of country specific Euro coins and bills by the choice of individual imprintings; cp. ECB [ed.] (2007).
906 Cp. Deroose, Hodson, Kuhlmann (2007), p. 800.
907 Cp. Ranyard (2007), p. 314.
908 Cp. Stavárek (2010), p. 82ff.
909 Cp. Bieling (2006), p. 420f.
910 Cp. Berbena, Jansen (2009), p. 3067.
911 Cp. Weber, Posner (2001), p. 140f.
912 Cp. Kumbhakar, Lozano-Vivas (2004), p. 507.
913 Cp. Yeh (2007), p. 81ff.
914 Cp. Serfaty (2010), p. 54ff.
915 Cp. Beetsma, Giuliodori (2010), p. 636f.
916 Cp. Garcia-Solanes, Maria-Dolores (2008), p. 655.

3.4.3 The European Central Bank

By integration of the EMU the ECB became the collective central bank as supranational institution and leading institution of the European System of Central Banks (ESCB)[917] for the execution of a common monetary policy in all EMU member countries and taking place at the centre of the Euro system.[918]

The ECB headquarter is situated in Frankfurt/Main (Germany) and the responsibilities refer to the Executive Board (EB) where the president, the vice president and the political leaders of the member countries take place. Further there is the Governing Council (GC), complying six persons from the EB, added by the governors of the national central banks as members of the ESCB.[919]

Every member country receives voting rights with respect to its participation in the GC and the EB, coordinating the ECB interest rates e.g. the ECB Main Refinancing Rate[920] which is illustrated in figure 11.[921]

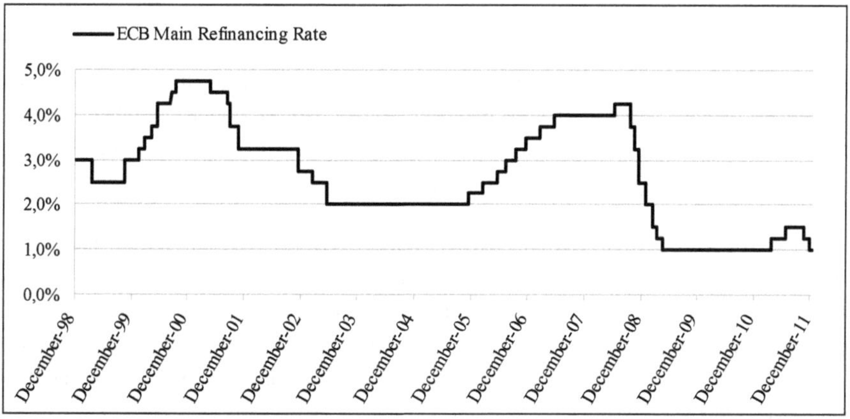

Figure 11: Development of the ECB Main Refinancing Rate[922]

The central banks major goal is to keep the price stability at about two percent within the EMU as the Bundesbank executed it in Germany prior to the formation of the monetary un-

917 Cp. Liebscher (2009), p. 382.
918 Cp. Bearce (2009), p. 582.
919 Cp. ECB [ed.] (2007) p. 36.
920 The ECB determines the common main refinancing rate as key interest rate for the EMU by the main refinancing operations; cp. Jansen, de Haan (2009), p. 1995ff.; Abbassi, Nautz (2008), p. 1ff.
921 Cp. Rostowski (2003), p. 1005.
922 Self-provided figure with reference to: Bloomberg [ed.] (2011a).

ion.[923] The development of the overall EMU inflation rate is illustrated in figure 12 with the help of a comparison towards the Harmonised Index of Consumer Prices (HICP) [924] and the target inflation rate of two percent per year.[925]

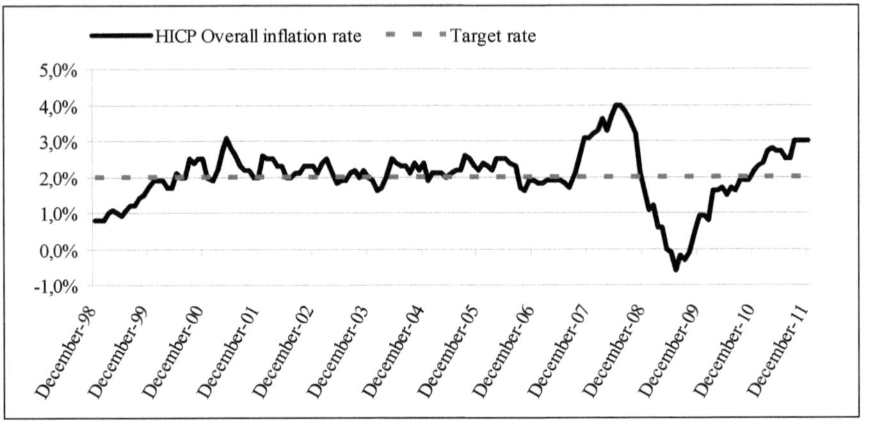

Figure 12: EMU overall inflation rate vs. inflation target[926]

Despite an average over the period from January 1998 to December 2011 of 1,95% is accommodated with the target rate but the maximum of four percent in June and July of the year 2008 are exactly twice as much as aimed. Hence, by its interest rate fixing, the ECB is not able to react to fast changes in the market inflation rate. [927]

According to former central bank policies of member countries like France, Italy and further southern European participants, it was obvious that their proceedings and economic circumstances differed conspicuously for example from Germany and its national bank policies.[928] Since the integration of a unique monetary policy, adopted by the GC and its segmented voting rights amongst the member countries in combination with the convergence criteria, they had to accommodate a consolidated approach.[929]

The common monetary policy is in line with the practice of one common and inflexible exchange rate which may provoke instability due to structural deficits or inconsistent national

923 Cp. Donnelly (2004), p. 59ff.
924 Cp. Astrin (1999), p. 123f.
925 Cp. Wynne, Rodriguez-Palenzuela (2004), p. 80f.
926 Self-provided figure in dependence of: ECB [ed.] (2011).
927 Cp. Cecchetti, Wynne (2003), p. 426f.
928 Cp. Cohen (2003), p. 575ff.
929 Cp. Dunn (2008), p. 86f.

developments between the central members of the EMU and its peripherals.[930] The neoliberal political independence of the ECB describes its autonomous monetary approach from national government decisions.[931]

Tsoukalis (2005) referred to the political independence of the ECB and stated that a profound and permanently intact integration of the member countries is only enforceable by a reconciliation of the ECB and centralised EMU politics.[932] Hodson (2009) argued that the EMU is no political union because national politicians still remain accountable for their individual and regional economic decisions, what can be interpreted as main contribution for an increasing removal from the aimed efficiency of a monetary and political union. A revision of the Lisbon Treaty is needed if an association of these differing views should be harmonised.[933] Strobel (2005) described the considerations of member country's politicians, leaving the EMU due to increasing impacts by the joint monetary policy, an inflation pressure and the interdependence with other members as real option whose price depends on the economical costs of leaving and operating independently or a subsequent re-entrance into the union.[934]

The recently increasing fiscal deficits in southern European countries are a succession of the financial market crisis[935] accompanied with negative GDP growth rates and the impossibility to depreciate their currencies in comparison to the Euro. These aspects provoke increasing systematic risk factors for every member country and the common union due to mutual dependencies.[936] Even before the inclusion of Greece it was foreseeable that politicians would be faced by important implications and challenges due to the EMU membership and the convergence criteria.[937]

In the meantime it has become obvious that Hellenic's financial figures never coincided with the SGP requirements although plenty of reforms have been accomplished. During the last years – at least since 1996, public debt ratios exceeded 100% of their respective GDP.[938] These kinds of excessive public debt ratios, even among some southern European countries,

---

930 Rodriguez-Fuentes and Dow (2003) described a distinction of central and peripheral regions in dependence of the respective income related to the GDP and the influences of economical shocks established by themonetary policy. They introduced an enhanced classification into: (1) most influenceable countries due to their monetary policy: Finland, Ireland and Spain; (2) countries susceptible to a lower extent: France, Italy and the Netherlands; (3) countries strongly related to the EMU averaged reaction: Austria, Belgium, Portugal, Germany and Luxemburg; cp. Rodriguez-Fuentes, Dow (2003), p. 976ff.

931 Cp. Verdun (2000), p. 5f.

932 Cp. Tsoukalis (2005), p. 159.

933 Cp. Hodson (2009), p. 522.

934 Cp. Strobel (2005), p. 1452.

935 Cp. Cortez, Ke (2010), p. 28.

936 Cp. Mayer (2006), p. 1.

937 Cp. Featherstone (2003), p. 930ff.

938 Cp. Becker (2005), p. 1f.

could enhance the political pressure on the ECB to lower interest rates[939] and decrease the state indebtedness by inflation – which is conflictive to the SGP and could risk the international confidence in the Euro and the EMU.[940]

Advertisements have appeared that e.g. Greece could drop out of the EMU and EU to remigrate to the drachma.[941] The subsequently arising problem is caused by additional costs for rising interest rates due to a further increased dept/GDP ratio and the present national debt dominated in Euro as foreign currency appreciating conspicuously against the drachma.[942] Though up to December 2011, no country has left the monetary union, the single country risks and their individual credit spreads[943] become visible within the developments of the elected 10 year governmental bond rates of Germany and Greece illustrated by figure 13.[944]

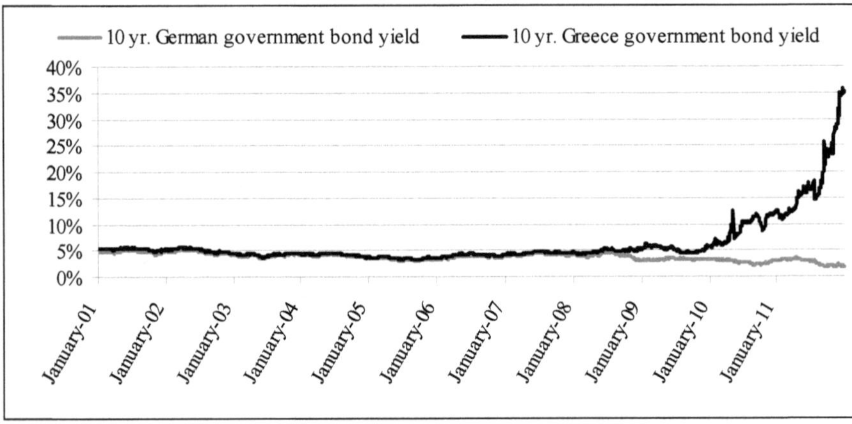

Figure 13: Comparison of 10 yr. German and Greek government bond yields[945]

The yield of Greece has maximally increased to 35,78% in comparison to the contemporaneous 1,93% paid by Germany at the equal date in December 2011. It is obvious that both countries had to pay comparable rates up to the beginning of the global financial crisis[946]. Since

939 On November 09th 2011, December 14th 2011 and July 11th 2012 the ECB lowered its Main Refinancing rate three times by respectively 25 bps to 0,75%; cp. ECB [ed.] (2012).

940 Cp. Heinen, Böttcher [ed.] (2009), p. 3.

941 Cp. Schwarzer (2007), p. 3.

942 Cp. Matthes (2009), p. 127.

943 Describing the risk adjusted yield between e.g. AAA-rated bonds and a competitive bond issued by an institution with an inferior financial reliability; cp. Kercheval, Goldberg, Breger (2003), p. 90.

944 Cp. Gärtner, Griesbach, Jung (2011), p. 298.

945 Self-provided figure in dependence of: Bloomberg [ed.] (2011aw); ibid. [ed.] (2011ax).

946 In July 2007 the global financial crisis developed as Subprime Crisis due to collapsing asset backed security portfolios and the US real estate market; cp. Tropeano (2011), p. 45; Lander, Barker, Zabelina, Williams (2009), p. 1ff.

this time Greece had to accomplish a permanently increasing premium as risk adjustment[947] in relation to the German AAA-rated[948] bonds with the same maturity. The rising costs of debt exacerbated the entire market based refinancing conditions up to their failure in the year 2010.[949]

Heinen (2011) is concerned with transfer payments originally obviated by EU and EMU regulations[950] to preclude moral hazard.[951] These vertical and horizontal payments to finance debt of southern European countries like Greece by direct or indirect payments of other countries, the ECB, the European Stabilisation Mechanism (ESM)[952], the European Financial Stability Facility (EFSF)[953] or the International Monetary Fund (IMF)[954] appear by recovery measures to avoid national insolvency because such events would provoke much higher financial burden for any remaining EMU member.[955] Ultimately these proceedings erode the pristine prevention of moral hazard[956] by widening the agreed conditionality for instance in the case of Greece, incorporated by joint and several liabilities of the payer countries and institutions.[957] Heinen concludes with a critical view to the stability criteria and consequently arising persistent and controversial challenges for EMU politicians, members and institutions.[958]

These explanations are evocative to the instability of the EMU accomplished by Sadeh (2009) during the time up to the conducted assimilations of the SGP due to violations by France and Germany.[959] The current issues are as such as problematic that economists have no advice how to proceed or to give confident advice, because it is impossible to calculate the financial consequences.

Finally the topic of the present evaluation is not the analysis of how to deal with exceeding public debt, but the challenges should have be commented to constitute the political, fiscal and economical asymmetries, the subsequent elaborations are aimed at.[960]

---

947 The rating agencies (1) S&P, (2) Moody's and (3) Fitch evaluate Greece as non-investment grade debtor-due to the described economical challenges and increasing public debt with ratings of (1) CCC, (2) C and (3) CCC; date: August 15th 2012; cp. Bloomberg [ed.] (2011dm).

948 German credit ratings: S&P AAA, Moody's Aaa, Fitch AAA; cp. Bloomberg [ed.] (2011dl).

949 Cp. Fildes (2010), p. 6; Colomer (2011), p. 10ff.

950 Cp. Article 125 of the Treaty on the Functioning of the European Union.

951 Cp. Bruce, Buck, Main (2005), p. 1494.

952 Cp. German Bundestag [ed.] (2011), p. 1f.

953 Cp. Heinen, Theiss (2011), p. 2ff.; Speyer (2011), p. 2f.

954 Cp. Risk (2010), p. 33ff.

955 Though a real test, which alternative is more expensive, will never be possible; cp. Schotter (2011), p. 3ff.

956 Cp. Robinson, Bingyong (2010), p. 968.

957 Cp. Mayer (2011), p. 2.

958 Cp. Heinen, Theiss (2011), p. 8ff.

959 Cp. Sadeh (2009), p. 560f.

960 Cp. Enderlein, Verdun (2009), p. 499.

3.4.4 Comparison of EMU Members versus STOXX Eurozone

In contrast to the composition of the EMU the STOXX Ltd. refers to the Eurozone as investment region with the Euro as common currency.[961] They define the area by the following twelve countries: Austria, Belgium, Finland, France, Germany, Greece, Ireland, Italy, Luxembourg, the Netherlands, Portugal and Spain.[962] Within table 6 a comparison of the STOXX Eurozone and the EMU membership is conducted.

EMU member countries	STOXX Eurozone membership
Austria	+
Belgium	+
Estonia	-
Finland	+
France	+
Germany	+
Greece	+
Ireland	+
Italy	+
Luxemburg	+
Malta	-
Netherlands	+
Portugal	+
Slovakia	-
Slovenia	-
Spain	+
Cyprus	-

Table 6: Comparison of EMU and STOXX Eurozone membership[963]

Puttonen and Seppä (2006) compared different types of European equity indices calculated by the index providers STOXX Ltd. and Morgan Stanley Capital International (MSCI) during the time from 2000 to 2005. They identified distinct dependencies of the analysed indices which are illustrated by correlation coefficients between 0,95 and 0,99. Hence, they concluded that the type of indexing and the selection universe as well as the selection process[964] do not reasonably influence the return attributes for investors.[965]

Parker (2011) expanded this analysis to indices, measured by the STOXX Ltd., Russell Indexes (RUBIX), Financial Times Stock Exchange (FTSE) and MSCI during the period form 2006 to 2010. He likewise determined a distinct similarity of index movements and returns. His calculated correlations vary between 0,950 and 0,997 but in his résumé he relegated an

961 Cp. Parker (2011), p. 9.
962 Cp. STOXX Ltd. [ed.] (2011b).
963 Self-provided table in dependence of: STOXX Ltd. [ed.] (2011d); Giannellis, Papadopoulos (2011), p. 39ff.
964 Cp. Arnott, Kuo (2011), p. 37ff.
965 Cp. Puttonen, Seppä (2006), p. 428.

investment advantage for indices comprising a great collectivism of single stocks. Hence, benchmark indices without constraints of the imbedded number of members are beneficial for investors.[966]

Following the findings by Puttonen and Seppä (2006) as well as Parker (2011), the subsequent explanations and portfolio allocations are constrained to the interpretation of the EMU following the STOXX Ltd. This serves to demonstrate the evidence of the Portfolio Selection Theory even within a unique and regionally limited allocation universe.

3.5 EMU Country versus Industry Allocation

Since the integration of the EMU and the Euro as common currency within the monetary union, investment conditions have changed conspicuously. The consequent impacts on the portfolio allocation approaches have been analysed in frequent investigations and a general summary is scheduled within the subsequent explanations.[967] After this review of the current state of research, an independent analysis is accomplished where equally weighted portfolios, composed by country and industry indices, are compared. The entire section serves as test of *(H2)*, where the null hypothesis of *(H2)* means a rejection of industry allocations being more feasible for the equity management of the Eurozone than conducting a country allocation.

3.5.1 Current State of Research Concerning Equity Allocations

Prior to the adoption of the EMU Heckman, Narayanan and Patel (1998) detected a positive connection of a company's market cap[968] and the diversification procedure. During 1989 to 1998 they identified the country allocation as more important for small cap portfolios and the industry factors as more crucial for large caps.[969]

The effect of diversification[970] in the Eurozone has decreased since the development of an integral currency and the accompanied increasing country correlations[971] due to interrelated dependencies.[972] Aspects of globalisation[973] and a universal liberalisation of the financial markets as well as industrial concentrations administrate a global intensification of the world trade and the turnover of capital.[974] The EMU and the attached strong interdependence of the

966 Cp. Parker (2011), p. 9f.
967 Cp. Berbena, Jansen (2009), p. 3067.
968 The (free float) market cap, serving as proxy for company size, is calculated by multiplying the number of (outstanding) shares with the current stock price; cp. Nawrocki, Carter (2010), p. 2856.
969 Cp. Heckman, Narayanan, Patel (1999), p. 29f.
970 Cp. Ferreira, Gama (2005), p. 196ff.
971 Cp. Phylaktis, Xia (2006), p. 647.
972 Cp. Yoshida, Carlos Leitao, Faustino (2009), p. 352.
973 Cp. Bekaert, Hodrick, Zhang (2009), p. 2593.
974 Cp. Gorman (1998), p. 32.

single economies account for a faster modification of correlations between the member countries. The Credit Suisse (2000) attested a faster accession of averaged correlations across the Eurozone than abroad. By tendency regional economic cycles were discovered discharging the global industry cycles.[975] During the considered time form 1990 to 1999 they established a good geographical diversification potential of industries, while the country allocation would feature exacting capabilities of improvement. Within a further analysis expected returns and correlations for countries and industries have been estimated. The results indicated diversified country portfolios as considerably more risky than industry allocations.[976]

Additional attributers of industry allocations in comparison to country specific portfolios are Phylaktis and Xia (2006) who accomplished an index based analysis from 1992 to 2001. They emphasised the outstanding industry effects for Europe in comparison to other areas due to the enhanced market integration[977]. They concluded that the significance of the industry and country impacts change with alterations of general market conditions[978] over time.[979]

Within a further evaluation Huber and Rieger (2004) deviated between integrated and segmented capital markets[980]. Within integrated markets as the EMU, investors have boundless access to the international security markets without administrative or fiscal barriers[981]. They detected the country (industry) allocation as less important (predominant) in integrated markets. Resmini (2007) constituted the overwhelming industry effects by possibilities of decentralisation and liberalisation illustrated by foreign investments and productions as well as international trade within open or integrated international areas.[982]

Nevertheless the country allocation does not remain irrelevant. For example service industries of the utility, bank or telecommunication businesses are subject to locally conditioned regulations.[983] Besides the monetary policy of the ECB, e.g. the SGP frames the national fiscal approaches.[984] Huge companies as Siemens or Daimler are less subject to their primary domestic market.[985] The elimination of interest rate differentials and foreign exchange rates by the Euro decreased the costs of capital[986].

---

975 Cp. Hargis, Jianping (2006), p. 320.
976 Cp. Döhnert, Kunz, Wälchi (2000), p. 15ff.
977 Cp. Berbena, Jansen (2009), p. 3067.
978 Cp. Kenjegalieva, Simper, Weyman-Jones (2009), p. 1532f.
979 Cp. Phylaktis, Xia (2006), p. 647.
980 For additional information according to the general distinctions of integrated and segmented markets even beyond the capital market implications; cp. Hansen, Nielsen (2010), p. 229ff.
981 Cp. Mardas, Nikas (2008), p. 356.
982 Cp. Resmini (2007), p. 760.
983 Cp. Gorman (1998), p. 72.
984 Cp. Ehling, Ramos, ECB [ed.] (2005), p. 7.
985 Cp. Freimann (1998), p. 32.
986 Cp. Bertomeu, Beyer, Dye (2011), p. 858.

Hence, further approximations of company returns from different member economies have arisen.[987] The survey leads to the result of widened industry effects in account of country matters. The industry diversification is recognised as more efficient. Prospectively a rising synchronicities of the global equity markets are predicted, further advocating the industry allocation.[988]

Moermann (2004) examined the time during 1995 and 2002 providing a major meaning of the industry than the country effects in the Eurozone. Thereby country, industry and mixed indices were compared. The most attractive investment strategy was arranged by the combination of industries and countries.[989]A study published by Ehling and Ramos (2005) acknowledged this conclusion. Their investigations generally challenged former studies favouring the industry allocations as impacted by any bear market trends[990] at the European stock markets.[991]

Urwyler and Homberger (2001) attributed industry allocations as more important than country diversifications. Their results go along with Cavaglia, Brightman and Aked (2000).[992] They further extinguished an outperformance of the active portfolio management, focussed on industries in contrast to country allocating managers.[993]

The listed results indicate a general restructuring of the European financial markets by the adoption of the EMU. Consequently the second largest stock market of the world was founded, dispositive to the number of listed companies and their common market cap. Several industries have consolidated and could develop to an expanded investment foundation. The former home bias[994] was assumed as developing to a new and regionally broader EMU bias[995].

Many researchers favour the industry instead of comparative country allocations but their results frequently depend on respectively predominant capital market circumstances and a consistent opinion is inexistent.[996]

The determination of the ECI will be based on the foundations of the following investigation, which enlarge the current status of research by a novel empirical analysis.

---

987 Cp. Darnell, Maramot, Vaughn (1998), p. 19; Coldiron, Kroner (1999), p. 39.
988 Cp. Huber, Rieger (2004), p. 25f.
989 Cp. Moerman (2004), p. 23f.
990 Cp. Roth (2009), p. 77.
991 Cp. Ehling, Ramos, ECB [ed.] (2005), p. 31.
992 Cp. Cavaglia, Brightman, Aked (2000), p. 41ff.
993 Cp. Urwyler, Homberger (2001), p. 23f.
994 Cp. Balli, Basher, Ozer-Balli (2010), p. 347ff.
995 Cp. Islam, DB Research [ed.] (1998), p. 1 ff.; Balli, Basher, Ozer-Balli (2010), p. 347ff.
996 Cp. Menchero, Morozov (2011), p. 58.

3.5.2 Implemented EMU Country Selection

According to the Eurozone defined by the STOXX Ltd. the twelve blue chip[997] country indices listed in table 7 are incorporated into the subsequent analysis.[998] The selected indices serve as representative barometers of the economical developments within the respective country.[999] They comprise 418 stocks and are calculated as price indices except for the German DAX[1000]. Following Chye, Meng, Gupta and Ramakrishna (2000) blue chip indices or respective portfolios are regarded as risk minimising equity investment opportunities[1001] or benchmarks for large scale companies.[1002]

No.	Index	Country	Symbol	Index Type	Members
1	Austrian Traded Index	Austria	ATX	Price	20
2	Belgiun 20 Index	Belgium	BEL20	Price	19
3	OMX Helsinki 25	Finnland	HEX25	Price	25
4	Cotation Assistée en Continu 40 Index	France	CAC	Price	40
5	Deutscher Aktien Index	Germany	DAX	Net Return	30
6	Athens Stock Exchange General Index	Greece	ASE	Price	40
7	Irish Stock Exchange Overall Index	Ireland	ISEQ	Price	51
8	FTSE MIB Index	Italy	FTSEMIB	Price	40
9	Luxembourg Stock Exchange LuxX Index	Luxembourg	LUXXX	Price	12
10	AEX-Index	Netherlands	AEX	Price	26
11	Portuguese Stock Index 20	Portugal	PSI20	Price	20
12	Iberia Index	Spain	IBEX	Price	35

Table 7: Data set of Eurozone country indices[1003]

The correlation matrix[1004] in table 8, illustrating monthly log-returns during the ten year period from January 01st 2001 to December 31st 2010, shows correlation coefficients between 0,42 (HEX vs. LUXX) and 0,94 (CAC vs. AEX) and an average of 0,65.

With reference to the former explanations according to table 1 the dependencies are predominantly located in the ranges of mean or strong interrelation.

997 Blue chip indices constitue the biggest listed companies with respect to their (free float) market cap of theentire market displaying the economical development of these most important operations; cp. Farzard (2006), p. 66f.

998 Cp. STOXX Ltd. [ed.] (2011b).

999 Cp. Cloyd, Siegel, Schoenfelder (2004), p. 65f.; Barbosa (2009), p. 37.

1000 The denotations of net return and performance index are used interchargeably.

1001 Cp. Bailey (1994), p. 20f.

1002 Cp. Chye, Meng, Gupta, Ramakrishna (2000), p. 19f.

1003 Self-provided table in dependence of: Bloomberg [ed.] (2011q) to ibid. (2011ab).

1004 Cp. Specht, Gohout (2009), p. 18.

	ATX	BEL20	HEX	CAC	DAX	ASE	ISEQ	FTSEMIB	LUXXX	AEX	PSI20	IBEX
ATX	1	0,64	0,51	0,64	0,57	0,54	0,62	0,65	0,54	0,62	0,63	0,65
BEL20		1	0,63	0,86	0,77	0,53	0,66	0,80	0,57	0,87	0,66	0,78
HEX			1	0,75	0,68	0,45	0,53	0,70	0,42	0,73	0,56	0,68
CAC				1	0,89	0,53	0,66	0,91	0,54	0,94	0,69	0,88
DAX					1	0,48	0,57	0,83	0,46	0,86	0,61	0,79
ASE						1	0,49	0,54	0,46	0,52	0,56	0,54
ISEQ							1	0,63	0,54	0,65	0,58	0,63
FTSEMIB								1	0,55	0,87	0,69	0,86
LUXXX									1	0,55	0,50	0,51
AEX										1	0,66	0,83
PSI20											1	0,73
IBEX												1

Table 8: Correlation matrix of Eurozone country indices[1005]

3.5.3 Implemented EMU Industry Selection

The STOXX Ltd. calculates five total market indices (TMI) for the Eurozone which are listed in table 9. Each index is computed as price and net return index, in Euro and US dollar.[1006] Subsequently the net return indices denominated in Euro are incorporated because they are practically more conventional.

No.	Index	Industry	Symbol	Index Type	Members*
1	EURO STOXX TMI Basic Materials	Basic Materials	TBSCT	Net Return	46
2	EURO STOXX TMI Consumer Goods	Consumer Goods	T3000T	Net Return	72
3	EURO STOXX TMI Consumer Services	Consumer Services	T5000T	Net Return	75
4	EURO STOXX TMI Financials	Financials	TFINT	Net Return	129
5	EURO STOXX TMI Industrials	Industrials	TIDUT	Net Return	147

Table 9: Data set of Eurozone TMI industry indices[1007]

The five benchmark indices combine 386 companies but are not limited to this quantity. If prospectively companies are added to (deleted from) an industry, they will be allocated in (discharged from) the respective index and the population is expanded (reduced), hence the indices serve as variable component benchmarks.[1008]

The correlations of the Euro STOXX TMI industry indices, shown in table 10 exhibit even higher values than the country indices. The lowest coefficient of the entire period is 0,70 comparing "Basic Materials"[1009] with "Consumer Goods"[1010] and "Consumer Goods" with

1005 Self-provided table in dependence of: Bloomberg [ed.] (2011e) to ibid. (2011p).
1006 Cp. STOXX Ltd. [ed.] (2011c).
1007 Self-provided table in dependence of: Bloomberg [ed.] (2011ac) to ibid. (2011al).
1008 Cp. Krein (2010), p. 20; Costa, Jakob (2010), p. 95.
1009 Dow Jones Euro STOXX TMI Basic Materials.
1010 Dow Jones Euro STOXX TMI Consumer Goods.

"Financials"[1011]. The average of 0,79 exceeds the average coefficient of 0,65 comparing the country indices conspicuously. Only the maximum correlation of the industries is marginally lower than the highest value, computed by the countries.[1012]

	EURO STOXX TMI Basic Materials	EURO STOXX TMI Consumer Goods	EURO STOXX TMI Consumer Services	EURO STOXX TMI Financials	EURO STOXX TMI Industrials
DJ EURO STOXX TMI Basic Materials	1	0,70	0,78	0,81	0,87
DJ EURO STOXX TMI Consumer Goods		1	0,77	0,70	0,73
DJ EURO STOXX TMI Consumer Services			1	0,84	0,84
DJ EURO STOXX TMI Financials				1	0,87
DJ EURO STOXX TMI Industrials					1

Table 10: Correlation matrix of Eurozone TMI industry indices[1013]

The TMI industry indices compose members of the respective Industry Classification Benchmark (ICB) Code[1014], independently of their market cap.[1015] Hence, opponent to the country specific blue chip indices, here any cap bias is avoided.[1016] Following Vermorken (2011) the choice of using the Global Industry Classification System (GICS) or the ICB industry relations does not allow to evaluate a superior allocation technique.[1017] Hence, the ICB Codes adopted by the STOXX Ltd. are maintained in the following analysis.

Each industry can be split into different supersectors again. One example for this subdivision is the DJ Euro STOXX TMI Financials, which is superordinated to the DJ Euro STOXX TMI supersectors (1) "financial services"[1018], (2) "insurance"[1019] and (3) "banks"[1020].

They can be adduced as representative example why the analysis refers to the TMI industry indices for the Eurozone in contrast to the supersectors.

1011 Dow Jones Euro STOXX TMI Financials.

1012 The DJ Euro STOXX TMI Industry indices Financials and Basic Materials display a correlation of 0,87. The highest coefficient of the country indices is 0,94, determined by the CAC and the AEX.

1013 Self-provided table in dependence of: Bloomberg [ed.] (2011am) to ibid. (2011av).

1014 Companies are allocated to one of 10 industries and 19 supersectors. Within the Eurozone only the mentioned five TMI industry indices are calculated by the STOXX Ltd.

1015 Cp. STOXX Ltd. [ed.] (2011i).

1016 Portfolios allocated with respect to market cap are inherently biased towards large caps. Within indexing Techniques, frequently a differentiation of small-, medium- and large-sized companies is accomplished. These capitalisation constraints are avoided by the use of TMI indices.

1017 Cp. Vermorken (2011), p. 43f.

1018 DJ Euro STOXX TMI Financial Services net return in Euro; cp. STOXX Ltd. [ed.] (2011g).

1019 DJ Euro STOXX TMI Insurance net return in Euro; cp. STOXX Ltd. [ed.] (2011g).

1020 DJ Euro STOXX TMI Banks net return in Euro; cp. STOXX Ltd. [ed.] (2011h).

As illustrated in figure 14 the rolling annual correlations among the three supersector indices almost exclusively exceed a factor of 0,5. Hence, the industry specific dependencies and interrelations, for example caused by an eternal regulation[1021], are also reflected in the price developments from January 01st 2001 to December 31st 2010.

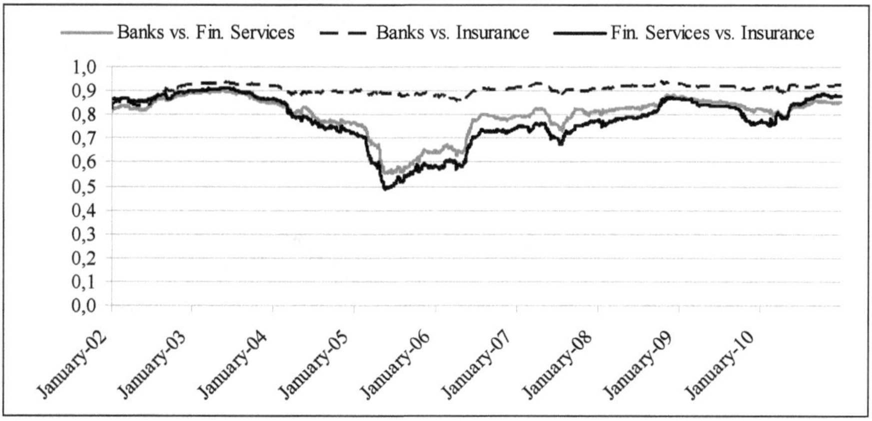

Figure 14: Rolling annual correlation of DJ Euro STOXX supersector indices[1022]

The average, minimum and maximum correlations among the supersectors are calculated and shown in table 11, emphasising the dominant interdependence and constituting the reference towards the expanded macro view of industries. The average correlations between the supersectors constantly display strong interrelations and even the minimum values between the indices insurance and financial services only temporary drop into the degree of mean interrelation.

average correlation	**Banks**	**Financial Services**	**Insurance**
Banks	1	0,83	0,89
Financial Services		1	0,83
Insurance			1

minimum/ maximum correlation	**Banks**	**Financial Services**	**Insurance**
Banks	1	0,55 0,90	0,82 0,94
Financial Services		1	0,49 0,91
Insurance			1

Table 11: Correlation matrixes of selected DJ Euro STOXX supersector indices[1023]

1021 Cp. Begg (2009), p. 1107.
1022 Self-provided figure in dependence of: Bloomberg [ed.] (2011ba) to ibid. (2011bc).
1023 Self-provided table in dependence of: Bloomberg [ed.] (2011ba) to ibid. (2011bc).

3.5.4 Development of an EMU Equity Allocation Approach

Two equally weighted portfolios[1024] are calculated, each with a base value of 100[1025] on January 01st 2001 and continuously computed until December 31st 2010 without any interim rebalancing[1026]. Each component of the country portfolio (industry portfolio) receives a weighting of one twelfth[1027] (one fifth[1028]). The portfolio developments are illustrated in figure 15, which serves to visualise a standardised comparison, that will be analysed within the following section.

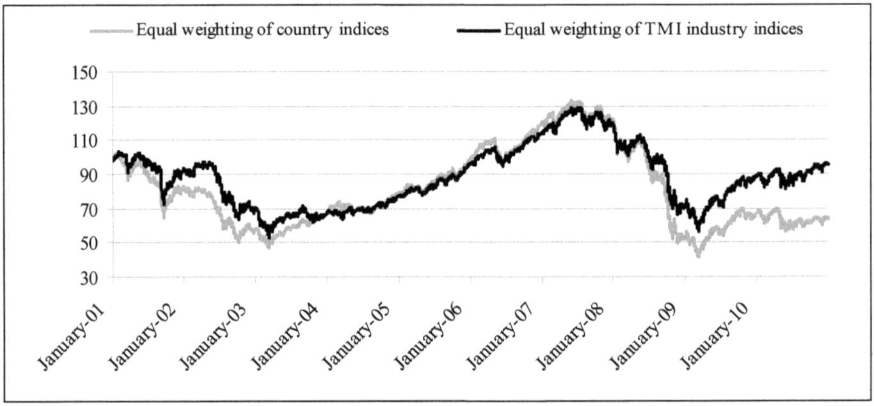

Figure 15: Standardised charts of the country and industry portfolio[1029]

According to the allocation procedures, both portfolios succeed a naive diversification[1030] as one of the simplest allocation approaches without respecting any fundamentals or economies of scale.[1031] According to this, the entire portfolio is divided into *n* portions of equal sizes and each is invested into one target asset, hence every security receives the weighting of *1/n*. This approach is practically only possible for a limited number of assets because in comparison to the assumptions of the CAPM, assets are not optionally separable.[1032]

1024 Cp. Bali, Cakici (2008), p. 31ff.
1025 Base values of indices are commonly assumed by 100 or 1000 index points, whereat the number simply serves as initial value for prospective calculations.
1026 The portfolios are not readjusted within the ten year lasting period of investigation.
1027 100% is devided by the number of twelve country indices, corresponding with approximately 8,33%.
1028 100% is devided by the number of five Euro STOXX TMI industry indices, corresponding with 20%.
1029 Self-provided figure in dependence of: Bloomberg [ed.] (2011e) to ibid. (2011al).
1030 Cp. Phillils, Cathcart, Teale (2007), p. 348.
1031 Cp. Benartzi, Thaler (2001), p. 79f.
1032 Cp. Hedesström, Svedsäter, Gärling (2009), p 405.

3.5.5 Analysis of the EMU Equity Allocation Approach

The conducted performance calculation and analysis is based on monthly log-returns[1033]. During the ten year lasting period[1034], the industry portfolio exhibits a loss of 5,05 index points[1035] in comparison to this, the country portfolio suffers a loss of 36,23 points[1036]. Due to the base value of 100, equal to 100%, these losses appear with 5,05% and 36,23%. Hence, it becomes obvious that a Eurozone equity driven buy and hold strategy[1037] has not become profitable over the last decade, though this is no prediction for future developments.[1038] The common opinion that stocks perform well in the long run, shapes up as precious misbelieve.[1039]

annual log-return	country portfolio	industry portfolio
2001	-18,01%	-6,85%
2002	-35,39%	-27,91%
2003	18,51%	0,18%
2004	16,96%	15,67%
2005	22,33%	21,63%
2006	20,44%	18,39%
2007	4,09%	6,44%
2008	-77,00%	-48,41%
2009	25,53%	24,26%
2010	-2,34%	8,41%
sum	-24,86%	11,80%
average	-2,49%	1,18%
max	25,53%	24,26%
min	-77,00%	-48,41%

Table 12: Annual log-returns of the country and industry portfolio[1040]

The annual log-returns, represented in table 12, show the superiority of the industry portfolio by an exceeding sum and average of returns. The most crucial annual loss[1041] of -48,41% is even conspicuously lower than the -77% of the country portfolio, though a loss of nearly half of the invested amount during one calendar year can not be regarded as essential prosperity.

The annual volatilities as most common measure of risk[1042], shown in table 13, are even lower in terms of the industry portfolio than the ratios of the country portfolio.

1033 Cp. Kerling (1998), p. 30ff.
1034 The investigation lasts from January 01st 2001 to December 31st 2010.
1035 The tart value is 100 points compared to the end value of 95,95 points.
1036 Again the start value is 100 points and the index's end value is at 63,77 points.
1037 Cp. Majumdar, Bouchaud (2008), p. 759f.
1038 Cp. Solow (2009), p. 64.
1039 Cp. Gannon, Blum (2006), p. 35.
1040 Self-provided table in dependence of: Bloomberg [ed.] (2011e) to ibid. (2011al).
1041 Representing a loss, with respect to the legal year, in contrast to the maximum drawdown for periods of less than a year, as represented in table 15.
1042 Cp. Yoon, Byun (2012), p. 59ff.

annual volatility	country portfolio	industry portfolio
2001	21,48%	19,22%
2002	25,60%	23,39%
2003	16,47%	19,29%
2004	9,42%	8,58%
2005	10,37%	10,78%
2006	10,65%	7,28%
2007	9,84%	8,58%
2008	28,38%	21,21%
2009	24,10%	21,15%
2010	18,62%	13,50%
average	17,49%	15,30%
max	28,38%	23,39%
min	9,42%	7,28%

Table 13: Annual volatilities of the country and industry portfolios[1043]

Exclusively during the year 2003 the return deviation of the industry allocation is disadvantageous but the average, maximum and minimum values provoke the positive discrimination of the industries even insofar as the superior return attributes of table 12 are aggregated to the evaluation.[1044] This takes place within the calculation of the Sharpe ratio as performance reference[1045] listed in table 14.

Sharpe ratio	country portfolio	industry portfolio
2001	-1,04	-0,58
2002	-1,51	-1,34
2003	0,98	-0,11
2004	1,58	1,58
2005	1,95	1,81
2006	1,65	2,13
2007	0,02	0,30
2008	-2,85	-2,47
2009	1,03	1,11
2010	-0,15	0,59
average	0,17	0,30
max	1,95	2,13
min	-2,85	-2,47

Table 14: Sharpe ratios of the country and industry portfolios[1046]

The Sharpe ratio, as comparison of the portfolio's excess return, superior to the riskless return, divided by the respective volatility, is the most commonly used performance meas-

1043 Self-provided table in dependence of: Bloomberg [ed.] (2011e) to ibid. (2011al).
1044 Cp. Shum, Tang (2010), p. 16.
1045 Cp. Mamoghli, Dabousi (2009), p. 101.
1046 Self-provided table in dependence of: Bloomberg [ed.] (2011e) to ibid. (2011al).

ure.[1047] Within the accomplished calculation the EONIA serves as proxy of the riskless rate of return for Eurozone money market investments.[1048]

Since the asset, presuming the highest Sharpe ratio, clarifies the best performance attributes, a categorisation is possible.[1049] The scheduled negative results appear by negative annual returns or lower values than the comparable EONIA of the respective period.[1050] Consequently to Scholz (2007) negative Sharpe ratios of single assets do not admit conclusions for meaningful evaluations of any investment decisions.[1051]

Regarding this facet a more profound consideration of single years is necessary, which reveals the predominance of the industry allocation. Seven of ten Sharpe ratios of the industry portfolio as well as their average exceed the measures of the country portfolio. Exclusively during the years 2003 and 2010 changes of singns appear amongst the different portfolios.

maximum drawdown	country portfolio	industry portfolio
high	133,06	129,00
date of high	01.06.07	16.07.07
following low	41,64	56,88
date of following low	09.03.09	09.03.09
Max DD (entire period)	68,71%	55,91%
Max DD 2001	36,76%	29,89%
Max DD 2002	39,10%	35,01%
Max DD 2003	4,69%	13,17%
Max DD 2004	9,26%	8,12%
Max DD 2005	5,84%	5,21%
Max DD 2006	20,28%	17,10%
Max DD 2007	12,48%	10,70%
Max DD 2008	59,46%	44,89%
Max DD 2009	26,47%	23,79%
Max DD 2010	18,42%	11,98%
average	23,28%	19,99%
max	59,46%	44,89%
min	4,69%	5,21%

Table 15: Maximum drawdowns of the country and industry portfolios[1052]

1047 Cp. Best, Hodges, Yoder (2007), p. 70.
1048 Cp. Zwick (2003), p. 19.
1049 Cp. McLeod, van Vuuren (2004), p. 15ff.
1050 The volatility, accounted in the denominator of the fraction, is inherently positive, hence the prefix of the entire ratio depends on the extension of the numerator where the annual portfolio's log-return is reduced by the contemporaneous EONIA.
1051 Cp. Scholz (2007), p. 356.
1052 Self-provided table in dependence of: Bloomberg [ed.] (2011e) to ibid. (2011al).

The maximum drawdowns that are shown in table 15 exhibit a loss appearing after reaching an interim highest price up to the following lowest level.[1053] These maximum losses of 55,91% (industry portfolio) and 68,71% (country portfolio) over the entire period, constitute extraordinary stress tests for every investor within the process of risk management[1054]. After these deficits frequently many positive years are required to compensate the negative impacts appearing in 21[1055] (22)[1056] months.[1057] Almost every calculated annual, average and aggregate maximum drawdown of the country portfolio is inferior to the industry allocation.[1058]

Additionally to the volatility and the maximum drawdowns, the downside deviation is calculated in table 16 as separation of negative return deviations[1059]. It becomes obvious that the industry portfolio is likewise as advantageous over the entire period with an average downside deviation of 10,33% in comparison to 12,00% and maximum annual values of 19,63% opponent to 25,89%.

downside deviation	country portfolio	industry portfolio
2001	13,47%	13,89%
2002	18,61%	19,62%
2003	2,87%	10,12%
2004	3,29%	3,55%
2005	4,88%	6,54%
2006	15,21%	9,98%
2007	5,90%	6,06%
2008	25,89%	17,83%
2009	15,50%	10,87%
2010	14,41%	4,86%
average	12,00%	10,33%
max	25,89%	19,62%
min	2,87%	3,55%

Table 16: Downside deviations of the country and industry portfolios[1060]

Besides the Sharpe ratio further performance measures can be implemented to interpret risk/return characteristics of asset price developments. Instead of various, the Sortino ratio is adopted to appraise the portfolio comparison by the disposal of excess returns[1061] in relation to the downside deviations. Table 17 shows the annual Sortino ratios.

1053 Cp. Pereira, Vaz de Melo Mendes (2005), p. 84.
1054 Cp. Vareman, Persson (2010), p. 687ff.
1055 Appearing during June 01st 2007 and March 09th 2009 by the country portfolio.
1056 Appearing during July 16th 2007 and March 09th 2009 by the industry portfolio.
1057 Cp. Pospisil, Vecer (2010), p. 626f.
1058 The only exception occurs during the year 2003.
1059 Cp. Miller, Leilein (1996), p. 92.
1060 Self-provided table in dependence of: Bloomberg [ed.] (2011e) to ibid. (2011al).
1061 According to the previous calculation of the Sharpe ratio, the excess return is calculated as annual portfolio return, compared to the EONIA.

Sortino ratio	country portfolio	industry portfolio
2001	-1,66	-0,81
2002	-2,08	-1,59
2003	5,63	-0,22
2004	4,53	3,82
2005	4,14	2,98
2006	1,16	1,56
2007	0,03	0,42
2008	-3,13	-2,94
2009	1,60	2,16
2010	-0,19	1,64
average	1,00	0,70
max	5,63	3,82
min	-3,13	-2,94

Table 17: Sortino ratios of the country and industry portfolios[1062]

An assimilable compilation to the Sharpe ratio is carried out whereby the Sortino ratios show differing outcomes. Here the country portfolio is marginally favourable to the industry allocation because the country portfolio displays higher measures.

As equity returns[1063] frequently do not follow the Gaussian distribution[1064], the analysis of skewness and kurtosis are completed by a Jarque-Bera test.

skewness	country portfolio	industry portfolio
2001	-0,37	-0,73
2002	-0,24	-0,64
2003	0,25	0,50
2004	-0,36	0,49
2005	-0,87	-0,84
2006	-1,72	-2,02
2007	-0,37	-0,54
2008	-0,52	-0,49
2009	-0,46	-0,13
2010	0,18	0,24
average	-0,46	-0,38

Table 18: Skewness of the country and industry portfolios[1065]

Investors generally prefer return distributions skewed to the right[1066] – exhibiting higher probabilities of positive returns – combined with thin tails[1067] which illustrate mean likeliness of

1062 Self-provided table in dependence of: Bloomberg [ed.] (2011e) to ibid. (2011al).
1063 Cp. Haas (2009), p. 1277; Baixauli, Alvarez (2006), p. 26.
1064 Cp. Xu, Song (2008), p. 570.
1065 Self-provided table in dependence of: Bloomberg [ed.] (2011e) to ibid. (2011al).
1066 Cp. Bergh, van Rensburg (2007), p. 104.
1067 Cp. Brigham, Kiesel (2002), p. 241.

extreme values.[1068] With the exception of five annual periods, the returns are skewed to the left as listed in table 18 and exhibit potential extreme negative spikes which are accommodated to the previous illustrations of returns and maximum drawdowns.

kurtosis	country portfolio	industry portfolio
2001	2,72	4,00
2002	2,69	2,70
2003	2,69	3,99
2004	1,77	3,35
2005	2,00	3,15
2006	6,90	7,73
2007	2,13	2,85
2008	2,32	1,60
2009	3,38	3,12
2010	1,70	1,46
average	2,86	3,41

Table 19: Kurtosis of the country and industry portfolios[1069]

The kurtosis coefficients shown in table 19 display the unlikely "fat tails"[1070]. The industry portfolio even tends conspicuously towards the leptokurtic[1071] return distribution and is consequently adversely assessed in comparison to the country portfolio.

Jarque-Bera test	country portfolio	industry portfolio
2001	0,31	1,58
2002	0,16	0,88
2003	0,17	0,99
2004	1,02	0,54
2005	2,01	1,41
2006	13,52	19,36
2007	0,64	0,59
2008	0,77	1,46
2009	0,50	0,04
2010	0,91	1,29
entire period	2,00	2,81

Table 20: Jarque-Bera test results for the country and industry portfolios[1072]

Concluding the distribution analysis of the available returns, the Jarque-Bera test for normality is occurred and the particular findings are listed in table 20.[1073] The results spell out that according to both portfolio return series, the assumption for normal distribution has to be re-

1068 Cp. Rojahn, Röhl, Frère (2010), p. 13.
1069 Self-provided table in dependence of: Bloomberg [ed.] (2011e) to ibid. (2011al).
1070 Cp. Focardi, Fabozzi (2003), p. 5.
1071 Cp. Yang (2008), 738f.
1072 Self-provided table in dependence of: Bloomberg [ed.] (2011e) to ibid. (2011al); the calculation complies for chi-values with two degrees of freedom and a confidence inverval of 95% exhibiting p-values of 5,991.
1073 Cp. Yazici, Yolacan (2007), p. 175f.

fused especially during the year 2006 where extreme results are calculated. Though, the negative attributes of return distributions are not as distinct as apprehendable due to the research listed before.[1074]

3.5.6 Conclusion for EMU Equity Allocations

In contrast to most previous investigations accomplished by various researchers the conducted analysis does not deal with one index or even single stocks but with naively diversified portfolios, consisting of industry and country indices irrespectively of any cap bias[1075] which establishes an enhancement of the current status of research. The appraisals clarify the predominance of selecting equity portfolios within the EMU in dependence of industry affiliations opponent to country allocations over different spaces of time[1076] and capital market circumstances[1077].

Advocates of the country selection may critically challenge the analysis due to the elected time series of ten years from January 01st 2001 to December 31st 2010, because during differing periods the results may perhaps adopt variant implications.[1078]

Within this space of time, plenty of capital market impacts like the attacks of the USA on September 11th 2001[1079], the proximate war on Iraq[1080] and the recent global financial crisis[1081] had to be converted. Hence, sufficient challenging capital market impacts are comprised as proof of this concept.

Concluding from the previous argumentation, the null hypothesis of *(H2)* has to be rejected because within the Eurozone the industry allocation is more feasible to diversify an equity portfolio in contrast to a country allocation approach. Hence, the subsequent ECI is allocated by the Euro STOXX TMI industry indices. For a validity of the reproval to the above mentioned results its analysis and execution within a multi asset portfolio will be accomplished for the identical temporal distance.

1074 Cp. Thadewald, Büning (2007), p. 88.
1075 Cp. Heckman, Narayanan, Patel (1999), p. 29f.
1076 Cp. Phylaktis, Xia (2006), p. 647.
1077 Cp. Menchero, Morozov (2011), p. 58.
1078 Cp. Ehling, Ramos, ECB [ed.] (2005), p. 31.
1079 Cp. Richman, Santos, Barkoulas (2005), p. 947ff.
1080 Cp. Beinart (2003), p. 6.
1081 Cp. Rojahn, Schyra (2010), p. 123.

4 Multi Asset Portfolio Construction within the EMU

4.1 Constraints of Selected Asset Classes

The entire investment universe of the following calculations is limited to four asset classes, in particular commodities, equities, German governmental bonds and cash. The former two are categorised as risky assets in contrast to German governmental bonds and cash, assessed as quasi riskless. Every subsequent allocation appears on the level of a strategical assortment by indices, hence an individual security selections according to the tactical asset allocation is precluded.

4.1.1 Cash

Equally to the integration of the Euro as bank money, since the beginning of the year 1999[1082], the EONIA serves as riskless investment opportunity or measure for the Sharpe and Sortino ratios according to calculate excess returns of assets.[1083] It is assessed as interbank money market interest rate for Euro determined over night transactions of international, EU and EMU panel banks[1084] by the European Banking Federation (EBF).[1085]

Within the subsequent analysis the EONIA investment alternative is made up as index of its daily calculated fixings. The progressional development of the interest rate is illustrated in figure 16.

The chart conveys that the interbank refinancing[1086] rate is not constant but deviates, conditioned by economical trends and general degrees of market interest rates[1087]. The dimension of the EONIA depends on the reciprocal confidence of the bank counterparts, whereby its peak during the Subprime Crisis[1088] can be explained by characteristics of the challenging interbank confidence and the market liquidity.[1089]

1082 Cp. Schröder (2003), p. 15.
1083 Cp. da Fonseca (2010), p. 728.
1084 The panel banks are listed on the EBF-website: www.euribor-ebf.eu/euribor-org/panel-banks.html.
1085 Cp. EBF [ed.] (2011).
1086 Cp. Ahlswede (2011), p. 2.
1087 Cp. Hooper, Mayer, Spencer, Slok (2011), p. 6.
1088 Cp. Hau, Thum (2009), p. 701ff.
1089 Cp. Becker (2007), p. 13.

Hence, the accomplished EMU money market interest rate is not fictitious but serves as practically perceived, most liquid and secure refinancing rate[1090] for the pricing of fixed income business deals.[1091]

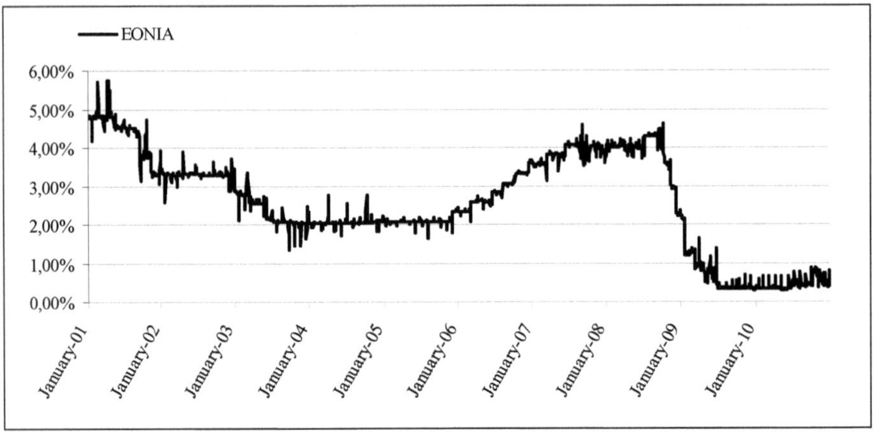

Figure 16: Daily EONIA fixings[1092]

4.1.2 German Governmental Bonds

As replication of the investment segment of quasi riskless governmental bonds, it has to be referred to an issuer with a robust AAA rating[1093] of the agencies Moody's, Standard & Poor's (S&P) and Fitch in the Eurozone, which has become challenging during times of financial market distortions and generally rising state indebtedness.[1094] Table 21 illustrates the different long-term sovereign ratings of the 17 EMU member countries per August 15th 2012.

The sample compassed the negative instances of Greece, with its non investment grade ratings (Moody's: C; S&P: CCC; Fitch: CCC), Portugal (Ba3; BB-; BB+), Ireland (Ba1; BBB+; A-) and Cyprus (Ba3; BB; BB-) up to the A, AA and AAA-rated debtors. It bekomes evident that EMU governmental bonds can not be systematically regarded as limited by risk and explicit distinctions have to be arranged by sorting the capable issuer for the above mentioned challenge.

1090 Cp. Hörth (1988), p. 1.
1091 Cp. Walter (2005), p. 7.
1092 Self-provided figure in dependence of: Bloomberg [ed.] (2011bd).
1093 Cp. Topp, Perl (2010), p. 47.
1094 Cp. Heinen, Böttcher [ed.] (2009), p. 3.

The objective of the prevailing asset class is to illustrate an investment opportunity that features comparatively mean loss risk. Hence, as second common approach of risk measurement, besides the volatility, the long-term credit rating is consulted to measure the degree of credit risk according to a respective bond issuer.[1095]

Country	Long-term governmental bond ratings		
	Moody's (outlook)	S&P (outlook)	Fitch (outlook)
Austria	Aaa (-)	AA+ (-)	AAA
Belgium	Aa3(-)	AA (-)	AA (-)
Cyprus	Ba3 (-)	BB (-)	BB- (-)
Estonia	A1	AA- (-)	A+
Finland	Aaa	AAA (-)	AAA
France	Aaa (-)	AA- (-)	AAA (-)
Germany	Aaa (-)	AAA	AAA
Greece	C	CCC (-)	CCC
Ireland	Ba1 (-)	BBB+ (-)	BBB+ (-)
Italy	Baa2 (-)	BBB+ (-)	A- (-)
Luxembourg	Aaa (-)	AAA (-)	AAA
Malta	A2 (-)	A- (-)	A+
Netherlands	Aaa (-)	AAA (-)	AAA
Portugal	Ba3 (-)	BB (-)	BB+ (-)
Slovakia	A2 (-)	A	A+
Slovenia	Baa2 (-)	A (-)	A- (-)
Spain	Baa3	BBB+ (-)	BBB (-)

Table 21: Long-term EMU sovereign ratings per 15th August 2012[1096]

The choice of Germany as most riskless issuer in the EMU is in accord with the findings by Afonso, Furceri and Gomes (2011), mentioning that even AAA-rated bonds, issued by countries, feature positive credit spreads[1097] in comparison to German governmental bonds with a maturity[1098] of ten years.[1099] Countries like Austria, France, Finland and Luxembourg exhibited similar ratings but they are frequently compared to German bonds even due to their disproportionate level of liquidity in contrast to different sovereign issues. Common to this aspect *ceteris paribus* an inferior credit rating provokes higher costs of (debt) capital.[1100] This clarifies the general evaluation of international or EMU sovereign bond yields, commonly appearing by confrontations with the German yield curves as proxy of riskless issuances.[1101]

1095 Cp. Weißbach, Tschiersch, Lawrenz (2009), p. 576.
1096 Self-provided table in dependence of: Bloomberg [ed.] (2012df) to ibid. (2012dv).
1097 Exhibiting a risk premium in comparison to the German governmental bond yield.
1098 Cp. Georgiev (2007), p. 615.
1099 Cp. Afonso, Furceri, Gomes (2011), p. 10ff.
1100 Cp. Herzog, Koziol, Thabe (2008), p. 237.
1101 Cp. Dietze, Entrop, Wilkens (2009), p. 196.

As every comprised asset class within the subsequent investigations is embodied by an index, the REXP[1102] is chosen as criterion for the exemplary development of retaining interest bearing investments into 30 German governmental bonds with maturities from one to ten years.[1103] The index portfolio comprehends bonds with interest rates of 6%, 7,5% and 9% that are mathematically not taxed and serially calculated since the year 1987.[1104]

Due to the growing state indebtedness of several EMU member countries, the rating agencies could prospectively downgrade any respective long-term sovereign ratings. The S&P press release by December 05th 2011[1105], of changing 15 of the 17[1106] EMU countries in the status of "credit watch negative"[1107] can be interpreted as one example and first step towards a more distinct deviation of financial strength and refinancing conditions in progression of the reached degree of political, economical and fiscal challenges that investors will be confronted with for an undefined time. Germany and the previously remaining five[1108] AAA rated countries have also been subject to this credit watch because of political and monetary deviances in the entire union. The implications of handling the international issues will frequently affect any subsequent rating reviews and changes of the sovereign credit gradings.[1109]

Even if the sovereign rating of Germany[1110] is lowered prospectively, the empirical investigation and acceptance of comparing any country's refinancing costs to the German yield curve[1111] will be maintained. Amongst others this is reasoned by the German proportion of the combined GDP[1112] in the EMU, representing the economically most powerful country within the union. This interpretation will furthermore be regarded as comparatively riskless.

1102 The Deutscher Rentenindex REX-Performanceindex (REXP) is conducted as combined measure of price and reinvested interest rate developments of the implied German governmental bonds.

1103 Cp. Deutsche Börse AG [ed.] (2004), p. 2f.

1104 Cp. Stehle (1999), p. 9ff.

1105 Cp. S&P [ed.] (2011a).

1106 Even before Cyprus was placed on the watchlist with negative outlook, Greece had been downgraded repeatedly to the rating of C by Moody's; cp. table 21.

1107 Cp. Stehle (1999), p. 9ff.

1108 Besides Germany also Austria, Finland, France. Luxembourg and the Netherlands are rated with a AAA.

1109 Cp. S&P [ed.] (2011b).

1110 Informationally: On January 13th 2012 S&P completed the EMU rating reviews, announced on December 05th 2011. They lowered the souvereign ratings of Cyprus, Italy, Portugal and Spain by two notches. Austria, France, Malta, Slovakia and Slovenia were reduced by one notch. The ratings of Belgium, Estonia, Finland, Germany, Ireland, Luxembourg and the Netherlands were affirmed; cp. S&P [ed.] (2012).

1111 Cp. Becker (2009), p. 1.

1112 Cp. Eurostat [ed.] (2011).

4.1.3 Commodities

Commodity investments tend to have an inflationary deviation[1113] because if prices for raw materials, that are necessary within the economical life, rise due to general market inflation and investors can thereby achieve a natural hedge.[1114] Prices for operationally required goods increase and are counterbalanced by investments in financial assets with similar price shifts.[1115]

Within the subsequent index and portfolio compositions as well as the previous correlation analysis the former named Thomson Reuters/Jefferies CRB index (since the year 2005: Reuters/Jefferies CRB index) is used. Following Brooks and Langerup (2011) who compared eight different commodity indices, including the CRB index, a choice of the outstanding commodity indices is difficult to determine because of different derivative strategies, weighting models and rolling methodologies[1116]. Their indentation of the CRB index, preparing a liquid tradable alternative as suitable access to the asset class[1117] of commodities, is further adopted.[1118]

Since the year 1957 the index is calculated as general and diversified measure for commodity price movements. It has been reallocated ten times[1119] to retain the economical pertinence within the choice and weighing of its member commodities.[1120] Genenrally commodities are traded in US Dollar[1121] but because of the designated EMU bias[1122] of the current elaboration, the incorporated index is converted into Euro by the respective daily EUR/USD exchange rate fixings[1123].

Former compositions allocated 27, 26, 25, 21 or 17 commodities via the spot or future markets.[1124] Since the year 2005, the final index composition comprises four groups under which 19 single commodities, calculated by future contracts, are combined and reallocated monthly:[1125] Group (1) petroleum or energy products, (2) highly liquid materials like precious metals, (3) diverse commodities for an enhancement of liquidity, (4) commodities for diversi-

1113 Cp. Saitta (1999), p. 36.
1114 Cp. Gupta (2011), p. 19.
1115 Cp. Mosser (1999), p. 36.
1116 For further allocation techniques, based on future investments; cp. Erhardt, Tucker (1990), p. 7ff.
1117 Cp. Freeman (2006), p. 3.
1118 Cp. Brooks, Langerup (2011), p. 32ff.
1119 Date: December 31st 2011.
1120 Cp. Acharya, Gentle, Paudel (2010), p. 1493.
1121 Cp. Brooks (2009), p. 38.
1122 Cp. Islam, DB Research [ed.] (1998), p. 1 ff.
1123 Cp. Dunis, Laws, Sermpinis (2009), p. 189.
1124 Cp. Bianco (1999), p. 51.
1125 Cp. Burke (2003), p. 34.

fication of the former groups.[1126] The current weighting scheme and the assignment of the raw materials are illustrated in table 22.

Group	Group weighting	Commodity	Commodity weighting
1	33%	WTI Crude Oil	23%
		Heating Oil	5%
		Gasoline	5%
2	42%	Natural Gas	6%
		Corn	6%
		Soybeans	6%
		Live Cattle	6%
		Gold	6%
		Aluminum	6%
		Copper	6%
3	20%	Sugar	5%
		Cotton	5%
		Coffee	5%
		Cocoa	5%
4	5%	Nickel	1%
		Wheat	1%
		Lean Hogs	1%
		Orange Juice	1%
		Silver	1%

Table 22: Composition scheme of the CRB index[1127]

4.1.4 EMU Equities

Since February 28th 1998[1128] the SX5E constitutes the most distinguished blue chip[1129] index within the Eurozone, wherefore it serves as representative equity proxy within the current explanations.[1130]

The index provider STOXX Ltd. was founded as joint venture[1131] by the Deutsche Börse AG, the Dow Jones & Company and the SWX Swiss Exchange in the year 1998. During the introduction of the Euro and the establishment of the Eurozone[1132], the DJ STOXX indices became Europe's most common equity indices.[1133] Within the context of this paper and the implemented empirical discussions, the primary attention appertains to the SX5E and the respective industry or supersector indices, but the general acceptance will be questioned critically.[1134]

1126 Cp. Blanch, Schels (2006), p. 34.
1127 Self-provided table in dependence of: Thomson Reuters [ed.] (2010), p. 8.
1128 The index is calculated back to December 31st 1986 and the base value of 1000 points was fixed on December 31st 1991; cp. STOXX Ltd. [ed.] (2011y).
1129 Cp. Chye, Meng, Gupta, Ramakrishna (2000), p. 20.
1130 Cp. Liedtke (1999), p. 7.
1131 Cp. Krishnan (2010), p. 439.
1132 Cp. STOXX Ltd. [ed.] (2011d).
1133 Cp. STOXX Ltd. [ed.] (2011t).
1134 Cp. Achleitner, Kaserer, Moldenhauer (2005), p. 121.

4.1.4.1 Allocation of the Dow Jones Euro STOXX 50

The SX5E serves as most accepted representation[1135] of the 50 companies with the highest capitalisations[1136] of the 19 supersectors in the Eurozone. Regionally the twelve countries of Austria, Belgium, Finland, France, Germany, Greece, Ireland, Italy, Luxembourg, the Netherlands, Portugal and Spain are comprised.[1137]

Despite the political divergences in the Eurozone, the index reflects the domestic market within these countries of the entirely more comprehensive region as union due to the joint currency.[1138] The adoption of the Euro as bank money on January 01st 1999 enabled the EMU to establish the second largest stock market with investment facilities avoiding any exchange rate risks behind the US American market.[1139]

The index rules arrange the substitution criteria and the dates, determining if former members are further approved or replaced by new company's shares. Hence, an extraordinary denotation is attached to the criterion of index transparency[1140]. Every market participant shall be enabled to comprehend the index reallocations[1141] by the generally published regulations. Exchanges of members should not be conducted without publicly available allocation notices.[1142] With some limitations the STOXX Ltd. achieves these specifications by the published guidelines of the index compositions and reallocations on their website www.stoxx.com. Especially European banks try to stay conformable to these guidelines and anticipate index changes to convey trading commendations[1143] according to the arising index effects.

The constraint of the information criteria, implemented on April 01st 2010, ever since access to weights of countries, supersectors, industries and company members, are complicated by the STOXX Ltd. and the request to sign a license agreement, liable to pay fees.[1144] Therefore exclusively the current index members and their native countries are illustrated, as visible in appendix 3, without their respective proportions of the index portfolio.

1135 Cp. Liedtke (1999), p. 7.

1136 In September 2000 the weighting criteria were changed from market cap to free float market cap in considerations of their trading liquidity according to the outstanding shares; cp. Domowitz, Glen, Madhavan (2001), p. 222; Wetzel (2000), p. 17.

1137 Cp. STOXX Ltd. [ed.] (2011u).

1138 Cp. Klein, Grimm, Röhl [ed.], Heussinger [ed.] (2006), p. 13.

1139 Cp. Berbena, Jansen (2009), p. 3067f.

1140 Cp. FTSE [ed.] (1996), p. 6; FTSE [ed.] (1999), p. 2.

1141 Cp. O'Brien (2006), p. 62.

1142 Cp. Schmitz-Esser (2001), p. 101ff.

1143 Cp. Jaisfeld, National-Bank AG [ed.] (2008), p. 4f.

1144 Cp. STOXX Ltd. [ed.] (2011a).

It is obvious that companies from Belgium (1)[1145], Finland (1), France (17), Germany (14), Ireland (1), Italy (6), Luxembourg (1), the Netherlands (3) and Spain (6) are comprised by a disequilibrium of quantity. Hence, Austria, Greece and Portugal remain unconsidered in, which is a distinct contrast to the economic centre of gravity by France and Germany, inserting cumulatively 31 of 50 index members.[1146]

The companies, listed in the SX5E, cover about 60% of the free float market cap[1147] of the respective benchmark[1148] index, the DJ Euro STOXX. This in turn demonstrates approximately 95%[1149] of the free float market cap of the entirely constituted Eurozone countries.[1150]

No.	Index	Symbol	Market cap (MLN EUR)	Portion
1	EURO STOXX Utilities	SX6E Index	306.567,41	10,29%
2	EURO STOXX Industrial Goods	SXNE Index	301.306,16	10,11%
3	EURO STOXX Banks	SX7E Index	288.743,00	9,69%
4	EURO STOXX Oil & Gas	SXEE Index	240.759,50	8,08%
5	EURO STOXX Food & Beverage	SX3E Index	218.502,09	7,33%
6	EURO STOXX Personal & Household Goods	SXQE Index	215.871,14	7,24%
7	EURO STOXX Chemicals	SX4E Index	184.722,59	6,20%
8	EURO STOXX Telecommunications	SXKE Index	184.400,28	6,19%
9	EURO STOXX Insurance	SXIE Index	169.527,19	5,69%
10	EURO STOXX Automobiles & Parts	SXAE Index	145.587,75	4,89%
11	EURO STOXX Health Care	SXDE Index	135.007,59	4,53%
12	EURO STOXX Technology	SX8E Index	128.490,96	4,31%
13	EURO STOXX Retail	SXRE Index	120.278,71	4,04%
14	EURO STOXX Construction & Materials	SXOE Index	100.369,83	3,37%
15	EURO STOXX Media	SXME Index	78.770,86	2,64%
16	EURO STOXX Basic Resources	SXPE Index	66.838,70	2,24%
17	EURO STOXX Real Estate	SX86E Index	35.656,71	1,20%
18	EURO STOXX Financial Services	SXFE Index	30.135,57	1,01%
19	EURO STOXX Travel & Leisure	SXTE Index	28.175,84	0,95%
Total			**2.979.711,87**	**100,00%**

Table 23: DJ Euro STOXX Supersector Indices[1151]

60 members of the 19 DJ Euro STOXX Supersector Indices[1152] listed in table 23 are weighted by their free float market cap and compose the selection list where from the members of the SX5E are elected. Due to the 40/60 rule, the first 40 companies are chosen directly as index members. The remaining ten positions are replenished by the former members, placed between the ranks 41 and 60 of the selection list. If thitherto less than 50 stocks achieve the aforementioned criteria, the biggest members of the selection list are chosen until 50 compa-

1145 The respective number of currently included stocks from each country is printed in brackets.
1146 Cp. Commerzbank [ed.] (2008), p. 140f.
1147 Cp. Chan, Yue-Cheong Chan, Fong (2004), p. 180.
1148 Cp. Frino, Gallagher, Neubert, Oetomo (2004), p. 89.
1149 Cp. STOXX [ed.] (2011w).
1150 Cp. STOXX [ed.] (2011i).
1151 Self-provided figure in dependence of: STOXX Ltd. [ed.] (2011x); Bloomberg [ed.] (2011cn) to ibid. (2011dd).
1152 Cp. STOXX Ltd. [ed.] (2011y).

nies are elected as further calculation base of the index.[1153] The operation of any index adjustment occurs rotationally on the third Friday in September when the weightings of the respective members are capped[1154] by ten percent, avoiding a disproportionate cap bias.[1155]

The SX5E is calculated in US dollar and Euro as price[1156] and performance[1157] index.[1158] The major public interest is directed towards the Euro dominated price index[1159], which is quoted every 15 seconds. In contrast to this calculation cycle, the performance indices are exclusively measured singularly a day.[1160]

4.1.4.2 Weightings of the Dow Jones Euro STOXX 50

Every company, serving as potential member of the SX5E, has to be located in the surrounding area of the Eurozone. A further weighting standard according to the origination, by minimum or maximum quantities of industry or country affiliations, is inexistent.

Table 24 clarifies the diverging capitalisations of the twelve country blue chip[1161] indices representing the selection universe. The predominance of Germany and France is particularly conspicuous, opponent to countries like Austria, Ireland, Portugal, Luxembourg and Greece. In retrospective to the previous section and appendix 3 this cap difference explains, why neglecting companies as members of the SX5E, that are originated in the mentioned lower capitalised countries.

No.	Index	Country	Symbol	Market cap (BLN EUR)	Portion
1	DAX INDEX	GERMANY	DAX Index	641.822,63	29,17%
2	CAC 40 INDEX	FRANCE	CAC Index	581.033,40	26,40%
3	IBEX 35 INDEX	SPAIN	IBEX Index	320.573,90	14,57%
4	AEX INDEX	NETHERLANDS	AEX Index	243.863,80	11,08%
5	FTSE MIB INDEX	ITALY	FTSEMIB Index	184.269,00	8,37%
6	OMX HELSINKI 25 INDEX	FINNLAND	HEX25 Index	67.925,55	3,09%
7	BEL 20 INDEX	BELGIUM	BEL20 Index	53.715,68	2,44%
8	IRISH OVERALL INDEX	IRELAND	ISEQ Index	39.763,14	1,81%
9	AUSTRIAN TRADED ATX INDX	AUSTRIA	ATX Index	29.214,09	1,33%
10	ATHEX COMPOSITE INDEX	GREECE	ASE Index	22.254,48	1,01%
11	PSI 20 INDEX	PORTUGAL	PSI20 Index	15.986,19	0,73%
12	LUXEMBOURG LUXX INDEX	LUXEMBOUR	LUXXX Index	49,21	0,00%
Total				**2.200.471,07**	**100,00%**

Table 24: Regional selection universe of the DJ Euro STOXX 50[1162]

1153 Cp. Jaisfeld, National-Bank AG [ed.] (2008), p. 3.
1154 Cp. Currier (2009), p. 222.
1155 Cp. Commerzbank [ed.] (2008), p. 141.
1156 Cp. Fava (2010), p. 23.
1157 Cp. Ernst, Vater (2005), p. 429.
1158 Cp. STOXX Ltd. [ed.] (2011d).
1159 According to its predominance, the Euro dominated price index is applied within the analysis.
1160 Cp. Commerzbank [ed.] (2008), p. 143.
1161 Cp. Farzard (2006), p. 66.
1162 Self-provided table in dependence of: Bloomberg [ed.] (2011cb) to ibid. (2011cm).

Due to the requirements of the disputed selection list, a predefined criterion of market cap is not available. Every current member of the SX5E is necessarily tabulated in this list, supporting the index continuity.[1163]

Adjacent to the constricted consideration of countries, a further challenge appears with respect to the levelling function of the index[1164]. As explained, generally EMU equity investments should be allocated by an adequate industry diversification.[1165] The regional selection of the Eurozone is classified as integrated capital market[1166], hence the conducted stock selection criteria appears as questionable.[1167]

The current allocation[1168] of the SX5E comprises 14 of 50 stocks, assigned to the financial industry as listed in table 25. Even though the percentile weight is not publicly available it is obvious that the index is biased by the industry groups financial services and REITS but especially banks and insurances, displaying a distinct reciprocal, statistical dependence.

No.	Company	Ticker	Industry	Industry Group
1	BANCO SANTANDER SA	SAN SQ Equity	Financials	Banks
2	BANCO BILBAO VIZCAYA ARGENTA	BBVA SQ Equity	Financials	Banks
3	BNP PARIBAS	BNP FP Equity	Financials	Banks
4	DEUTSCHE BANK AG-REGISTERED	DBK GY Equity	Financials	Banks
5	INTESA SANPAOLO	ISP IM Equity	Financials	Banks
6	SOCIETE GENERALE	GLE FP Equity	Financials	Banks
7	UNICREDIT SPA	UCG IM Equity	Financials	Banks
8	DEUTSCHE BOERSE AG-NEW	63DU GY Equity	Financials	Financial Services
9	ALLIANZ SE-REG	ALV GY Equity	Financials	Insurance
10	AXA SA	CS FP Equity	Financials	Insurance
11	ASSICURAZIONI GENERALI	G IM Equity	Financials	Insurance
12	ING GROEP NV-CVA	INGA NA Equity	Financials	Insurance
13	MUENCHENER RUECKVER AG-REG	MUV2 GY Equity	Financials	Insurance
14	UNIBAIL-RODAMCO SE	UL FP Equity	Financials	REITS

Table 25: DJ Euro STOXX 50 members of the financial industry[1169]

The three supersectors banks, insurance and financial services comprise 16,39% of the entire market cap according to the 19 supersectors.[1170] This coherent denotation explains the disproportionate number of companies associated with the financial industry what again should not be interpreted as positive endorsement. Such an overwhelming level of single companies deriving form one industry does not coincide with the intrinsic representativeness by the information function, but is recognised according to several indices illustrating a region with an

1163 Cp. Schmitz-Esser (2001), p. 108.
1164 Cp. Amenc, Goltz, Martellini (2011), p. 11.
1165 Cp. Freimann (1998), p. 32.
1166 Cp. Galati, Tsatsaronis (2003), p. 11ff.
1167 Cp. Garz, Günther, Moriabadi (2006), p. 42ff.
1168 Date: December 31st 2011.
1169 Self-provided figure in dependence of: Bloomberg [ed.] (2011ca).
1170 Cp. table 22.

economically failing, but distinct financial industry.[1171] Consequently the economical meaning of the Eurozone is rather adulterated and an irrational standard is interceded. Because of the enlisted restraints, the admission of the SX5E as predominant equity index for the EMU remains questionable.[1172]

4.2 Index Effects in the EMU

Stocks that are included into (deleted from) an index frequently exhibit a conspicuously deviating return in comparison to the entire market or the respective index. This abnormal return characteristic is denoted as index effect.[1173] The current section serves as test of *(H3)*, where the null hypothesis of *(H3)* assumes that the SX5E is not subject to index effects and pure indexing is unable to outperform stock picking biased by the assumption of these effects.

4.2.1 Current State of Research Concerning Index Effects

Index reallocations, subject to changing memberships of the US equity market[1174] and especially the S&P 500[1175], have frequently been analysed by global researchers.[1176] Active portfolio managers[1177] try to achieve an outperformance in comparison to the benchmark index by anticipating the selection criteria[1178] and precocious portfolio reallocations. Commonly stocks that tend to be added to (deleted from) the index are bought (sold) before their effective addition (deletion).[1179] After the announcement date portfolio managers assume downward (upward) sloping demand curves of stocks, deleted from (added to) indices.[1180] These suppositions coincide with the short-term price impacts[1181] due to interim abnormal returns, resulting from the decreasing (increasing) amounts of demand orders[1182] which are attended by the price pressure hypothesis[1183] (PPH).[1184]

A further explanation of the demand curve movements, biased by any changes of index memberships is described by the information hypothesis (IH)[1185] combined with the liquidity hy-

1171 Cp. Schmitz-Esser (2001), p. 27.
1172 Cp. Klein, Grimm, Röhl [ed.] Heussinger [ed.] (2006), p. 13.
1173 Cp. Elton, Gruber, Busse (2004), p. 270; Wetzel (2000), p. 6; Goetzmann, Massa (1999), p. 2.
1174 Cp. Collins, Wansley, Robinson (1995), p. 329ff.; Beneish, Whaley (1996), p. 1909ff.
1175 Cp. Denis, McConnell, Ovtchinnikov, Yu (2003), p. 1821.
1176 Cp. Chen (2006), p. 409f.
1177 Cp. Clarke, de Silva, Thorley (2002), p. 48ff.
1178 Index changes are precociously released on the announcement date.
1179 Cp. Bechmann (2004), p. 3f.
1180 Cp. Chen, Noronha, Singal (2004), p. 1901f.
1181 Cp. Kogan, Ross, Wang, Westerfield (2006), p. 196.
1182 Cp. Schmitz-Esser (2001), p. 303; Denis, McConnell, Ovtchinnikov, Yu (2003), p. 1822.
1183 Cp. Schlumpf, Schmid, Zimmermann (2008), p. 965.
1184 Cp. Lidén (2007), p. 254.
1185 Cp. Malhotra, Thenmozhi, Kumar (2007), p. 224ff.

pothesis (LH)[1186]. The LH assumes the trading liquidity of stocks as positively correlated to index memberships.[1187] Within informational efficient capital markets, investors appreciate index changes instantly before the effective date and convert their conclusion into orders, generating a new market balance, influencing stock price liquidity by enhanced trading activities.[1188] These aspects are closely connected to the explanations by Chen, Noronha and Singal (2004) who denominated index members as well-established[1189] within the investor's recognition in the sense of the investor's awareness hypothesis (IAH).[1190] Docking and Dowen (2006) acknowledged these results by their discovery of predominantly persistent[1191] excess (minor) returns by added (deleted) stocks at the US small cap market.[1192]

Mazouz and Saadouni (2007) analysed short- and long-term index effects according to the FTSE 100. They supposed excess (minor) returns of added (deleted) stocks in comparison to the index, if active managers place orders before the announcement of the composition changes because passive index funds[1193] replace stocks primary on the implementation date[1194] to avoid an increasing tracking error.[1195] Their findings proved the information of stock additions (deletions) to be imputed in asset prices even before the announcement date due to the PPH and the publicly available index guidelines[1196]. The index effects lasted only divertingly from a time compendiously prior to the announcement until about two weeks after the effective change of the indexportfolio.[1197] They also mentioned a coherence with the information effect hypothesis which was subdivided by Sokulsky, Brooks and Davidson (2008) within the content of changing index membership: (1) the added stock is verified and recommended by the index contractor in dependence on the certification hypothesis and (2) the index membership provokes a superior growth by the supervision according to the information content hypothesis[1198] and the IAH.[1199]

1186 Cp. Jaemin (2005), p. 2ff.
1187 Cp. Schmidt-Tank (2005), p. 133; Deininger, Kaserer, Roos (2002), p. 262ff.
1188 Cp. Vespro (2006), p. 104f.
1189 According to the demand information hypothesis, the degree of dispersed information by a company deliminates the demand for its listed stock; cp. Hoje, Yongtae, Park (2008), p. 263.
1190 Cp. Chen, Noronha, Singal (2004), p. 1901ff.
1191 The persistence of superior returns of index members is attended by the attention hypothesis; cp. Hyland, Swidler (2002), p. 302.
1192 Cp. Docking, Dowen (2006), p. 113.
1193 Cp. Chen, Huang (2010), p. 1155ff.
1194 Usually the implementation date appears one trading day before the effective change.
1195 Cp. Dunham, Simpson (2010), p. 58ff.
1196 Cp. Farzard (2011), p. 49.
1197 Cp. Mazouz, Saadouni (2007), p. 501ff.
1198 Cp. Cai (2007), p. 113ff.
1199 Cp. Sokulsky, Brooks, Davidson (2008), p. 605f.

Vespro (2006) detected confirmations of the PPH in coherence with the index rebalancing but rejected the imperfect substitution hypothesis[1200], the LH and the IH for European and US stock indices. She explained her findings by the higher elasticity of long-run demand curves in contrast to the short-term demand.[1201] If a stock is included into an index the demand curve for this asset slopes downward shortly after the effective date because some investors anticipate the inclusion and index fund managers are constrained to pay higher prices at the efficient index inclusion.[1202]

Masse, Hanrahan, Kushner and Martinello (2000) examined the index effects of the Canadian TSE 300 index which are positive for additions in the short- and long-run whereby the mentioned positive attributes[1203] of announced index memberships are validated. Contrary to these sustained effects, the returns of deleted stocks are designated as marginally negative.[1204] The marginal verifiability could administrate the notion that stocks, having been former members of indices, pursue their beneficial attributes even after a deletion. Though this consideration is disputing the presumption that profoundly regulated and index listed stocks are emphasised as more liquid marketable.[1205] In respect of the liquidity preference hypothesis[1206] they exhibit an enduring liquidity premium[1207], resulting in rising prices.[1208]

Cooper and Woglom (2003) challenged the enduring increase of stocks, added to the S&P 500. They declared a positive but exclusively temporary price effect after the announcement date, accompanied by rising volatilities. The increased risk causes a subsequent decline of the stock price due to higher, risk adjusted discount rates of the prospective earnings, resulting in a decreased present value, identical to the asset price.[1209]

Assimilable unsustainable effects were identified by Gerke, Arneth and Fleischer (2001) for the German DAX. Their dataset features an average excess (minor) return at the announcement date for added (deleted) stocks. Both types of return abnormalities are adjusted to the market return during the consequent variation of time.[1210] The temporary price reactions in combination to the index composition are constituted with the help of portfolio modifications of passive asset managers.[1211] In addition to them Schmitz-Esser (2001) engaged an analysis

1200 Cp. Zhou (2011), 72.
1201 Cp. Vespro (2006), p. 126.
1202 Cp. Schleifer (1986), p. 579ff.
1203 E.g. by an enhanced analyst's coverage; cp. Denis, McConnell, Ovtchinnikov, Yu (2003), p. 133f.
1204 Cp. Masse, Hanrahan, Kushner, Martinello (2000), p. 357.
1205 Cp. Galariotis, Giouvris (2007), p. 385.
1206 Cp. Wray (2004), p. 310.
1207 Cp. Nguyen, Mishra, Suchismita, Ghosh (2007), p. 380.
1208 Cp. Erwin, Miller (1998), p. 144.
1209 Cp. Cooper, Woglom (2003), p. 68.
1210 Cp. Gerke, Arneth, Fleischer (2001), p. 45f.
1211 Cp. Lynch, Mendenhall (1997), p. 351ff.; Harris, Gurel (1986), p. 815ff.; Wetzel (2000), p. 8.

of index effects at the broader European market. Contradictory, he emphasised every appearing index effect as statistically significant and permanent, whereat retrograde tendencies have to be acknowledged according to the FTSE 100, the CAC 40 and the DAX 30.[1212]

Comparable decreasing levels of index effects were substantiated by Dash and Blitzer (2004) according to the S&P 500.[1213] The diminishment was expounded by precocious and improved capabilities of anticipating and acting by investors already during the early initiation of possible index changes.[1214]

Generally the appearing and inconstant abnormal return characteristics can be regarded in association with the selection criteria hypothesis, which constitutes the stock selection of index providers as driven by the historical price and capitalisation[1215] developments.[1216]

4.2.2 Empirical Investigation by the Dow Jones Euro STOXX 50

The following analysis enlarges the former mentioned status of research by a short- and long-term investigation of deleted and added stocks according to the SX5E. During the years 2001 to 2010 eleven stocks were added to or respectively deleted from the index. The process and the critical dates are listed in table 26 which illustrates that during the years 2005 and 2006 the index membership has not been changed.

year	cut-off date	announcement	implementation	change effective	addition	deletion
2001	31.08.2001	03.09.2001	21.09.2001	24.09.2001	St. Gobain	KPN
2002	30.08.2002	02.09.2002	20.09.2002	23.09.2002	Lafarge	Pinault Printemps Redoute
2003	29.08.2003	01.09.2003	19.09.2003	22.09.2003	Iberdrola	Bayerische Hypo & Vereinsbank
2004	31.08.2004	01.09.2004	17.09.2004	20.09.2004	Credit Agricole	Volkswagen
2005	31.08.2009	01.09.2005	16.09.2005	19.09.2005	--	--
2006	31.08.2006	01.09.2006	15.09.2006	18.09.2006	--	--
2007	31.08.2007	03.09.2007	21.09.2007	24.09.2007	Arcelor Mittal	Ahold
					Schneider Electronic	Allied Irish Banks
					Vinci	Lafarge
2008	29.08.2008	01.09.2008	19.09.2008	22.09.2008	Alstom	Alcatel Lucent
2009	31.08.2009	31.08.2009	18.09.2009	21.09.2009	Anheuser-Busch Inbev	Fortis
					CRH	Renault
2010	31.08.2010	31.08.2010	17.09.2010	20.09.2010	BMW	AEGON

Table 26: Composition changes of the DJ Euro STOXX 50[1217]

Since the entire thesis is aligned to the denotation of indices as benchmark in the broader scope of the portfolio management, the subsequent evaluation is targeted towards the consideration of stock picking[1218], affected by index reallocations versus EMU index investing in a

1212 Cp. Schmitz-Esser (2001), p. 241ff.; Schmidt-Tank (2005), p. 133f.
1213 Cp. Soe, Dash, S&P [ed.] (2008), p. 3ff.
1214 Cp. Blitzer, Dash, Murphy, S&P [ed.] (2004), p. 1ff.
1215 Cp. Ferguson, Leistikow, Rentzler, Yu (2009), p. 69.
1216 Cp. Becker-Blease, Paul (2010), p. 325.
1217 Self-provided table in dependence of: STOXX [ed.] (2011j) to ibid. (2011s).
1218 Cp. Ferruz, Munoz, Vargas (2010), p. 408.

bipartite long and short maturity. The main aspect of the executed investigation aims on the differentiation if the returns of added (deleted) stocks deviate from the index return and if the added (deleted) stocks exhibit an excess (a minor) return in the short- and long-run. The short period is determined as price change in the time frame between the announcement[1219] and the effective date[1220] of any composition changes.

The price variation in the long-run is observed as differentiation between the effective change of a membership and the price on September 30th one year after the actual stock addition or deletion.[1221] Table 27 concentrates the results of the eleven stocks, added to the SX5E.

	stock price development (announcement vs. effective)	return DJ Euro STOXX 50 (announcement vs. effective)	active return (announcement vs. effective)	short term index effect	stock price development (effective vs. end of September +1 year)	return DJ Euro STOXX 50 (effective vs. end of September +1 year)	active return (effective vs. ultimo September +1 year)	long term index effect
St. Gobain (2001)	-16,06%	-18,51%	2,44%	positive	-46,95%	-33,06%	-13,89%	negative
Lafarge (2002)	-7,38%	-17,41%	10,03%	positive	-38,73%	7,74%	-46,47%	negative
Iberdrola (2003)	-3,66%	-3,39%	-0,26%	negative	10,54%	8,10%	2,43%	positive
Credit Agricole (2004)	5,53%	3,09%	2,44%	positive	10,67%	21,11%	-10,44%	negative
Arcelor Mittal (2007)	12,36%	1,49%	10,87%	positive	-44,73%	-36,14%	-8,60%	negative
Schneider Electronic (2007)	-7,30%	1,49%	-8,79%	negative	-41,54%	-36,14%	-5,41%	negative
Vinci (2007)	3,29%	1,49%	1,79%	positive	-51,20%	-36,14%	-15,06%	negative
Alstom (2008)	-8,44%	-5,58%	-2,86%	negative	-28,32%	-10,22%	-18,10%	negative
Anheuser-Busch Inbev (2009)	7,27%	3,45%	3,82%	positive	28,70%	-4,43%	33,13%	positive
CRH (2009)	0,05%	3,45%	-3,40%	negative	0,93%	-4,43%	5,36%	positive
BMW (2010)	16,43%	6,63%	9,80%	positive	1,76%	-25,14%	26,90%	positive

Table 27: Index effects by additions to the DJ Euro STOXX 50[1222]

[1219] It is located at the monthly allowance of August to September within each year, except 2005 and 2006.

[1220] The date is on a Monday between September 18th and 24th of any respective year.

[1221] During both maturities the respective beta factors, measuring the company risk compared to the index, remain unconsidered because practically portfolio managers likewise do not adopt their allocation procedures or stock pickings by such systematic attributes but focus exclusively on the return aberration between the stocks and the index.

[1222] Self-provided table in dependence of: Bloomberg [ed.] (2011b) to ibid. (2011bo).

During both maturities the index and the stock price changes are calculated and compared. The index effect is signified as positive (negative) if the stock (index) investment would have been predominant. In seven of eleven short-term inspections a positive effect is existent.

Within the time of less than one month, an average return according to the entire eleven composition changes of 2,35% is realised in the interval of +10,87% according to ArcelorMittal (2007)[1223] and -8,79% in the case of Schneider Electronic (2007). In accord to Cooper and Woglom (2003) the effects are not permanent[1224] because the relation of positive vs. negative effects has inverted from seven/four to four/seven. At the end of September – one year after the index inclusion – only the excess returns by Anheuser-Busch InBev (2009) and BMW (2010) still remain and have even increased conspicuously[1225]. Even the average return becomes negative by -4,56%, inside the extreme values of +33,13% of Anheuser-Busch InBev (2009) and -46,47% by Lafarge (2002).

Consequently the results are in line with the findings of Mazouz and Saadouni (2007)[1226]. In the short-run index additions can provoke an enhanced return though the current outcome of seven[1227] positive and four[1228] negative effects is not entitled as positively significant.

The long-term results illustrate a rather random effect, though the returns of the added stocks with positive effects in the short-run are furthermore surpassing. The evaluation of the stock additions to the SX5E has to be concluded as shortly possible but in the long-run indexing tends to be more effective than the stock picking[1229] based on index additions.

Every stock addition depends on a further company leaving the index, hence table 28 displays the deleted SX5E members by the equal schedule as the aforementioned analysis of stock additions. In dependence of Masse, Hanrahan, Kushner and Martinello (2000) the long- and short-term excess returns of active portfolio managers, selling deleted stocks at the announcement date, are insignificant.[1230] Within seven of eleven circumstances the effect would have been positive at least in the short-run.[1231] During this period the average return would have been marginally positive by 1,98% between the extreme values of 32,86%[1232] and -18,84%[1233]. The ratio of positive vs. negative index effects changes from seven/four to

1223 The respective year of addition/deletion is printed in brackets.
1224 Cp. Cooper, Woglom (2003), p. 68.
1225 In the case of Anheuser-Busch InBev (BMW) from 3,82% (9,80%) to 33,13% (26,90%).
1226 Cp. Mazouz, Saadouni (2007), p. 501ff.
1227 63,64% as confirmation of excess returns by the added stocks.
1228 36,36% as rejection of excess returns by the added stocks.
1229 Cp. Ferruz, Munoz, Vargas (2010), p. 408.
1230 Cp. Masse, Hanrahan, Kushner, Martinello (2000), p. 357.
1231 KPN (2001), Bayerische Hypo & Vereinsbank (2003), Ahold (2007) and Aegon (2010).
1232 Alcatel Lucent (2008).
1233 KPN (2001).

five/six. This seems incidental and does not serve as affirmation for a long-term success of the deleted stocks. Though the average excess return has decreased to -9,52%[1234].

	stock price development (announcement vs. effective)	return DJ Euro STOXX 50 (announcement vs. effective)	active return (announcement vs. effective)	short term index effect	stock price development (effective vs. end of September +1 year)	return DJ Euro STOXX 50 (effective vs. end of September +1 year)	active return (effective vs. ultimo September +1 year)	long term index effect
KPN (2001)	0,34%	-18,51%	-18,84%	negative	66,10%	-33,06%	-99,16%	negative
Pinault Printemps Redoute (2002)	-19,63%	-17,41%	2,22%	positive	4,94%	7,74%	2,79%	positive
Bayerische Hypo & Vereinsbank (2003)	10,54%	-3,39%	-13,93%	negative	15,86%	8,10%	-7,76%	negative
Volkswagen (2004)	2,35%	3,09%	0,74%	positive	46,17%	21,11%	-25,06%	negative
Ahold (2007)	6,71%	1,49%	-5,22%	negative	-25,43%	-36,14%	-10,71%	negative
Allied Irish Banks (2007)	-12,02%	1,49%	13,51%	positive	-64,46%	-36,14%	28,32%	positive
Lafarge (2007)	-5,46%	1,49%	6,95%	positive	-38,57%	-36,14%	2,44%	positive
Alcatel Lucent (2008)	-38,44%	-5,58%	32,86%	positive	4,21%	-10,22%	-14,43%	negative
Fortis (2009)	-2,34%	3,45%	5,79%	positive	-32,79%	-4,43%	28,36%	positive
Renault (2009)	1,74%	3,45%	1,71%	positive	16,67%	-4,43%	-21,10%	negative
Aegon (2010)	10,63%	6,63%	-4,01%	negative	-38,24%	-25,14%	13,10%	positive

Table 28: Index effects by deletions from the DJ Euro STOXX 50[1235]

The mentioned statistical significance is checked by a two-tailed t-test assuming different variances, though eleven index changes are actually rarely able to detect considerable results. Short-term (long-term) additions and deletions are compared to their respective mean to detect the respective deviations.[1236] Both detailed statistics are visible in appendices 4 and 5. The t-values for two-tailed inspections of 0,36 (short-term) and 0,28 (long-term) acknowledge the refusal of statistically significant excess returns by changes of index memberships.[1237]

1234 Average of the extreme loss of -99,16% by KPN (2001) and the gain of 28,36% by Fortis (2006).

1235 Self-provided table in dependence of: Bloomberg [ed.] (2011b) to ibid. (2011bz).

1236 T-tests normally serve as test of significance for a sample of at least 15 inspections; cp. Büning, Trenkler (1994), p. 116f.

1237 The critical values are 2,11 (long-term) and 2,14 (short-term); cp. Kobelt, Steinhausen (2000), p. 354ff.

4.2.3 Conclusion Regarding EMU Index Effects

Concluding the previous appraisal associated with the quoted research acknowledges the hypothesis of index investments within the Eurozone effecting superior returns[1238] in comparison to stock picking[1239], conducted by variations of index memberships[1240]. Although the entire investigation is only based on respectively eleven index additions and deletions, affecting the explanatory power according to its force of expression to the challenged data set, the null hypothesis of *(H3)* has to be rejected. Hence, the investigation illustrates that in the long-term pure indexing is more feasible than stock picking biased by the anticipation of index effects.

The ordinary possibilities to obtain short-term excess returns via precocious portfolio implementations of index assimilations have to be admitted but in the long-run the positive performance attributes disappear. The long-term success by asset allocations[1241], focussed on index effects are released as principally random[1242].

4.3 Development of the EMU Correlation Index

As illustrated previously, the correlation between the CRB [in EUR] and the SX5E is mostly detrimental for investors in comparison to the further dependencies of the incorporated asset classes. Hence, the purpose of the ECI is to reduce the interdependence drawbacks with the commodity index for enhancing the diversification opportunities of the arranged multi asset portfolio. The subsequent explanations serve as first reference towards testing the null hypothesis of *(H4)*, assuming the Portfolio Selection Theory as inappropriate for current capital market circumstances and portfolio management approaches.

4.3.1 Allocation Criteria of the EMU Correlation Index

The index is calculated as index of indices, comprising no single stocks but the five DJ Euro STOXX TMI industry indices, listed in table 9. In comparison to a conceivable application of the country indices, the industry indices are used as members because of their relative historical advantage. The superordinated index is reallocated semi-annually[1243] respectively at the first trading day in January and July.

1238 As superior return to the index ignoring risk adjustments; cp. Herold, Maurer (2008), p. 150.
1239 Cp. Duan, Hu, McLean (2009), p. 1.
1240 Corresponding to the SX5E.
1241 Cp. Evensky, Clark, Boscaljon (2010), p. 32.
1242 Cp. Lima, Tabak (2007), p. 255.
1243 The trade-off between practically appearing transaction costs and the dynamics of the portfolio reactions towards the market alteration has to be verified by prospective research and e.g. a robustness test.

	Correlation rank	Weight of TMI industry index
lowest correlation to the CRB [in EUR]	1	33,33%
...	2	26,67%
...	3	20,00%
...	4	13,33%
highest correlation to the CRB [in EUR]	5	6,67%
	15	**100,00%**

Table 29: Correlation weighting of DJ Euro STOXX TMI industry indices[1244]

The industry indices are weighted by their respective historical correlation towards the CRB [in EUR] during the half-year prior to the reallocation. Semi-annually one trading day before the reallocation, the industry indices are ranked from one[1245] to five[1246] in dependence of their correlation towards the commodity index. The respective weights are scaled by the inverted rankings as listed in table 29. The summation of ranks equals 15, hence the reciprocal order ascribes the weight of five (one) fifteenths for rank one (five) und analogically to the intermediates.

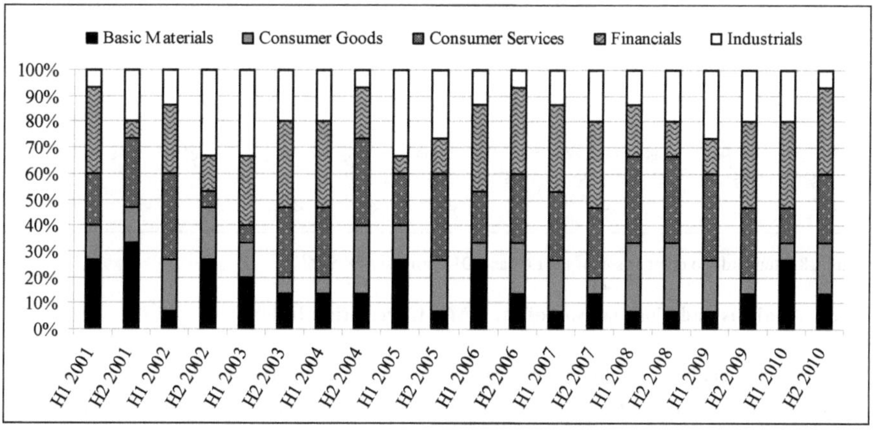

Figure 17: Semi-annual weighting of the DJ Euro STOXX TMI industry indices[1247]

The deviation of the respective industry index quantities in the continuous time frames are illustrated in figure 17. Due to the aim of a broad industry diversification[1248] accompanied by the weighting algorithm, no index is weighted with zero and the time varying impacts of the members caused by inconsistently fluctuating[1249] prices of commodities and equities become evident.

1244 Self-provided table in dependence of: own calculations.
1245 The industry index with the lowest correlation towards the CRB [in EUR].
1246 The industry index with the highest correlation towards the CRB [in EUR].
1247 Self-provided table in dependence of: own calculations.
1248 Cp. Hansen, Nielsen (2010), p. 229ff.
1249 Cp. Ball, Torous (2000), p. 373ff.

4.3.2 Backtesting of the EMU Correlation Index

The backtesting[1250] and the subsequent performance appraisal[1251] compare the ECI and the SX5E. Figure 18 roughly demonstrates the ECI as predominant. During the time from January 01st 2001 to December 31st 2010 both indices suffer losses from their base value[1252] of 100 but the ECI ends at 84,70 index points in contrast to the SX5E with a value of 43,14. Hence, the ECI loses 15,3% in comparison to 56,86% of the SX5E. The ECI proceeds serially above the SX5E but the more profound analysis occurs within the following section.

Figure 18: Standardised comparison of the ECI and DJ Euro STOXX 50[1253]

4.3.3 Analysis and Comparison of the EMU Correlation Index

The conducted analysis equals the previous procedure of comparing the industry and country portfolios for the EMU and will be recovered within the reporting to the subsequent multi asset allocation. Every measure is calculated by monthly log-returns due to their positive characteristics for long-term empirical analysis.[1254]

1250 Cp. Barone-Adesi, Giannopoulos, Vosper (2002), p. 31.
1251 Cp. Hung, Jan (2005), p. 75.
1252 Cp. Ganser (2008), p. 16.
1253 Self-provided figure in dependence of: Bloomberg [ed.] (2011b) to ibid. (2011al).
1254 Cp. Steiner, Bruns (2007), p. 51.

annual log-return	DJ Euro STOXX 50	EMU Correlation Index
2001	-21,13%	-16,16%
2002	-46,68%	-36,77%
2003	14,18%	20,37%
2004	7,06%	11,32%
2005	18,96%	23,98%
2006	14,08%	23,10%
2007	6,68%	3,99%
2008	-58,60%	-57,01%
2009	19,06%	27,83%
2010	-5,52%	7,24%
sum	-51,90%	7,88%
average	-5,19%	0,79%
max	19,06%	27,83%
min	-58,60%	-57,01%

Table 30: Annual log-returns of ECI and DJ Euro STOXX 50[1255]

Initiating to exploit the annual log-returns[1256], shown by table 30, the assumed predominance of the ECI presented by the charts in figure 18 has to be confirmed. Exclusively during the year 2007 the SX5E is marginally more profiting but during every other period and the confrontation of the extreme values, the ECI is more successful.

annual volatility	DJ Euro STOXX 50	EMU Correlation Index
2001	23,02%	23,68%
2002	32,48%	30,64%
2003	20,71%	21,09%
2004	8,96%	9,13%
2005	11,33%	12,30%
2006	8,53%	9,63%
2007	8,78%	10,95%
2008	23,80%	26,09%
2009	25,93%	24,61%
2010	19,48%	18,90%
average	18,30%	18,70%
max	32,48%	30,64%
min	8,53%	9,13%

Table 31: Volatilities of ECI and DJ Euro STOXX 50 [1257]

The superior returns of the ECI are accompanied by slightly higher annual volatilities as shown in table 31. But the narrow difference of risk is not rudimentary assimilable to the mentioned distinction of returns[1258].

1255 Self-provided table in dependence of: Bloomberg [ed.] (2011b) to ibid. (2011al).
1256 Cp. Sydsaeter, Hammond (2009), p. 412f.
1257 Self-provided table in dependence of: Bloomberg [ed.] (2011b) to ibid. (2011al).
1258 Cp. Zimmerer (2008), p. 129.

Sharpe ratio	DJ Euro STOXX 50	EMU Correlation Index
2001	-1,11	-0,87
2002	-1,54	-1,31
2003	0,57	0,85
2004	0,56	1,01
2005	1,49	1,78
2006	1,32	2,10
2007	0,32	0,01
2008	-2,63	-2,34
2009	0,71	1,10
2010	-0,31	0,36
average	-0,06	0,27
max	1,49	2,10
min	-2,63	-2,34

Table 32: Sharpe ratios of ECI and DJ Euro STOXX 50[1259]

As performance measures[1260], the annual Sharpe ratios[1261], listed in table 32, clarify the comparison of risk and excess return to the EONIA and represents the previously indicated superiority of the ECI. The slightly inferior measures of volatility calculated for the ECI are adjusted by considerably higher returns; hence the Sharpe ratios of the ECI are likewise more favourable for investors.[1262]

The meaning of inferior annual prosperity according to the SX5E can be assigned to the maximum drawdowns listed in table 33 as second measure of risk exhibiting the greatest loss since reaching an interim highest price level.[1263]

Only during the years 2005, 2006 and 2007 the ECI is unfavourable but within any remaining period even more conspicuous losses appear in the shape of the SX5E, whereby this has to be attributed as distinctly fraught with risk. The appearing extreme losses clarify a challenge for every risk management system as described by Pereira and Vaz de Melo Mendes (2005).[1264]

1259 Self-provided table in dependence of: Bloomberg [ed.] (2011b) to ibid. (2011al).
1260 Cp. Hung, Jan (2005), p. 75.
1261 Cp. Poddig, Brinkmann, Seiler (2009), p. 610f.
1262 Cp. Dempsey (2009), p. 156.
1263 Cp. Füss, Rehkugler, Disch (2005), p. 48f.
1264 Cp. Pereira, Vaz de Melo Mendes (2005), p. 83.

maximum drawdown	DJ Euro STOXX 50	EMU Correlation Index
high	101,74	133,52
date of high	17.01.01	01.06.07
following low	29,37	49,28
date of following low	09.03.09	09.03.09
Max DD (entire period)	-71,13%	-63,09%
Max DD 2001	41,06%	38,79%
Max DD 2002	46,76%	42,54%
Max DD 2003	27,64%	8,46%
Max DD 2004	13,36%	9,47%
Max DD 2005	6,50%	7,35%
Max DD 2006	12,73%	13,70%
Max DD 2007	11,24%	15,00%
Max DD 2008	53,19%	51,14%
Max DD 2009	30,72%	26,49%
Max DD 2010	18,81%	17,74%
average	26,20%	23,07%
max	53,19%	51,14%
min	6,50%	7,35%

Table 33: Maximum drawdowns of ECI and DJ Euro STOXX 50[1265]

The downside deviation as limitation of negative volatility is the first measure exhibiting meaningful disutility of the ECI because the SX5E features return deviations below zero that are only adversely within the years 2009 and 2010.[1266] Comparing the average values of 11,18% (SX5E) and 12,14% (ECI), listed in table 34, modifies the validity because the measures do not differ crucially.

downside deviation	DJ Euro STOXX 50	EMU Correlation Index
2001	14,18%	18,06%
2002	22,73%	25,62%
2003	2,70%	4,50%
2004	3,41%	4,40%
2005	6,17%	6,97%
2006	12,40%	13,37%
2007	4,99%	6,33%
2008	20,55%	22,88%
2009	16,01%	11,57%
2010	8,68%	7,69%
average	11,18%	12,14%
max	22,73%	25,62%
min	2,70%	4,40%

Table 34: Downside deviation of ECI and DJ Euro STOXX 50[1267]

1265 Self-provided table in dependence of: Bloomberg [ed.] (2011b) to ibid. (2011al).
1266 Cp. Kochman, Badarinathi (1996), p. 381.
1267 Self-provided table in dependence of: Bloomberg [ed.] (2011b) to ibid. (2011al).

Continuing the analysis with the Sortino ratios quoted in table 35 by using the downside deviations as relation of risk.[1268] The results are comparable to the Sharpe ratios as discussed before. Hence, the more attractive returns of the ECI overcompensate the detrimental downside deviations to the superior Sortino measures and the previously described disadvantage can be balanced again.

Sortino ratio	DJ Euro STOXX 50	EMU Correlation Index
2001	-1,80	-1,14
2002	-2,20	-1,57
2003	4,38	4,00
2004	1,46	2,10
2005	2,73	3,14
2006	0,90	1,51
2007	0,56	0,01
2008	-3,04	-2,66
2009	1,14	2,34
2010	-0,69	0,88
average	0,34	0,86
max	4,38	4,00
min	-3,04	-2,66

Table 35: Sortino ratios of ECI and DJ Euro STOXX 50[1269]

As frequently known equity returns do not follow the Gaussian distribution.[1270] This is regarded as general limitation for asset allocations by Amnec, Martellini, Milhau and Ziemann (2010) supposing every asset manager to assume constant return movements according to normal distributions.[1271]

skewness	DJ Euro STOXX 50	EMU Correlation Index
2001	-0,19	-0,79
2002	-0,01	-0,49
2003	0,38	0,34
2004	-0,67	-0,85
2005	-0,77	-0,98
2006	-1,94	-1,87
2007	-0,17	-0,27
2008	-0,43	-0,40
2009	-0,48	-0,04
2010	0,12	0,21
average	-0,48	-0,60

Table 36: Skewness of ECI and DJ Euro STOXX 50[1272]

1268 Cp. Casarin, Lazzarin, Pelizzon, Sartore (2005), p. 302f.
1269 Self-provided table in dependence of: Bloomberg [ed.] (2011b) to ibid. (2011al).
1270 Cp. Haas (2009), p. 1277.
1271 Cp. Sheikh, Qiao (2010), p. 8.
1272 Self-provided table in dependence of: Bloomberg [ed.] (2011b) to ibid. (2011al).

Ceteris paribus investors prefer returns skewed to the right. As visible by the skewness measures in table 36 even the correlation optimisation is not able to influence the return distribution positively because for both indices only the return series of the years 2003 and 2010 are favourable for investors.[1273]

kurtosis	DJ Euro STOXX 50	EMU Correlation Index
2001	1,90	3,89
2002	3,03	2,45
2003	2,83	2,36
2004	1,69	2,25
2005	2,15	2,74
2006	7,40	7,26
2007	2,56	1,98
2008	1,92	1,53
2009	2,94	3,02
2010	1,22	1,38
average	2,93	3,06

Table 37: Kurtosis of ECI and DJ Euro STOXX 50[1274]

According to investor's preferences, equity portfolios are commonly not able to achieve these requirements because they tend towards fat-tailed distributions and extreme spikes of negative returns.[1275] The kurtosis results in table 37 clarify that leptokurtic and platykurtic return distributions are arranged quite accidentally. Both average ratios are as close to three illustrating the critical value that a clear determination or even the consideration of superiority is impossible.[1276]

As further confirmation according to rejecting the assumption of normal return distribution, the Jarque-Bera test[1277] is conducted. The results are listed in table 38 whereby the skewness and kurtosis results were even distinct and have to be acknowledged especially during the year 2006. Both indices partially follow disadvantageous return successions as characteristically for a risky asset class.[1278]

1273 Cp. Kaiser, Thießen (2007), p. 426f.
1274 Self-provided table in dependence of: Bloomberg [ed.] (2011b) to ibid. (2011al).
1275 Cp. Baixauli, Alvarez (2006), p. 26.
1276 Cp. Toutenburg, Heumann (2008), p. 81ff.
1277 Cp. Bera, Jarque (1981), p. 314f.
1278 Cp. Boutahar (2010), p. 196ff.

Jarque-Bera test	DJ Euro STOXX 50	EMU Correlation Index
2001	0,68	1,63
2002	0,00	0,63
2003	0,31	0,44
2004	1,76	1,73
2005	1,54	1,97
2006	17,19	16,07
2007	0,16	0,67
2008	0,95	1,41
2009	0,46	0,00
2010	1,62	1,40
entire period	2,47	2,60

Table 38: Jarque-Bera test results of ECI and DJ Euro STOXX 50[1279]

4.3.4 Conclusion of Correlation Weighted Equity Indexing

Within the conducted analysis the correlation weighted[1280] ECI, comprising five DJ Euro STOXX TMI industry indices, is compared to the free float market cap weighted[1281] SX5E. The unusual kind of implying industry indices as members of the superordinated index instead of singles stocks in combination with quantifying them by correlations towards a different risky asset class is targeted on enhanced diversification benefits of a subsequently allocated multi asset composition. The prospective asset classes of the EMU multi asset portfolios will be equities, commodities, German governmental bonds and cash, whereupon the previous calculations exhibited the statistical dependence between the risky assets of equities and commodities comparatively as disadvantageously conspicuous with a correlation coefficient of 0,3 over the entire decade, which should be improved by the ECI.

Due to the explanations by Markowitz in the 1950s, assets should be comprised and weighted in a well diversified[1282] portfolio with reference to their reciprocal correlations to enhance chances and decrease the unsystematic[1283] portion of portfolio risk.[1284] This aspect has exclusively been considered by calculating the ECI as EMU equity portion of the subsequently allocated entire portfolio. The conducted indexing approach should demonstrate a practical reference to the Markowitz criteria in the superior portfolio context. Though, in the case of an alternative portfolio and a different choice of securities, the allocation conception can be adopted by a simple exchange of the asset prices whereat the general reproval remains unchanged.

1279 Self-provided table in dependence of: Bloomberg [ed.] (2011b) to ibid. (2011al); the calculation complies for chi-values with two degrees of freedom and a confidence inverval of 95%, exhibiting p-values of 5,991.

1280 Weighting the members is conducted by their relative correlation towards the CRB [in EUR].

1281 Cp. Lam, Lin, Michayluk (2011), p. 55.

1282 Cp. Willenbrock (2011), p. 42.

1283 Cp. Shum, Tang (2010), p. 25.

1284 Cp. Markowitz (1952), p. 77ff.

The primary goal of the ECI was not implicitly the improving of the allocation drawbacks according to the SX5E but as comfortable secondary action, the risk and return characteristics of the ECI are even predominant to the SX5E[1285].

The present results allow an interim and partial reference to reject the null hypothesis of *(H4)*. The explanations reprehend to the Portfolio Selection Theory[1286] and their perpetual validity, if special practical references are achieved as conducted in the allocation process of the ECI.

4.4 Allocation of Dynamic Multi Asset Portfolios

The subsequent allocation of a dynamic[1287] multi asset portfolio, which is again enhanced[1288] in a further stage, is similar to the "reverse optimisation"[1289] by Sharpe. A mean-variance investment procedure according to the primary developments by Markowitz is implicated.[1290] Hence, the results should acknowledge the Portfolio Selection Theory as valid for multi asset portfolio allocations of investors, dominated in the Eurozone and intending to place their assets in Euro currency. After calculating the ECI as correlation weighted practical equity reference the subsequent sections serve as final evaluation of *(H4)*, where the null hypothesis of *(H4)* assumes the Portfolio Selection Theory as inappropriate for a multi asset portfolio management during the current capital market circumstances.

4.4.1 Allocation Criteria of the Multi Asset Portfolios

The primary dynamic EMU Multi Asset Portfolio (EMA) as well as the enhanced EMU Multi Asset Portfolio (EEMA) are calculated and back tested for the time series from January 01st 2001 to December 31st 2010 as conducted by every previous analysis. According to the interim results, the unsteady flows of asset returns, volatilities and correlations have to be considered within the allocation process.[1291] These parameters are incorporated by a dynamic[1292] sampling of the portfolio compositions.

1285 Cp. Garz, Günther, Moriabadi (2006), p. 42ff.
1286 Cp. Markowitz (1987), p. 47ff.
1287 Cp. Kohn, Papazoglu-Statescu (2006), p. 173.
1288 The enhancement is imbedded by a loss constriction.
1289 Sharpe (2007), p. 18f.
1290 Cp. Markowitz (1952), p. 77ff.
1291 Cp. Arshanapalli, Nelson (2010), p. 34ff.
1292 Cp. Chen, Glasserman (2007), p. 155.

In terms of Markowitz, who constituted his investment maturity by a not further verified term of a one-period model, this incoherent denomination is converted into a period of half a year.[1293] The portfolios are reallocated semi-annually at the first trading day in January and July, which provokes a dynamic alteration of portfolio weights in contrast to the static naïve diversification.

The progressional weightings of the index members are quantified by measuring the maximum Sharpe ratio[1294] portfolios for the return series of the former half-year. Hence, the frequently predefined percentile maximum portfolio influences[1295] of assets or asset classes are avoided because the portfolios should serve as flexible long-term[1296] investment vehicles. If investors compare their historical portfolio achievements to market barometers[1297], they frequently marvel why the outcomes differ significantly[1298]. Hence, in positive equity market trends[1299] they desire to participate of these gains and in market downturns[1300] they require a portfolio comprising exclusively riskless assets.

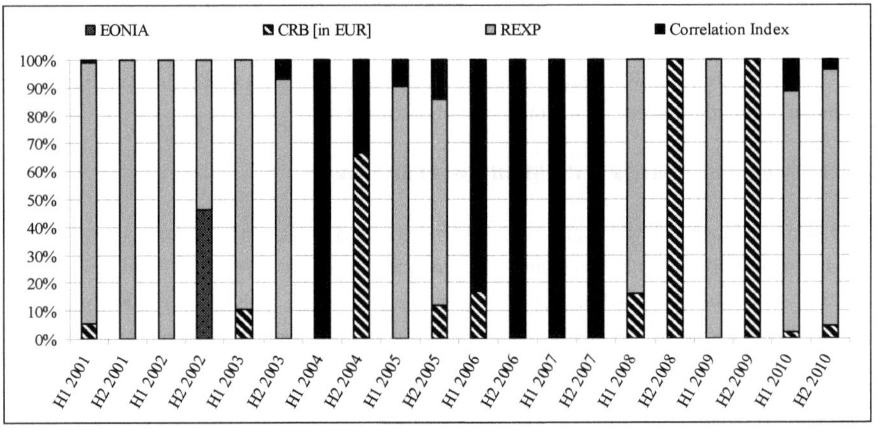

Figure 19: EMA and EEMA portfolio compositions at the reallocation dates[1301]

1293 Cp. Steinbach (2001), p. 32.
1294 Cp. Christensen, Platen (2007), p. 1340.
1295 Cp. Dolvin, Templeton, Riebe (2010), p. 60.
1296 Cp. Gintschel, Scherer (2008), p. 215.
1297 Cp. Barbosa (2009), p. 37.
1298 Cp. Xiong, Ibbotson, Idzorek, Chen (2010), p. 7.
1299 Cp. Wong, Shum (2010), p. 1615.
1300 Cp. Buraschi, Porchia, Trojani (2010), p. 395.
1301 Self-provided figure in dependence of: Bloomberg [ed.] (2011c) to ibid. (2011bd).

Hence, the security compositions should be trend[1302] dependent and not predefined by specific proportions. The portfolio modifications are illustrated in figure 19, where this trend dependency becomes obvious. The relative asset quantities are chosen on the reallocation dates, whereby in particular the maximum Sharpe ratio portfolios in half-year two (H2) 2001, half-year one (H1) 2002, H1 2004, H2 2006, H1 2007, H2 2007, H2 2008, H1 2009 and H2 2009 are biased by solely one asset class.

Using the return progressions of the previous half-year to calculate the subsequent portfolio constitutions assumes the past performance to serve as predictor for the prospective asset price developments as described by Jacobsen (2010).[1303]

Aberrations from the Markowitz concept are pretended by the regional limitation of the EMU in contrast to a potential global diversification[1304] and the number of exclusively four assets, opponent to an abstractly boundless[1305] quantity of securities.

Within the allocation process of the EEMA, a comprehension of stop loss[1306] constraints is applied for considerations of return series, impacted by third[1307] and fourth moments[1308] and especially the appearing negative extreme values[1309]. According to Lei and Li (2009) these loss restrictions should not necessarily serve as return enhancement but rather as risk diminution and behavioural[1310] encouragement against prospective loss aversion.[1311]

1302 Cp. Cohen (2011), p. 45f.
1303 Cp. Jacobsen (2010), p. 53.
1304 Cp. Ferris, Sen, Nguyen (2010), p. 1028.
1305 Cp. Bai, Liu, Wong (2009), p. 640.
1306 Cp. James, Yang (2010), p. 2.
1307 Cp. Bao, Ullah (2009), p. 233.
1308 Cp. Fang, Lai (1997), p. 293.
1309 Cp. Darkiewicz, Deelstra, Dhaene, Hoedemakers, Vanmaele (2009), p. 848.
1310 Cp. Mittal, Vyas (2009), p. 27.
1311 Cp. Lei, Li (2009), p. 49.

Effective date	Return without loss restriction (only implied assets)	Worst return since reallocation (only implied assets)	Respective asset	Date of loss restriction
02.01.2001	-0,42%	-12,71%	EMU Correlation Index	23.03.2011
02.07.2001	0,02%	-0,20%	REXP	--
02.01.2002	0,09%	-1,13%	REXP	--
01.07.2002	0,06%	-0,20%	REXP	--
02.01.2003	0,09%	-9,51%	CRB [in EUR]	--
01.07.2003	-0,24%	-2,23%	REXP	--
02.01.2004	-0,33%	-4,10%	EMU Correlation Index	--
01.07.2004	-0,50%	-8,83%	CRB [in EUR]	--
03.01.2005	0,21%	-0,58%	EMU Correlation Index	--
01.07.2005	0,17%	-2,77%	CRB [in EUR]	--
03.01.2006	1,31%	-2,21%	EMU Correlation Index	--
03.07.2006	-0,10%	-4,46%	EMU Correlation Index	--
02.01.2007	0,66%	-1,96%	EMU Correlation Index	--
02.07.2007	0,01%	-13,08%	EMU Correlation Index	17.08.2007
02.01.2008	-0,32%	-3,73%	CRB [in EUR]	--
01.07.2008	0,01%	-49,40%	CRB [in EUR]	24.07.2008
02.01.2009	-0,07%	0,00%	REXP	--
01.07.2009	0,02%	-5,93%	CRB [in EUR]	--
04.01.2010	-0,08%	-13,80%	EMU Correlation Index	08.02.2010
01.07.2010	0,06%	-2,52%	CRB [in EUR]	--

Table 39: Loss restrictions of the EEMA[1312]

During every investment period and for every comprised asset the stop loss limit is established at a deficit of ten percent[1313] since the last reallocation because a double-digit loss appears to be maximally tolerable for an allocation even admitting to invest the entire portfolio into risky assets. This procedure permits a maximum loss per biannual investment period of ten percent according to the entire portfolio[1314]. If the loss barrier is hit or crossed, the asset is sold and reinvested into cash on the following trading day. Table 39 indicates that the loss restraint has intervened four times[1315] during the 20 allocation cycles.

1312 Self-provided table in dependence of: Bloomberg [ed.] (2011c) to ibid. (2011bd).

1313 The extent of the stop loss limit can be elected individually, depending on the respective loss aversion of the investor; cp. Jagd, Madsen (2009), p. 1384.

1314 Though this negative extreme value is only provoked if the entire portfolio is exclusively allocated by any-losing assest, which hit the stop loss barriere and subsequently cash does not obtain any gains.

1315 The restrictions intervene respectively three times for the ECI and once for the CRB [in EUR].

4.4.2 Backtesting of the Multi Asset Portfolios

Subsequently the EMA[1316] and the EEMA[1317] are confronted with an equally weighted[1318] portfolio of the four comprised assets. The naïvely diversified[1319] portfolio is not subject to any rebalancings[1320] and serves as measure of comparison whereat the performance measures and the backtesting results are declared.[1321]

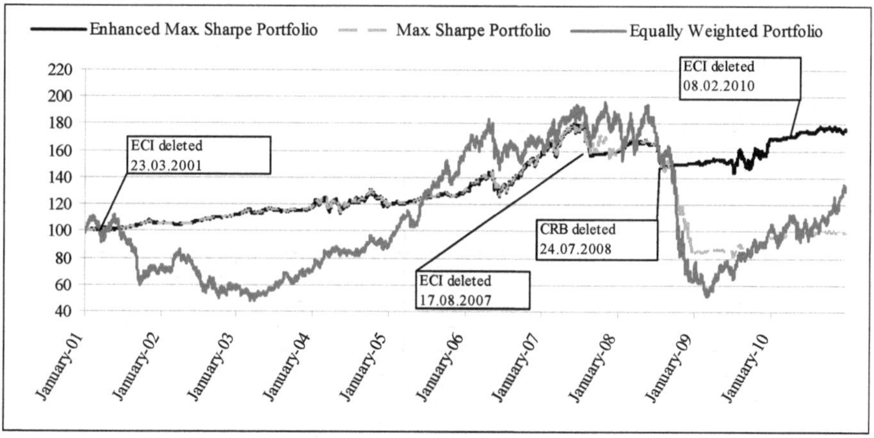

Figure 20: Standardised charts of the EMA, EEMA and equal weighting[1322]

Figure 20 illustrates the charts of the three objects for analysis together with the remarks of the deleted assets according to the stop loss mechanism of the EEMA. The portfolio developments are standardised to the base value[1323] of 100 on January 01st 2001. Prior to the detailed performance evaluation, the predominance of the EEMA becomes evident, even by a simple examination of the charts. Solely the EMA suffers a marginal loss with its final value[1324] of 98,88 opponent to 130,39 of the equal weighting and the maximum of 175,69 ac-

1316 For reasons of a better perceivability within the following tables and figures, the EMA is denominated as Max Sharpe Portfolio.

1317 For reasons of a better perceivability within the following tables and figures, the EEMA is denominated as Enahnced Max Sharpe Portfolio.

1318 Cp. Block, French (2002), p. 20.

1319 Cp. Hamza, Kortas, L'Her, Roberge (2007), p. 103.

1320 Cp. Willenbrock (2011), p. 45.

1321 Cp. McQuarrie (2008), p. 30.

1322 Self-provided figure in dependence of: Bloomberg [ed.] (2011c) to ibid. (2011bd).

1323 Cp. Ganser (2008), p. 16.

1324 At the end of the investigation period on December 31st 2010.

cording to the EEMA. Hence, the stop loss processing[1325] does not only cause a behavioural[1326] loss reduction[1327] but coexistently a return optimisation.

4.4.3 Analysis and Comparison of the Multi Asset Portfolios

The performance analysis depends on the monthly log-returns of the EMA, the EEMA and the equal weighting that are annualised[1328] and listed in table 40.

annual log-return	Max Sharpe Portfolio	Enhanced Max Sharpe Portfolio	Equal weighting
2001	5,03%	4,98%	-27,46%
2002	6,45%	6,45%	-21,39%
2003	4,48%	4,48%	27,29%
2004	2,44%	2,44%	23,92%
2005	8,03%	8,03%	63,57%
2006	20,29%	20,29%	4,98%
2007	2,00%	1,80%	12,04%
2008	-58,41%	-4,89%	-93,18%
2009	12,19%	12,19%	50,27%
2010	3,69%	3,60%	28,42%
sum	6,20%	59,39%	68,45%
average	0,62%	5,94%	6,85%
max	20,29%	20,29%	63,57%
min	-58,41%	-4,89%	-93,18%

Table 40: Annual log-returns of the EMA, EEMA and the equal weighting[1329]

Especially the distinction of returns during the year 2008[1330] is conspicuous. The inherent loss restriction of the EEMA provokes the avoidance of obvious losses, appearing in the case of the EMA and the equal weighting. Consequently to the stop loss[1331] mechanism and the occasional selling of equities or commodities and their exchange into cash conserves the EEMA of further losses and affects a comparatively compliant annual loss of 4,89% during the year 2008. As illustrated by the charts of figure 20, this aspect is the main reason for the predominant success of the EEMA during the entire investment period.

1325 Cp. Osler (2003), p. 1793.
1326 Cp. Levy (2010), p. 1021.
1327 Cp. Harris (2010), p. 38.
1328 Cp. Chang, DuPoyet, Prakash (2008), p. 1635.
1329 Self-provided table in dependence of: Bloomberg [ed.] (2011c) to ibid. (2011bd).
1330 During the year 2008, commodity prices declined distinctly; cp. Mitchell (2010), p. 42.
1331 Cp. Ng (2005), p. 624.

annual volatility	Max Sharpe Portfolio	Enhanced Max Sharpe Portfolio	Equal weighting
2001	3,05%	3,07%	31,38%
2002	2,21%	2,21%	32,41%
2003	3,67%	3,67%	27,14%
2004	9,81%	9,81%	14,71%
2005	3,28%	3,28%	24,69%
2006	9,32%	9,32%	12,95%
2007	11,21%	12,03%	15,66%
2008	25,94%	11,52%	44,06%
2009	8,02%	8,02%	26,25%
2010	3,43%	3,47%	21,09%
average	7,99%	6,64%	25,04%
max	25,94%	12,03%	44,06%
min	2,21%	2,21%	12,95%

Table 41: Annual volatilities of the EMA, EEMA and the equal weighting[1332]

Comparing the annual volatilities[1333] in table 41 emphasises the effectiveness of the EMA and especially the EEMA because their return deviations are conspicuously lower than those of the equal weighting. The results of the EMA depict that even without the stop loss approach the allocation procedure induces a discrete risk reduction[1334]. The average volatilities of 7,99% (EMA) and 6,64% (EEMA) are merely a third of the 25,05% by the equal weighting. Both portfolios maintain their distribution advantage over any analysed year. This can be interpreted as indicator of the past performance, impairing the future return developments; hence the allocation, based on historical price movements, seems to have an explanatory power for the prospective progressions.[1335] These findings provoke the supposition that the EMU[1336] capital markets are not even exceeding the weak level of information efficiency.

The performance measures of Sharpe[1337], listed in table 42, exhibit assimilable but inconstant results, denoting an advantage of the EMA and especially the EEMA. At least their average "risk reward ratios"[1338] exceed the equal weighting, though during the selected periods the equal weighting features comparable or even superior values.

1332 Self-provided table in dependence of: Bloomberg [ed.] (2011c) to ibid. (2011bd).
1333 Cp. Gerard, Guojun (2006), p. 2204.
1334 Cp. Fletcher (2009), p. 953.
1335 Cp. Jacobsen (2010), p. 53.
1336 Cp. Patra, Poshakwale (2008), p. 1409.
1337 Cp. Israelsen (2001), p. 51.
1338 Amenc, Goltz, Martellini (2011), p. 14.

Sharpe ratio	Max Sharpe Portfolio	Enhanced Max Sharpe Portfolio	Equal weighting
2001	0,21	0,19	-1,02
2002	1,39	1,39	-0,76
2003	0,58	0,58	0,92
2004	0,04	0,04	1,48
2005	1,80	1,80	2,49
2006	1,87	1,87	0,16
2007	-0,17	-0,18	0,52
2008	-2,40	-0,77	-2,20
2009	1,43	1,43	1,89
2010	0,95	0,91	1,33
average	0,57	0,73	0,48
max	1,87	1,87	2,49
min	-2,40	-0,77	-2,20

Table 42: Sharpe ratios of the EMA, EEMA and the equal weighting[1339]

Equally to every further calculated return, risk or performance ratio, the EMA and the EEMA differ only during the years with the four stop loss interventions of the EEMA because the intrinsic interim start allocations are equal.

maximum drawdown	Max Sharpe Portfolio	Enhanced Max Sharpe Portfolio	Equal weighting
high	180,90	180,83	196,54
date of high	01.06.2007	04.06.2007	31.10.2007
following low	80,99	144,03	51,60
date of following low	08.07.2009	08.08.2009	09.03.2009
Max DD (entire period)	55,23%	20,35%	73,74%
Max DD 2001	2,69%	2,69%	47,31%
Max DD 2002	1,75%	1,75%	42,59%
Max DD 2003	2,38%	2,38%	12,82%
Max DD 2004	9,89%	9,89%	10,43%
Max DD 2005	2,24%	2,24%	11,85%
Max DD 2006	12,73%	12,73%	20,61%
Max DD 2007	15,67%	13,64%	18,71%
Max DD 2008	50,27%	12,52%	67,86%
Max DD 2009	8,94%	8,94%	17,34%
Max DD 2010	2,41%	2,41%	17,52%
average	10,90%	6,92%	26,70%
max	50,27%	13,64%	67,86%
min	1,75%	1,75%	10,43%

Table 43: Maximum drawdowns of the EMA, EEMA and the equal weighting[1340]

1339 Self-provided table in dependence of: Bloomberg [ed.] (2011c) to ibid. (2011bd).
1340 Self-provided table in dependence of: Bloomberg [ed.] (2011c) to ibid. (2011bd).

In addition to the volatility, the second calculated risk measure of annual and entire period's maximum drawdowns[1341], specified in table 43, prove the equal weighting as most risky and both portfolio allocations as risk minimising[1342]. Again the risk reduction technique of the EEMA is emphasised as predominant because it delivers the best results and lowest maximum losses since reaching an interim high during the entire investigation.[1343] In addition to Lei and Li (2009) the expectation of comprising the stop loss barriers provokes superior results because of the reduction of extreme losses[1344], which are evoked by the adverse return distribution[1345] as described in the subsequent accomplishments.[1346]

downside deviation	Max Sharpe Portfolio	Enhanced Max Sharpe Portfolio	Equal weighting
2001	1,04%	1,04%	24,23%
2002	1,90%	1,90%	17,98%
2003	1,47%	1,47%	23,81%
2004	5,18%	5,18%	5,40%
2005	NA	NA	1,66%
2006	12,71%	12,71%	10,41%
2007	6,47%	10,94%	12,87%
2008	25,17%	18,78%	25,50%
2009	2,94%	2,94%	21,13%
2010	1,40%	1,40%	9,08%
average	6,47%	6,26%	15,21%
max	25,17%	18,78%	25,50%
min	1,04%	1,04%	1,66%

Table 44: Downside deviations of the EMA, EEMA and the equal weighting[1347]

The downside deviations, listed in table 44, serve as confirmation of the negative volatilities[1348] which could only be calculated for years with negative monthly return deviations that do not exist for the EMA and the EEMA during the year 2005. They are applied because investors frequently regard any risk exclusively in the context of negative aberrations beneath a certain benchmark return, which is assumed with zero.[1349]

1341 Cp. Pospisil, Vecer (2010), p. 617.
1342 Cp. Mainik, Rüschendorf (2010), p. 608.
1343 Cp. Heidorn, Kaiser, Roder (2009), p. 89.
1344 Cp. de Melo Mendes (2006), p. 594.
1345 Cp. Athavale, Gaebel (2011), p. 39.
1346 Cp. Lei, Li (2009), p. 49.
1347 Self-provided table in dependence of: Bloomberg [ed.] (2011c) to ibid. (2011bd).
1348 Cp. Miller, Leiblein (1996), p. 92.
1349 Cp. Trachtenberg (2001), p. 76.

Using the downside deviation as risk measure in the denominator of the Sortino ratio[1350], as alternative performance measure to the common use of the Sharpe index, the respective ratios are given in table 45.[1351]

In contrast to the Sortino[1352] measure, the Sharpe ratio is used as allocation principle because it refers directly to the mean-variance[1353] criteria of Markowitz and according to Beach (2006) the entire consideration of volatility as connotation of risk is more valuable than the simple limitation towards the downside risk.[1354]

Sortino ratio	Max Sharpe Portfolio	Enhanced Max Sharpe Portfolio	Equal weighting
2001	0,61	0,57	-1,31
2002	1,63	1,63	-1,38
2003	1,44	1,44	1,05
2004	0,07	0,07	4,04
2005	NA	NA	37,09
2006	1,37	1,37	0,20
2007	-0,29	-0,19	0,63
2008	-2,48	-0,47	-3,81
2009	3,90	3,90	2,34
2010	2,32	2,26	3,08
average	0,95	1,18	0,54
max	3,90	3,90	4,04
min	-2,48	-0,47	-3,81

Table 45: Sortino ratios of the EMA, EEMA and the equal weighting[1355]

The Sortino results are in line with the above specified criteria, mentioning the EEMA as predominant to the EMA and the equal weighting.[1356] The average data already marks the EEMA (1,18) as best, the EMA (0,95) as second and the equal weighting (0,54) as worst ranked.

The stop loss restriction was introduced to manage the extreme losses appearing the by not normally distributed[1357] returns due to third and fourth moments.[1358] Tables 46 and 47 represent the skewness and kurtosis parameters of the three portfolios.

1350 Cp. Chaudhry, Johnson (2008), p. 486.
1351 Cp. Leggio, Lien (2003), p. 82.
1352 Cp. Scherer (2004), p. 5.
1353 Cp. Mukherji (2003), p. 62.
1354 Cp. Beach (2006), p. 16.
1355 Self-provided table in dependence of: Bloomberg [ed.] (2011c) to ibid. (2011bd).
1356 Cp. Eling, Farinelli, Rossello, Tibiletti (2011), p. 267.
1357 Cp. Zakamouline, Koekebakker (2009), p. 938.
1358 Cp. Fang, Lai (1997), p. 293; Bao, Ullah (2009), p. 233.

skewness	Max Sharpe Portfolio	Enhanced Max Sharpe Portfolio	Equal weighting
2001	-0,50	-0,51	-0,90
2002	-0,98	-0,98	0,18
2003	0,27	0,27	-0,96
2004	-0,36	-0,36	0,68
2005	-2,20	-2,20	-1,61
2006	-1,67	-1,67	-0,83
2007	-0,24	-1,03	-0,85
2008	-0,98	-2,81	0,12
2009	1,32	1,32	-0,56
2010	0,78	0,84	-0,43
average	-0,46	-0,71	-0,52

Table 46: Skewness of the EMA, EEMA and the equal weighting[1359]

The skewness[1360] and kurtosis[1361] figures are volatile and disadvantageous for risk-averse[1362] investors because extreme negative risk levels[1363] have to be supposed and regarded within the consideration of any general investment decision.[1364]

kurtosis	Max Sharpe Portfolio	Enhanced Max Sharpe Portfolio	Equal weighting
2001	2,63	2,62	4,26
2002	3,80	3,80	2,10
2003	1,88	1,88	3,18
2004	1,58	1,58	3,03
2005	9,00	9,00	4,51
2006	6,69	6,69	4,38
2007	1,88	4,34	3,78
2008	3,03	12,00	2,27
2009	5,74	5,74	4,00
2010	3,92	3,91	2,68
average	3,81	5,24	3,44

Table 47: Kurtosis of the EMA, EEMA and the equal weighting[1365]

Especially during the years 2005, 2006, 2008 and 2009 the rejection of a log-normal return distribution[1366] is proved by the Jarque-Bera test[1367] results, as listed in table 48.

1359 Self-provided table in dependence of: Bloomberg [ed.] (2011c) to ibid. (2011bd).
1360 Cp. Leggio, Lien (2003a), p. 213.
1361 Cp. Botha (2007), p. 464.
1362 Cp. Gemmill, Soosung, Salmon (2006), p. 192.
1363 Cp. Kida, Moreno, Smith (2010), p. 24.
1364 Cp. Bharathi (2010), p. 34.
1365 Self-provided table in dependence of: Bloomberg [ed.] (2011c) to ibid. (2011bd).
1366 Cp. De La Grandville, Pakes, Tricot (2002), p. 26.
1367 Cp. Thadewald, Büning (2007), p. 88.

An essential superiority does not have to be declared between the EMA and the EEMA because both reflect the common perspective of risky asset returns deviating conspicuously from the Gaussian distribution.[1368] Only the returns of the equal weighting are distributed advantageous over the entire period.

Jarque-Bera test	Max Sharpe Portfolio	Enhanced Max Sharpe Portfolio	Equal weighting
2001	0,58	0,60	2,39
2002	2,23	2,23	0,46
2003	0,77	0,77	1,86
2004	1,28	1,28	0,92
2005	27,68	27,68	6,29
2006	12,41	12,41	2,32
2007	0,74	3,03	1,76
2008	1,93	56,25	0,29
2009	7,26	7,26	1,12
2010	1,63	1,83	0,42
entire period	5,65	11,33	1,78

Table 48: Jarque-Bera test results of the EMA, EEMA and the equal weighting[1369]

4.4.4 Conclusion Concerning the Multi Asset Portfolios

Analysing the three portfolios serves to measure the applicability of the EMA and the EEMA as efficient portfolio combinations for commodities, EMU equities, German governmental bonds and cash without any weighting restrictions[1370].

The exclusive allocations of a maximum Sharpe ratio portfolio[1371] is predominant to the equal weighting but the enhancement by a stop loss[1372] mechanism, to constrain losses, even outperforms both standards of comparison. Without this amplification the return outliers[1373], due to science-based third[1374] and fourth moments[1375], evoke above average losses that can only be balanced during several years and defeat potential previous gains.

1368 Cp. Haas, Mittnik, Paolella (2006), p. 1145.
1369 Self-provided table in dependence of: Bloomberg [ed.] (2011c) to ibid. (2011bd); the calculation complies for chi-values with two degrees of freedom and a confidence inverval of 95%, exhibiting p-values of 5,991.
1370 Cp. Pfau (2010), p. 60.
1371 Cp. Christensen, Platen (2007), p. 1339ff.
1372 Cp. James, Yang (2010), p. 2.
1373 Cp. Darkiewicz, Deelstra, Dhaene, Hoedemakers, Vanmaele (2009), p. 848.
1374 Cp. Bao, Ullah (2009), p. 233.
1375 Cp. Fang, Lai (1997), p. 293.

The extent of the supposed stop loss limits can be elected individually in dependence of the respective investor's loss aversion.[1376] If the loss restriction intervenes and the concerned asset's weight is rearranged into cash, the investment risk is automatically reduced. This procedure assumes cash as single asset class[1377] which has to be incorporated in the asset allocations especially as portfolio coverage.[1378]

The consideration of the performance analysis induces the conclusion to reject the null hypothesis of *(H4)* because the allocation approach implicated by means of the EEMA is a qualified modification of the Portfolio Selection Theory[1379]. The application of an entire market portfolio[1380] comprising any risky asset of the global market is an exclusively hypothetical approach but as identified by the EEMA even a definite diminution of composition delivers appealing returns. The diversification[1381] requirements can even be conformed by the limited market portfolio of the chosen four indices displaying diverse asset classes.[1382] Especially the correlation weighting of the equity portion enhances the principle of diversification benefits[1383] conspicuously due to regarding price dependencies[1384] of the comprised most risky members of the final portfolio.[1385]

The criticism of the Markowitz approach seems to be unjustified and motivated by investors featuring portfolios, biased by exceedingly weighted risky elements whose risk premiums[1386] are interdependent but this aspect remains unconsidered.[1387] Hence, security accounts are not sufficiently diversified and do not incorporate a dynamic mean-variance[1388] composition of uncorrelated risky and riskless fractions. As exemplary approach, the EEMA encompasses the specified reasons why investors can assail the Markowitz approach[1389]. The performance analysis illustrates that its consideration together with the implied loss constrictions, as specification of practical requirements, performed well even during the financial crisis.[1390]

1376 Cp. Jagd, Madsen (2009), p. 1384.
1377 Cp. Rojahn, Röhl, Frère (2010), p. 5.
1378 Cp. Kritzman, Page, Turkington (2010), p. 32f.
1379 Cp. Markowitz (1952), p. 77ff.
1380 Cp. Hwang, Satchell (2002), p. 775.
1381 Cp. Willenbrock (2011), p. 191.
1382 Cp. McCormick (2011), p. 20f.
1383 Cp. Baltussen, Post (2010), p. 1464.
1384 Cp. Statman, Scheid (2008), p. 132.
1385 Cp. Eling (2006), p. 32.
1386 Cp. Kim (2011), p. 170.
1387 Cp. Patchett, Horgan (2011), p. 37.
1388 Cp. Mitra, Mitra, Di Bartolomeo (2009), p. 887.
1389 Cp. Curtis (2004), p. 16.
1390 Cp. Khademian (2011), p. 841ff.

5 Conclusion and Outlook

5.1 Recapitulation of Achievements and Hypotheses

After initiating the thesis with the introduction, including the initial situation, the definition of the problem and the four assumed hypotheses, the second chapter exemplifies the principles of portfolio management[1391] conditions. This deals with a great scope of indexing approaches[1392] as well as their economical denotations, complemented by several explanations of the portfolio selection[1393] and capital market theories[1394] as well as a deduction of the practical denotations of correlation[1395].

Section 2.2.4 deals with the falsification of the null hypothesis according to *(H1)* where it could be clarified that correlations between financial assets, in the case of commodities and EMU equities, depend negatively on equity market trends[1396]. This phenomenon is expressed during the time of ten years from 2001 to 2010, which is divided into bullish and bearish equity market tendencies by means of the SX5E. During market downturns (upturns) the analysed correlations increase (decrease), whereat investors especially depend on low statistical dependencies of security prices during market turmoil to enhance their potential portfolio diversification benefits[1397].

Chapter 2 expires with determinations of the elected performance[1398] parameters as risk[1399], return[1400] and liquidity[1401], which are further disposed in the differentiation and consideration of the selected performance measures[1402] as reprehension of the subsequent allocation approaches and performance evaluations[1403].

The empirical investigation of comparing the EMU equity allocation approaches by countries or industries with reference to *(H2)* is conducted in chapter 3.[1404] Prior to this, the allocation framework is constituted by distinctions of the information efficiency[1405], the principal-agent

---

1391 Cp. Gülpinar, Katata, Pachamanova (2011), p. 68.
1392 Cp. Ganser (2008), p. 15.
1393 Cp. Markowitz (1952), p. 77ff.
1394 Cp. Stock (2002), p. 41.
1395 Cp. D'Antonio, Johnsen (2011), p. 37.
1396 Cp. Buraschi, Porchia, Trojani (2010), p. 395.
1397 Cp. Ang, Chen (2002), p. 444.
1398 Cp. Chamberlain (2011), p. 18.
1399 Cp. Scholz, Wilkens (2006), p. 1278.
1400 Cp. Gregoriou, Pascalau (2010), p. 189.
1401 Cp. Steiner, Bruns (2007), p. 77.
1402 Cp. Heidorn, Hoppe, Kaiser (2006), p. 571.
1403 Cp. Guojin, Li, Shin (2011), p. 1012.
1404 Cp. Döhnert, Kunz, Wälchi (2000), p. 15ff.
1405 Cp. Perridon, Steiner (2004), p. 344ff.; Fama (1970), p. 383; Stock (2002), p. 19ff.

conflicts[1406] and general asset allocation[1407] procedures as well as the specific implications of the regional qualifications by the EMU. In section 3.5 the null hypothesis of *(H2)* is falsified because the consequence of the arranged naïvely diversified EMU country and industry portfolios constrain the industry allocation as advantageous in comparison to the country diversification.[1408]

In chapter 4 firstly proxies of the four incorporated asset classes[1409] are delineated by indices restricting the investment universe. Accordingly the null hypothesis of *(H3)* is experimentally rejected by identifying the EMU equity indexing as more promising than stock picking according to the SX5E[1410] determined by anticipating changes of its index memberships[1411]. Subsequently the ECI is calculated and tested *qua novel* equity indexing approach[1412] by weighting index members with reference to their correlation towards commodity prices as the remaining risky asset class of the insinuated investment framework.

Finally the EMA and the EEMA are engineered as dynamic multi asset portfolios[1413] and sampling of *(H4)*. Both maximum Sharpe ratio[1414] allocations are calculated due to considerations of the former capital market developments serving as prospect of future trends with a risk restriction by means of the EEMA. The achievements point out the rejection of the null hypothesis of *(H4)* because the calculations of the EMA as well as the EEMA refer to practical amplifications of the Markowitz technique[1415] and feature beneficial evolutions for EMU investors during the challenging capital market conditions[1416] of the years 2001 to 2010. *(H4)* expresses the main objective of this thesis as verification of the Portfolio Selection Theory[1417] and their availability according to the current capital market circumstances.[1418] This purpose is confirmed even within a conspicuously constricted portfolio of the EMU comprising exclusively four asset classes.

1406 Cp. Gauld (2007), p. 18.
1407 Cp. Ibbotson (2010), p. 1.
1408 Cp. Berbena, Jansen (2009), p. 3067.
1409 Cp. Freeman (2006), p. 3.
1410 Cp. Ferruz, Munoz, Vargas (2010), p. 408.
1411 Cp. Elton, Gruber, Busse (2004), p. 270.
1412 Cp. Ganser (2008), p. 15.
1413 Cp. McCormick (2011), p. 20f.
1414 Cp. Christensen, Platen (2007), p. 1340.
1415 Cp. Curtis (2004), p. 16.
1416 Cp. Khademian (2011), p. 841.
1417 Cp. Markowitz (1952), p. 77ff.
1418 Cp. Beinart (2003), p. 6; Richman, Santos, Barkoulas (2005), p. 947ff.

Hence, the ordinary criticism[1419] of the theory is refuted. Frequently apperaing portfolio losses during the global financial crisis[1420] are in fact constituted by disregarding the changeability of the asset price movements and their statistical dependencies[1421]. Portfolios did not comprise sufficient real time techniques of risk management[1422] and investors featured overconfidence in their own abilities[1423].

5.2 Future Prospects

The common practical application of static, single asset benchmarks[1424] for actively managed multi asset portfolios is identified as missing investor's targets[1425]. Hence, portfolio managers should adopt dynamic[1426], risk adjusted[1427] benchmarks that are actually suitable to their management approaches. Otherwise any benchmarking effort is senseless and incapable to compare risk/return attributes of investments with the active ability of the portfolio manager. A respective systematic measure of comparison even secures the investor to be affected by moral hazard[1428] if the manager gathers disproportionate portions of risk during times markets do not compensate them by adjusted returns.[1429] The enhanced acceptance of variable and systematically allocated benchmarks depends on the professional eligibility of investors and managers which has to be expanded by additional research.

It has to be expected that Markowitz's intention of building efficiently[1430] diversified portfolios did not contain the optional acceptance of including securities exhibiting extreme losses[1431]. Allocating portfolios with regard to the asset's intercorrelation[1432] and combination of risky assets like equities or commodities can evoke extreme outliers due to their pricing characteristics biased by skewness and kurtosis.[1433] Hence, gains of portfolio portions are frequently overcompensated by negative price developments of ulterior members reasoning in distinct and enduring portfolio losses. The changing capital market conditions cause a progressional process of empirical research to enable investors to handle appearing and variable risk factors adequately.

1419 Cp. Mitra, Mitra, Di Bartolomeo (2009), p. 887.
1420 Cp. Khademian (2011), p. 841ff.
1421 Cp. Statman, Scheid (2008), p. 132.
1422 Cp. D'Antonio, Johnsen (2011), p. 37.
1423 Cp. Horvitz, Wilcox (2007), p. 43.
1424 Cp. Amenc, Goltz, Martellini (2011), p. 11.
1425 Cp. Curtillet, Dieudonné (2007), p. 410.
1426 Cp. Gèrber, Hens, Woehrmann (2010), p. 370.
1427 Cp. Rompolis, Tzavalis (2010), p. 129ff.
1428 Cp. Kuhnen (2009), p. 2185f.
1429 Cp. Krein (2010), p. 20.
1430 Cp. Hu, Kercheval (2010), p. 91.
1431 Cp. Lescourret, Robert (2006), p. 223.
1432 Cp. Eling (2006), p. 32.
1433 Cp. Bao, Ullah (2009), p. 233.

The allocated mean-variance[1434] optimised EEMA comprises a stop loss mechanism as behavioural[1435] control and risk restriction[1436] which can be individualised respecting the investor's loss aversion.[1437] The dynamic portfolio approach serves as one possibility and adoption of several static allocations towards the fast moving alterability of financial markets including frequent incidents of market turmoil. Equally to Markowitz the portfolio is allocated using the volatility as indicator of risk[1438] expanded by the Sharpe ratio[1439]. Though both parameters remain contradictory if returns of the comprised assets are not normally distributed[1440] and the past is adducted as prospective allocation criteria, the portfolio is effective even during the challenging years 2007 and 2008[1441]. Additional research will be focussed on different performance attributes which prepare the investment community with an improved prediction of future market developments.

The entire elaboration should be regarded as proposal to terminate the global discussion of passive[1442] vs. active[1443] portfolio management. The implementations suggest that both approaches are advantageous as reciprocal completion. Passive investments can be applied as strategicall[1444] long-term inducements expanded by active, tactical[1445] short-run implications reducing losses and enhancing returns. The practical appreciation of this combined perspective of both standards of portfolio management depends on further research which should illustrate their interrelation as well as their reciprocal benefit.

Analogically to the affirmed validity of the Portfolio Selection Theory the model is assumed to maintain available even if the EMU[1446] is subject to prospective composition changes because the attested decade was already impaired by this apprehension[1447]. The explanations demonstrate that correlation[1448] based systematical diversification[1449] approaches are able to offer additional benefits for investors in the long-run. Neither the exploitation of any anticipated index effect[1450] nor a buy and hold strategy[1451] are approximately as prosperous.

1434 Cp. Mukherji (2003), p. 62.
1435 Cp. Mittal, Vyas (2009), p. 27.
1436 Cp. Darkiewicz, Deelstra, Dhaene, Hoedemakers, Vanmaele (2009), p. 848.
1437 Cp. Xiong, Idzorek (2011), p. 23ff.
1438 Cp. Kaplanski, Kroll (2002), p. 1ff.
1439 Cp. Sharpe (1975), p. 29ff.
1440 Cp. Füss, Rehkugler, Disch (2005), p. 46.
1441 Cp. Khademian (2011), p. 841.
1442 Cp. Milonas, Rompotis (2010), p. 97.
1443 Cp. Duan, Hu, McLean (2009), p. 56ff.
1444 Cp. Sharpe (1987), p. 27.
1445 Cp. Winchester, Huston, Finke (2011), p. 48.
1446 Cp. Giannellis, Papadopoulos (2011), p. 39ff.
1447 Cp. Heinen, Böttcher [ed.] (2010), p. 3.
1448 Cp. Williams, Zumbo, Ross, Zimmermann (2003), p. 296ff.
1449 Cp. Willenbrock (2011), p. 191.
1450 Cp. Elton, Gruber, Busse (2004), p. 270.
1451 Cp. Ruggiero (2009), p. 42ff.

Within further research the investigation can be complemented by implications from the behavioural finance[1452] as reference towards the irrational behaviour of investors which is disregarded by the Portfolio Selection Theory.[1453] Further a robustness test combined to a sensitivity analyses should validate the findings. In doing so exchanges of the Sharpe ratio by varying performance measures[1454] as well as different stop loss limits[1455] of the EEMA, ulterior allocation cycles, comprehensions of additional asset classes, the consideration of deviant currencies and especially a global investment environment[1456] ought to be assumed.

A further analysis has to substantiate the essential existence of a riskless rate of return[1457]. Capital market theories like the CAPM[1458] are founded by assuming the existence of a risk-free yield[1459] or at least the possibility to create it by collateralising claims. The constrictions of the interbank refinancing[1460] and any appearing counterpart risks[1461] constitute this acceptance as dignified to scrutinize, whereat a prospective rejection would provoke an entire reorientation of several existent capital market and portfolio theories.

1452 Cp. Singh (2010), p. 1ff.
1453 Cp. Roßbach (2001), p. 3ff.
1454 Cp. Barton, Hansen, Pownall (2010), p. 754.
1455 Cp. Heidorn, Kaiser, Roder (2009), p. 5; James, Yang (2010), p. 1ff.
1456 Cp. Bai, Liu, Wong (2009), p. 640.
1457 Cp. Hamada, Valdez (2008), p. 388.
1458 Cp. Wang, Xia (2002), p. 145.
1459 Cp. da Fonseca (2010), p. 728.
1460 Cp. Colomer (2011), p. 10ff.
1461 Cp. Martin, Reitz, When (2006), p. 22f.

Appendix

Monitoring of the budgetary discipline by the commission

annual announcement dates:
- 01. March or
- 01. September

Excessive deficite procedures are discharged if:
- public deficit/GDP ratio equals or exceeds 3%
- public debt/GDP ratio equals or exceeds 60%
- consideration of discretionary decisions according to maceration of the pact

Comment to the Ecofin

- Not binding commendation to the counsil

Counsil

Decision about the exceeding deficit
- commendation of the commission
- consultation of the respective member country
- proof of the economic circumstances

in the case of an exceeding deficit

Obligatory commendation and deadline of six months
- by the recommendation of the commission
- corrective measures
- amendment of deficit in the next year (with reference to the revaluation of the pact)

after the expiring date

Publication of the recommendations

if futher inaction

Obligartory communication of delay
- deadline of two months since the notice of inaction and publication notice
- requirements of financial restructuring
- reportings by the member country

in the case of noncompliance

Sanctions
- depositation of interest-free contribution to capital (at least 2% of the GDP)
- deposits can be changed into retribution after two years

Appendix 1: Simplified excessive deficit procedures[1462]

[1462] Self-provided figure in dependence of: Heinen, Böttcher [ed.] (2009), p. 5.

	Original version of the Stability and Growth Pact	Reconditioned version of the Stability and Growth Pact
Interim, low exceeding of the state indebedness guidelines	- during extraordinary incidents (e.g. natural catastrophes) - within recessions of GDP downturns exceeding 2% - "different relevant criteria"	additional fiscal exporsures due to structural reforms lprovoked by… - research - European political goals - international solidarity - investment plans - pension reforms - consolidation pools - special EU-fees
Possibility of exceeding deficites	- GDP downturn exceeding 2% - GDP downturn exceeding 0,75% if… … during sudden economic slumps … productivity shortfalls or further extraordinary circumstances appear	supplemented by… - sustained economical stagnation - pretty fragile growth
Time for deficite diminishment	- during the year of establishment	supplemented by… - savings exceeding 0,5% of the GDP are accounted in the first period - under certain conditions the second year can be regarded as the first period - extension of the period if efforts are visible and during lown economical growth
Implementation of correction suggestions	- during four months	- enlarged to six months
Intermediate-term balance goals	- equated balance or overplus	- 1% deficit in the case of low debt and exalted potential of economic growth
Saving and debt reduction during economical revivals	---	- 0,5% reduction per year without nonrecurring tasks - unexpected additional receipts for debt reduction - early-warning indicators

Appendix 2: Comparison of „Stability and Growth Pacts I and II“[1463]

[1463] Self-provided table in dependence of: Becker (2005), p. 9.

No.	Company	Ticker	ISIN	Home country
1	AIR LIQUIDE SA	AI FP Equity	FR0000120073	FRANCE
2	ALLIANZ SE-REG	ALV GY Equity	DE0008404005	GERMANY
3	ANHEUSER-BUSCH INBEV NV	ABI BB Equity	BE0003793107	BELGIUM
4	ARCELORMITTAL	MT NA Equity	LU0323134006	LUXEMBOURG
5	AXA SA	CS FP Equity	FR0000120628	FRANCE
6	BANCO SANTANDER SA	SAN SQ Equity	ES0113900J37	SPAIN
7	BASF SE	BAS GY Equity	DE000BASF111	GERMANY
8	BAYER AG-REG	BAYN GY Equity	DE000BAY0017	GERMANY
9	BAYERISCHE MOTOREN WERKE AG	BMW GY Equity	DE0005190003	GERMANY
10	BANCO BILBAO VIZCAYA ARGENTA	BBVA SQ Equity	ES0113211835	SPAIN
11	BNP PARIBAS	BNP FP Equity	FR0000131104	FRANCE
12	CARREFOUR SA	CA FP Equity	FR0000120172	FRANCE
13	CRH PLC	CRH ID Equity	IE0001827041	IRELAND
14	DAIMLER AG-REGISTERED SHARES	DAI GY Equity	DE0007100000	GERMANY
15	DANONE	BN FP Equity	FR0000120644	FRANCE
16	DEUTSCHE BANK AG-REGISTERED	DBK GY Equity	DE0005140008	GERMANY
17	DEUTSCHE BOERSE AG-NEW	63DU GY Equity	DE000A1KRND6	GERMANY
18	DEUTSCHE TELEKOM AG-REG	DTE GY Equity	DE0005557508	GERMANY
19	E.ON AG	EOAN GY Equity	DE000ENAG999	GERMANY
20	ENEL SPA	ENEL IM Equity	IT0003128367	ITALY
21	ENI SPA	ENI IM Equity	IT0003132476	ITALY
22	FRANCE TELECOM SA	FTE FP Equity	FR0000133308	FRANCE
23	GDF SUEZ	GSZ FP Equity	FR0010208488	FRANCE
24	ASSICURAZIONI GENERALI	G IM Equity	IT0000062072	ITALY
25	IBERDROLA SA	IBE SQ Equity	ES0144580Y14	SPAIN
26	INDITEX	ITX SQ Equity	ES0148396015	SPAIN
27	ING GROEP NV-CVA	INGA NA Equity	NL0000303600	NETHERLANDS
28	INTESA SANPAOLO	ISP IM Equity	IT0000072618	ITALY
29	KONINKLIJKE PHILIPS ELECTRON	PHIA NA Equity	NL0000009538	NETHERLANDS
30	L'OREAL	OR FP Equity	FR0000120321	FRANCE
31	LVMH MOET HENNESSY LOUIS VUI	MC FP Equity	FR0000121014	FRANCE
32	MUENCHENER RUECKVER AG-REG	MUV2 GY Equity	DE0008430026	GERMANY
33	NOKIA OYJ	NOK1V FH Equity	FI0009000681	FINLAND
34	REPSOL YPF SA	REP SQ Equity	ES0173516115	SPAIN
35	RWE AG	RWE GY Equity	DE0007037129	GERMANY
36	COMPAGNIE DE SAINT-GOBAIN	SGO FP Equity	FR0000125007	FRANCE
37	SANOFI	SAN FP Equity	FR0000120578	FRANCE
38	SAP AG	SAP GY Equity	DE0007164600	GERMANY
39	SCHNEIDER ELECTRIC SA	SU FP Equity	FR0000121972	FRANCE
40	SIEMENS AG-REG	SIE GY Equity	DE0007236101	GERMANY
41	SOCIETE GENERALE	GLE FP Equity	FR0000130809	FRANCE
42	TELECOM ITALIA SPA	TIT IM Equity	IT0003497168	ITALY
43	TELEFONICA SA	TEF SQ Equity	ES0178430E18	SPAIN
44	TOTAL SA	FP FP Equity	FR0000120271	FRANCE
45	UNIBAIL-RODAMCO SE	UL FP Equity	FR0000124711	FRANCE
46	UNICREDIT SPA	UCG IM Equity	IT0000064854	ITALY
47	UNILEVER NV-CVA	UNA NA Equity	NL0000009355	NETHERLANDS
48	VINCI SA	DG FP Equity	FR0000125486	FRANCE
49	VIVENDI	VIV FP Equity	FR0000127771	FRANCE
50	VOLKSWAGEN AG-PFD	VOW3 GY Equity	DE0007664039	GERMANY

Appendix 3: Members of the DJ Euro STOXX 50[1464]

[1464] Self-provided table in dependence of: Bloomberg [ed.] (2011ca).

two sample t-test for short-term index effects by assumption of different variances (probability error of 5%)	short-term stock additions	short-term stock deletions
mean	0,023537454	-0,019808766
variance	0,00380696	0,019019859
number of inspections	11	11
hypothetical difference of mean values	0	
degrees of freedom (df)	14	
t-statistic	0,951535244	
P(T<=t) one-tailed	0,178736214	
critical t-value for one-tailed inspections	1,761310115	
P(T<=t) two-tailed	0,357472428	
critical t-value for tow-tailed inspections	2,144786681	

Appendix 4: Two sample t-test for short-term index effects[1465]

two sample t-test for long-term index effects by assumption of different variances (probability error of 5%)	long-term stock additions	long-term stock deletions
mean	-0,045567646	0,093822851
variance	0,047468848	0,121117276
number of inspections	11	11
hypothetical difference of mean values	0	
degrees of freedom (df)	17	
t-statistic	-1,125948681	
P(T<=t) one-tailed	0,137915983	
critical t-value for one-tailed inspections	1,739606716	
P(T<=t) two-tailed	0,275831967	
critical t-value for tow-tailed inspections	2,109815559	

Appendix 5: Two sample t-test for long-term index effects[1466]

[1465] Self-provided table in dependence of: Own calculations.
[1466] Self-provided table in dependence of: Own calculations.

List of Literature

Abbassi, Puriya; Nautz, Dieter (2008): The Information Content of the ECB's Main Refinancing Operations: Evidence from the Money Market, Frankfurt a. M. 2008.

Abbring, Jaap H.; Heckman, James J.; Chiappori, Pierre-André; Pinquet, Jean (2003): Adverse Selection and Moral Hazard in Insurance: Can Dynamic Data Help to Distinguish?, in: Journal of the European Economic Association, Vol. 1, No. 2/3, pp. 512-521.

Acar, Emmanuel; James Shane (1997): Maximum Loss and Maximum Drawdown in Financial Markets, in: Proceedings of International Conferences on Foreign Financial Markets, London 1997.

Acharya, Ram N.; Gentle, Paul F.; Paudel, Krishna P. (2010): Examining the CRB index as a leading indicator for US inflation, in: Applied Economics Letters, Vol. 17, No. 15, pp. 1493-1496.

Adjoute, Kpate; Danthine, Jean-Pierre (2000): EMU and Portfolio Diversification Opportunities, FAME - International Centre for Financial Asset Management and Engineering, Research Paper No. 31, April 2000.

Afonso, António; Furceri, Davide; Gomes, Pedro (2011): Sovereign Credit Ratings and Financial Markets Linkages – Application to European Data, ECB Working Paper Series, No. 1347.

Ahlswede, Sophie (2011): Wie Banken in der EU Wohnimmobilienkredite refinanzieren, in: DB Research, Frankfurt a. M. 2011.

Aizenman, Joshua; Spiegel, Mark M. (2006): Institutional Efficiency, Monitoring Costs and the Investment Share of FDI, in: Review of International Economics, Vol. 14, No. 4, pp. 683-697.

Albala-Bertrand, Jose Miguel (2010): A contribution to estimate a benchmark capital stock. An optimal consistency method, in: International Review of Applied Economics, Vol. 24, No. 6, pp. 715-729.

Alexakis, Christos; Patra, Theophano; Poshakwale, Sunil (2010): Predictability of stock returns using financial statement information: evidence on semi-strong efficiency of emerging Greek stock market, in: Applied Financial Economics, Vol. 20, No. 16, pp. 1321-1326.

Alexander, Gordon J. (2009): From Markowitz to modern risk management, in: European Journal of Finance, Vol. 15, No. 5/6, pp. 451-461.

Alexander, Gordon J.; Baptista, Alexandre M. (2003): Portfolio Performance Evaluation Using Value at Risk, in: Journal of Portfolio Management, Vol. 29, No. 4, pp. 93-102.

Allen, Douglas W.; Lueck, Dean (1995): Risk preferences and the economics of contracts, in: American Economic Review, Vol. 85, No. 2, pp. 447-451.

Altavilla, Carlo (2004): Do EMU Members Share the Same Business Cycle?, in: Journal of Common Market Studies, Vol. 42, No. 5, pp. 869-896.

Ambachtsheer, Keith (2005): Beyond Portfolio Theory: The Next Frontier, in: Financial Analysts Journal, Vol. 61, No. 1, pp. 29-33.

Amenc, Noël; Goltz, Felix; Martellini, Lionel (2011): A comparison of index weighting schemes, in: Journal of Indexes, January/February 2011, pp. 10-19.

Amenc, Noël; Martellini, Linonel; Milhau, Vincent; Ziemann, Volker (2010): Asset-Liability Management in Private Wealth Management, in: Journal of Portfolio Management, Vol. 36, No. 1, pp. 100-120.

Amihud, Yakov; Mendelson, Haim (1986): Asset Pricing and the Bid-Ask Spread, in: Journal of Financial Economics, Vol. 17, pp. 223-249.

Anderson, Hamish D.; Cooper, Sapphire; Prevosi, Andrew K. (2006): Block Trade Price Asymmetry and Changes in Depth: Evidence from the Australian Stock Exchange, in: Financial Review, Vol. 41, No. 2, pp. 247-271.

Andréani, Gilles (2001): What Future for Federalism?, in: Centre for European Reform, London 2001.

Andreou, Panayiotis C.; Pierides, Yiannos A. (2008): Empirical investigation of stock index futures market efficiency: the case of the Athens Derivatives Exchange, in: European Journal of Finance, Vol. 14, No. 3, pp. 211-223.

Ang, Andrew; Chen, Joseph (2002): Asymmetric Correlations on Equity Portfolios, in: Journal of Financial Economics, Vol. 63, No. 2, pp. 443-494.

Ang, James S.; Boyer, Carol M. (2010): Knightian uncertainty: evidence of uncertainty premium in the capital market, in: Applied Economics Letters, Vol. 17, No. 10, pp. 945-949.

Ang, James S.; Cole, Rebel A.; Lin, James Wuh (2000): Agency Costs and Ownership Structure, in: Journal of Finance, Vol. 55, No. 1, pp. 81-106.

Angel, James; McCabe, Douglas (2009): The Business Ethics of Short Selling and Naked Short Selling, in: Journal of Business Ethics, Vol. 85, February 2009, pp. 239-249.

Anson, Mark (2004): Strategic versus Tactical Asset Allocation, in: Journal of Portfolio Management, Vol. 30, No. 2, pp. 8-22.

Antzoulatos, Angelos A. (2010): Greece in 2010: A Tragedy Without (?) Catharsis, in: International Advances in Economic Research, Vol. 17, No. 3, pp. 241-257.

Arnold, Tom; Nail, Lance A.; Nixon, Terry D. (2006): Getting More Out of Two-Asset Portfolios, in: Journal of Applied Finance, Vol. 16, No. 1, pp. 72-81.

Arnott, Robert D. (2005): Disentangling Size and Value, in: Financial Analysts Journal, September/October 2005, pp. 12-15.

Arnott, Robert D.; Hsu, Jason; Moore, Philippe (2005): Fundamental Indexation, in: Financial Analysts Journal, Vol. 61, No. 2, pp. 83-99.

Arnott, Robert D.; Kalesnik, Vitali; Moghtader, Paul; Scholl, Craig (2010): Beyond Cap Weight, in: Journal of Indexes, January/February 2010, pp. 16-29.

Arnott, Robert D.; Kuo, Li-Lan (2011): Selection Bias, in: Journal of Indexes, September/October 2011, pp. 36-44.

Arnott, Robert D.; West, John M. (2006): Fundamental Indexes: Current and Future Applications, in: ETF and Indexing, Fall 2006, pp. 111-121.

Arrow, Kenneth J. (1985): The Economics of Agency, in: Pratt, John; Zeckhauser, Richard [ed.]: Principals and Agents: The Structure of Business, Boston 1985, pp. 37-51.

Arshanapalli, Bala; Nelson, William (2010): Yes Virginia, diversification is still a free lunch, in: Journal of Wealth Management, Vol. 13, No. 2, pp. 34-40.

Artzner, Philippe; Delbaen, Freddy; Health, David (1997): Thinking Coherently, in: Risk, Vol. 10, pp. 68-71.

Asai, Manabu; Dashzeveg, Ulziijargal (2008): A Distribution-Free Test for Symmetry with an Application to S&P Index Returns, in: Applied Economics Letters, Vol. 15, No. 4-6, pp. 461-464.

Astrin, John (1999): The European Union Harmonised Indices of Consumer Prices (HICP), in: Statistical Journal of the UN Economic Commission for Europe, Vol. 16, No. 2/3, pp. 123-135.

Athavale, Manoj; Goebel, Joseph M. (2011): A Safer Safe Withdrawl Rate Using Various Return Distributions, in: Journal of Financial Planning, Vol. 24, No. 7, pp. 36-43.

Atkinson, Colin; Storey, Emmeline (2010): Building an Optimal Portfolio in Discrete Time in the Presence of Transaction Costs, in: Applied Mathematical Finance, Vol. 17, No. 4, pp. 323-357.

Aussenegg, Wolfgang; Grünbichler, Andreas (1999): Der Size-Effekt am österreichischen Aktienmarkt, in: Zeitschrift für betriebswirtschaftliche Forschung, Vol. 51, pp. 636-661.

Avellaneda, Marco; Lee, Jeong-Hyun (2010): Statistical arbitrage in the US equity market, in: Quantitative Finance, Vol. 10, No. 7, pp. 761-782.

Bai, Zhidong; Liu, Huixia; Wong, Wing-Keung (2009): Enhancement of the Applicability of Markowitz's Portfolio Optimization by Utilizing Random Matrix Theory, in: Mathematical Finance, Vol. 19, No. 4, pp. 639-667.

Bailey, Alice (1994): How to Keep a Good Company, in: Investors' Chronicle, Vol. 109, pp. 20-21.

Baixauli, Samuel J.; Alvarez, Susana (2006): Evaluating effects of excess kurtosis on VaR estimates: Evidence for international stock indices, in: Review of Quantitative Finance & Accounting, Vol. 27, No. 1, pp. 27-46.

Balassone, Fabrizio; Franco, Daniele; Rizza, Pietro (2009): Fiscal Sustainability and EMU: An Evolving Relationship, in: Proceedings of the Annual Conference on Taxation, Vol. 8, pp. 231-2138.

Bali, Turan G.; Cakici, Nusret (2008): Idiosyncratic Volatility and the Cross Section of Expected Returns, in: Journal of Financial and Quantitative Analysis, Vol. 43, No. 1, pp. 29-58.

Ball, Clifford; Torous, Walter (2000): Stochastic correlation across international stock markets, in: Journal of Empirical Finance, Vol. 7, No. 5, pp. 373-388.

Balli, Faruk; Basher, Syed Abul; Ozer-Balli, Hatice (2010): From home bias to Euro bias: Disentangling the effects of monetary union on the European financial markets, in: Journal of Economics & Business, Vol. 62, No. 5, pp. 347-366.

Baltussen, Guido; Post, Gerrit T. (2010): Irrational Diversification: An Examination of Individual Portfolio Choice, in: Journal of Financial & Quantitative Analysis, Vol. 46, No. 5, pp. 1463-1491.

Bamberg, Günter; Baur, Franz (1996): Statistik, Vol. 9, Oldenburg, Munich, Vienna 1996.

Banal-Estanol, Albert; Heidhues, Paul; Nitsche, Rainer; Seldeslachts, Jo (2010): Screening and Merger Activity, in: Journal of Industrial Economics, Vol. 58, No. 4, pp. 794-817.

Bao, Yong; Ullah, Aman (2009): On skewness and kurtosis of econometric estimators, in: Economics Journal, Vol. 12, pp. 232-247.

Barbosa, Andreza (2009): Equity Indexing, Saarbrücken 2009.

Barney, Lee (2010): Index Providers Turn To the Wild Frontier, in: Money Management Executive, Vol. 18, No. 47, pp. 1-8.

Barone-Adesi, Giovanni; Giannopoulos, Kostas; Vosper, Les (2002): Backtesting Derivative Portfolios with Filtered Historical Simulation (FHS), in: European Financial Management, Vol. 8, No. 1, pp 31-58.

Barras, Laurent; Scaillet, Oliver; Wermers, Russ (2010): False Discoveries in Mutual Fund Performance: Measuring Luck in Estimated Alphas, in: Journal of Finance, Vol. 65, No. 1, pp. 179-216.

Barton, Jan; Hansen, Thomas Bowe; Pownall, Grace (2010): Which Performance Measures Do Investors Around the World Value the Most - and Why?, in: Accounting Review, Vol. 85, No. 3, pp. 753-789.

Basu, Devraj; Oomen, Roel; Stremme, Alexander (2010): International Dynamic Asset Allocation and Return Predictability, in: Journal of Business Finance & Accounting, Vol. 37, No. 7/8, pp. 1008-1025.

Beach, Steven L. (2006): Why Emerging Market Equities Belong in a Diversified Investment Portfolio, in: Journal of Investing, Vol. 15, No. 4, pp. 12-18.

Beach, Steven L. (2007): Semivariance in Asset Allocations: Longer Horizons Can Handle Riskier Holdings, in: Journal of Financial Planning, Vol. 20, No. 1, pp. 60-69.

Bearce, David H. (2009): EMU: the last stand for the policy convergence hypothesis, in: Journal of European Public Policy, Vol. 16, No. 4, pp. 582-600.

Bechmann, Ken L. (2004): Price and Volume Effects Associated with Changes in the Danish Blue-Chip Index: The KFX Index, in: Multinational Finance Journal, Vol. 8, No. 1/2, pp. 3-34.

Becker, Sebastian (2007): Globale Liquiditätsschwemme und Vermögenspreisinflation: Fakt oder Fiktion?, in: DB Research, Frankfurt a. M. 2007.

Becker, Sebastian (2009): EMU sovereign spread widening – Reasonable market reaction or exaggeration?, in: DB Research, Frankfurt a. M. 2009.

Becker, Werner (2005): Reform des Stabilitätspakts – Lizenz zur Verschuldung, in: DB Research, Frankfurt a. M. 2005.

Becker-Blease, John, R.; Paul, Donna L. (2010): Does Inclusion in a Smaller S&P Index Create Value?, in: Financial Review, Vol. 45, No. 2, pp. 307-330.

Beckers, Stan; Connor, Gregory; Curds, Ross (1996): National versus Global Influences on Global Equities, in: Financial Analysts Journal, Vol. 52, No. 2, pp. 31-39.

Beckers, Stan; Grinold, Richard; Rudd, Andrew; Stefek, Dan (1992): The Relative Importance of Common Factors Across the European Equity Markets, in: Journal of Banking and Finance, Vol. 16, pp. 75-95.

Beetsma, Roel; Giuliodori, Massimo (2010): The Macroeconomic Costs and Benefits of the EMU and Other Monetary Unions: An Overview of Recent Research, in: Journal of Economic Literature, Vol. 48, No. 3, pp. 603-641.

Begg, Iain (2009): Regulation and Supervision of Financial Intermediaries in the EU: The Aftermath of the Financial Crisis, in: Journal of Common Market Studies, Vol. 47, No. 5 2009, pp. 1107-1128.

Beinart, Peter (2003): Counting Heads, in: New Republic, 04.07.2003, p. 6.

Bekaert, Geert; Hodrick, Robert J.; Zhang, Xiaoyan (2009): International Stock Return Comovements, in: Journal of Finance, Vol. 64, No. 6, pp. 2591-2626.

Bekkers, Niels; Doeswijk, Ronald Q.; Lam, Trevin W. (2009): Strategic Asset Allocation: Determining the Optimal Portfolio with Ten Asset Classes, in: Journal of Wealth Management, Vol. 12, No. 3, pp. 61-77.

Belkhir, Mohamed (2009): Board structure, ownership structure and firm performance: evidence from banking, in: Applied Financial Economics, Vol. 19, No. 19, pp. 1581-1593.

Benartzi, Shlomo; Thaler, Richard H. (2001): Naive Diversification Strategies in Defined Contribution Saving Plans, in: American Economic Review, Vol. 91, No. 1, pp. 79-98.

Beneish, Messod D.; Whaley, Robert E. (1996): An Autonomy of the "S&P Game": The Effects of Changing the Rules, in: Journal of Finance, Vol. 51, pp. 1909-1930.

Benson, Karen L.; Gallagher, David R.; Teodorowski, Patrick (2007): Momentum investing and the asset allocation decision, in: Accounting & Finance, Vol. 47, No, 7, pp. 571-598.

Benz, Matthias; Frey, Bruno S. (2007): Corporate Governance: What Can We Learn From Public Governance?, in: Academy of Management Review, Vol. 32, No. 1, pp. 92-104.

Bera, Anil K.; Jarque Carlos M. (1981): Efficient tests for normality, homoscedasticity and serial independence of regression residuals, in: Economics Letters, Vol. 7, pp. 313-318.

Berbena, Robert-Paul; Jansen, W. Jos (2009): Bond market and stock market integration in Europe: a smooth transition approach, in: Applied Economics, Vol. 41, No. 24, pp. 3067-3080.

Bergh, Greg; van Rensburg, Paul (2007): Hedge funds and higher moment portfolio selection, in: Journal of Derivatives & Hedge Funds, Vol. 14, No. 2, pp. 102-126.

Bergmann, Michael D.; Howard, C. Thomas (2003): Estimating Asset Class Standard Deviations and Correlations, in: Journal of Wealth Management, Vol. 6, No. 3, pp. 11-18.

Bernhard, Jan (2005): International Diversification across Countries and Industries, St. Gallen 2005.

Bernhard, German; Höcht, Stephan; Neugebauer, Michael; Neumann, Michael; Zagst, Rudi (2011): Asset Correlations in Turbulent Markets and the Impact of Different Regimes on Asset Management, in: Asia-Pacific Journal of Operational Research, Vol. 28, No. 1, pp. 1-23.

Bernstein, William J. (2006): Fundamental Indexing and the Three-Factor Model, in: Fundamental Indexing, 2006, pp. 1-3.

Bertomeu, Jeremy; Beyer, Anne; Dye, Ronald A. (2011): Capital Structure, Cost of Capital, and Voluntary Disclosures, in: Accounting Review, Vol. 86, No. 7, pp. 857-886.

Best, Ronald; Hodges, Charles W.; Yoder, James A. (2007): The Sharpe Ratio and Long-Run Investment Decisions, in: Journal of Investing, Vol. 16, No. 2, pp. 70-76.

Bharathi, N. (2010): Decision Making: Equity Investment, in: SCMS Journal of Indian Management, Vol. 7, No. 1, pp. 34-43.

Bhargava, Vivek; Malhotra, Davinder Kumar (2006): Do Price-Earnings Ratios Drive Stock Values?, in: Journal of Portfolio Management, Vol. 33, No. 1, pp. 86-92.

Bianco, James A. (1999): The CRB's unknown double bottom, in: Futures; News, Analysis & Strategies for Futures, Options & Derivatives Traders, Vol. 28, No. 7 1999, pp. 50-52.

Bieling, Hans-Jürgen (2006): EMU, financial integration and global economic governance, in: Review of International Political Economy, Vol. 13, No. 3, pp. 420-448.

Bikker, Jacob A.; Spierdijk, Laura; van der Sluis, Pieter-Jelle (2010): What factors increase the risk of incurring higher market impact costs?, in: Applied Economics, Vol. 42, No. 3, pp. 369-387.

Bird, Ron; Gallagher, David R. (2002): The evaluation of active manager returns in a non-symmetrical environment, in: Journal of Asset Management, Vol. 2, No. 4, pp. 303-324.

Birkner, Christine (2010): Stock indexes: Up in the air, in Futures; News, Analysis & Strategies for Futures, Options & Derivatives Traders, Vol. 39, No. 8, pp. 24-27.

Black, Fischer; Litterman, Robert (1992): Global Portfolio Optimization, in: Financial Analysts Journal, Vol. 48, No. 5, pp. 28-43

Black, Fischer; Scholes, Myron (1974): From theory to a new financial product, in: Journal of Finance, Vol. 29, pp. 399-412.

Blanch, Francisco; Schels, Sabine (2010): Selecting a commodity index, in: Merrill Lynch Global Commodity Paper, Vol. 4, pp. 1-39.

Bleymüller, Josef (1966): Theorie und Technik der Aktienkursindizes, Wiesbaden 1966.

Bleymüller, Josef; Gehlert, Günter; Gülicher, Herbert (2008): Statistik für Wirtschaftswissenschaftler, Vol. 15, Munich 2008.

Blitz, David C.; van Vliet, Pim (2008): Global Tactical Cross-Asset Allocation: Applying Value and Momentum across Asset Classes, in: Journal of Portfolio Management, Vol. 35, No. 1, pp. 23-38.

Blitzer, David M. (2011): Sorting and Digging, in: Journal of Indexes, January/ February 2011, pp. 50-51.

Blitzer, David M.; Dash, Srikant; Murphy, Philip; S&P [ed.] (2004): Equity Duration – Update Duration of the S&P 500, in: Standard & Poor's Working Paper Series, July 2008.

Block, Stanley B.; French, Dan W. (2002): The Effect of Portfolio Weighting on Investment Performance Evaluation: The Case of Actively Managed Mutual Funds, in: Journal of Economics & Finance, Vol. 26, No. 1, pp. 16-30.

Bloomberg [ed.] (2011a): EURR002W Index HP 01.01.1998-31.12.2011, date: 31.12.2011.

Bloomberg [ed.] (2011b): SX5E Index HP 01.01.2001-31.12.2010, date: 12.11.2011.

Bloomberg [ed.] (2011c): CRY Index HP EUR 01.01.2001-31.12.2010, date: 12.11.2011.

Bloomberg [ed.] (2011d): REXP Index HP 01.01.2001-31.12.2010, date: 12.11.2011.

Bloomberg [ed.] (2011e): ATX Index HP 01.01.2001-31-12-2010, date: 14.11.2011.

Bloomberg [ed.] (2011f): BEL20 Index HP 01.01.2001-31-12-2010, date: 14.11.2011.

Bloomberg [ed.] (2011g): HEX25 Index HP 01.01.2001-31-12-2010, date: 14.11.2011.

Bloomberg [ed.] (2011h): CAC Index HP 01.01.2001-31-12-2010, date: 14.11.2011.

Bloomberg [ed.] (2011i): DAX Index HP 01.01.2001-31-12-2010, date: 14.11.2011.

Bloomberg [ed.] (2011j): ASE Index HP 01.01.2001-31-12-2010, date: 14.11.2011.

Bloomberg [ed.] (2011k): ISEQ Index HP 01.01.2001-31-12-2010, date: 14.11.2011.

Bloomberg [ed.] (2011l): FTSEMIB Index HP 01.01.2001-31-12-2010, date: 14.11.2011.

Bloomberg [ed.] (2011m): LUXXX Index HP 01.01.2001-31-12-2010, date: 14.11.2011.

Bloomberg [ed.] (2011n): AEX Index HP 01.01.2001-31-12-2010, date: 14.11.2011.

Bloomberg [ed.] (2011o): PSI20 Index HP 01.01.2001-31-12-2010, date: 14.11.2011.

Bloomberg [ed.] (2011p): IBEX Index HP 01.01.2001-31-12-2010, date: 14.11.2011.

Bloomberg [ed.] (2011q): ATX Index DES, date: 14.11.2011.

Bloomberg [ed.] (2011r): BEL20 Index DES, date: 14.11.2011.

Bloomberg [ed.] (2011s): HEX25 Index DES, date: 14.11.2011.

Bloomberg [ed.] (2011t): CAC Index DES, date: 14.11.2011.

Bloomberg [ed.] (2011u): DAX Index DES, date: 14.11.2011.

Bloomberg [ed.] (2011v): ASE Index DES, date: 14.11.2011.

Bloomberg [ed.] (2011w): ISEQ Index DES, date: 14.11.2011.

Bloomberg [ed.] (2011x): FTSEMIB Index DES, date: 14.11.2011.

Bloomberg [ed.] (2011y): LUXXX Index DES, date: 14.11.2011.

Bloomberg [ed.] (2011z): AEX Index DES, date: 14.11.2011.

Bloomberg [ed.] (2011aa): PSI20 Index DES, date: 14.11.2011.

Bloomberg [ed.] (2011ab): IBEX Index DES, date: 14.11.2011.

Bloomberg [ed.] (2011ac): TBSCE Index HP 01.01.2001-31-12-2010, date: 14.11.2011.

Bloomberg [ed.] (2011ad): TBSCT Index HP 01.01.2001-31-12-2010, date: 14.11.2011.

Bloomberg [ed.] (2011ae): T3000E Index HP 01.01.2001-31-12-2010, date: 14.11.2011.

Bloomberg [ed.] (2011af): T3000T Index HP 01.01.2001-31-12-2010, date: 14.11.2011.

Bloomberg [ed.] (2011ag): T5000E Index HP 01.01.2001-31-12-2010, date: 14.11.2011.

Bloomberg [ed.] (2011ah): T5000T Index HP 01.01.2001-31-12-2010, date: 14.11.2011.

Bloomberg [ed.] (2011ai): TFINE Index HP 01.01.2001-31-12-2010, date: 14.11.2011.

Bloomberg [ed.] (2011aj): TFINT Index HP 01.01.2001-31-12-2010, date: 14.11.2011.

Bloomberg [ed.] (2011ak): TIDUE Index HP 01.01.2001-31-12-2010, date: 14.11.2011.

Bloomberg [ed.] (2011al): TIDUT Index HP 01.01.2001-31-12-2010, date: 14.11.2011.

Bloomberg [ed.] (2011am): TBSCE Index DES, date: 14.11.2011.

Bloomberg [ed.] (2011an): TBSCT Index DES, date: 14.11.2011.

Bloomberg [ed.] (2011ao): T3000E Index DES, date: 14.11.2011.

Bloomberg [ed.] (2011ap): T3000T Index DES, date: 14.11.2011.

Bloomberg [ed.] (2011aq): T5000E Index DES, date: 14.11.2011.

Bloomberg [ed.] (2011ar): T5000T Index DES, date: 14.11.2011.

Bloomberg [ed.] (2011as): TFINE Index DES, date: 14.11.2011.

Bloomberg [ed.] (2011at): TFINT Index DES, date: 14.11.2011.

Bloomberg [ed.] (2011au): TIDUE Index DES, date: 14.11.2011.

Bloomberg [ed.] (2011av): TIDUT Index DES, date: 14.11.2011.

Bloomberg [ed.] (2011aw): GGGB10YR Index HP 01.01.2000-15.11.2011, date: 15.11.2011.

Bloomberg [ed.] (2011ax): GDBR10 Index HP 01.01.2000-15.11.2011, date: 15.11.2011.

Bloomberg [ed.] (2011ay): CBQD Germany, date: 15.11.2011.

Bloomberg [ed.] (2011az): CBQD Greece, date: 15.11.2011.

Bloomberg [ed.] (2011ba): BFST Index HP 01.01.2000-31.12.2010, date: 15.11.2011.

Bloomberg [ed.] (2011bb): BINT Index HP 01.01.2000-31.12.2010, date: 15.11.2011.

Bloomberg [ed.] (2011bc): BBAT Index HP 01.01.2000-31.12.2010, date: 15.11.2011.

Bloomberg [ed.] (2011bd): EONIA Index HP EUR 01.01.2001-31.12.2010, date: 21.11.2011.

Bloomberg [ed.] (2011be): SGO FP Equity HP EUR 31.08.2001-30.09.2002, date: 28.11.2011.

Bloomberg [ed.] (2011bf): LG FP Equity HP EUR 30.08.2002-30.09.2003, date: 28.11.2011.

Bloomberg [ed.] (2011bg): IBE SM Equity HP EUR 29.08.2003-30.09.2004, date: 28.11.2011.

Bloomberg [ed.] (2011bh): ACA FP Equity HP EUR 31.08.2004-30.09.2005, date: 28.11.2011.

Bloomberg [ed.] (2011bi): MT NA Equity HP EUR 31.08.2007-30.09.2008, date: 28.11.2011.

Bloomberg [ed.] (2011bj): SU FP Equity HP EUR 31.08.2007-30.09.2008, date: 28.11.2011.

Bloomberg [ed.] (2011bk): DG FP Equity HP EUR 31.08.2007-30.09.2008, date: 28.11.2011.

Bloomberg [ed.] (2011bl): ALO FP Equity HP EUR 29.08.2008-30.09.2009, date: 28.11.2011.

Bloomberg [ed.] (2011bm): ABI BB Equity HP EUR 31.08.2009-30.09.2010, date: 28.11.2011.

Bloomberg [ed.] (2011bn): CRH ID Equity HP EUR 31.08.2009-30.09.2010, date: 28.11.2011.

Bloomberg [ed.] (2011bo): BMW GR Equity HP EUR 31.08.2010-30.09.2011, date: 28.11.2011.

Bloomberg [ed.] (2011bp): KPN NA Equity HP EUR 31.08.2001-30.09.2002, date: 28.11.2011.

Bloomberg [ed.] (2011bq): PP FP Equity HP EUR 30.08.2002-30.09.2003, date: 28.11.2011.

Bloomberg [ed.] (2011br): HVM GR Equity HP EUR 29.08.2003-30.09.2004, date: 28.11.2011.

Bloomberg [ed.] (2011bs): VOW GR Equity HP EUR 31.08.2004-30.09.2005, date: 28.11.2011.

Bloomberg [ed.] (2011bt): AH NA Equity HP EUR 31.08.2007-30.09.2008, date: 28.11.2011.

Bloomberg [ed.] (2011bu): ALBK ID Equity HP EUR 31.08.2007-30.09.2008, date: 28.11.2011.

Bloomberg [ed.] (2011bv): LG FP Equity HP EUR 31.08.2007-30.09.2008, date: 28.11.2011.

Bloomberg [ed.] (2011bw): ALU FP Equity HP EUR 29.08.2008-30.09.2009, date: 28.11.2011.

Bloomberg [ed.] (2011bx): FBAVP BB Equity HP EUR 31.08.2009-30.09.2010, date: 28.11.2011.

Bloomberg [ed.] (2011by): RNO FP Equity HP EUR 31.08.2009-30.09.2010, date: 28.11.2011.

Bloomberg [ed.] (2011bz): AGN NA Equity HP EUR 31.08.2010-30.09.2011, date: 28.11.2011.

Bloomberg [ed.] (2011ca): SX5E Index MEMB, date: 02.12.2011.

Bloomberg [ed.] (2011cb): DAX Index DES, date: 02.12.2011.

Bloomberg [ed.] (2011cc): CAC Index DES, date: 02.12.2011.

Bloomberg [ed.] (2011cd): IBEX Index DES, date: 02.12.2011.

Bloomberg [ed.] (2011ce): AEX Index DES, date: 02.12.2011.

Bloomberg [ed.] (2011cf): FTSEMIB Index DES, date: 02.12.2011.

Bloomberg [ed.] (2011cg): HEX25 Index DES, date: 02.12.2011.

Bloomberg [ed.] (2011ch): BEL20 Index DES, date: 02.12.2011.

Bloomberg [ed.] (2011ci): ISEQ Index DES, date: 02.12.2011.

Bloomberg [ed.] (2011cj): ATX Index DES, date: 02.12.2011.

Bloomberg [ed.] (2011ck): ASE Index DES, date: 02.12.2011.

Bloomberg [ed.] (2011cl): PSI20 Index DES, date: 02.12.2011.

Bloomberg [ed.] (2011cm): LUXXX Index DES, date: 02.12.2011.

Bloomberg [ed.] (2011cn): SX6E Index DES, date: 02.12.2011.

Bloomberg [ed.] (2011co): SXNE Index DES, date: 02.12.2011.

Bloomberg [ed.] (2011cp): SX7E Index DES, date: 02.12.2011.

Bloomberg [ed.] (2011cq): SXEE Index DES, date: 02.12.2011.

Bloomberg [ed.] (2011cr): SX3E Index DES, date: 02.12.2011.

Bloomberg [ed.] (2011cs): SXQE Index DES, date: 02.12.2011.

Bloomberg [ed.] (2011ct): SX4E Index DES, date: 02.12.2011.

Bloomberg [ed.] (2011cu): SXKE Index DES, date: 02.12.2011.

Bloomberg [ed.] (2011cv): SXIE Index DES, date: 02.12.2011.

Bloomberg [ed.] (2011cw): SXAE Index DES, date: 02.12.2011.

Bloomberg [ed.] (2011cx): SXDE Index DES, date: 02.12.2011.

Bloomberg [ed.] (2011cy): SX8E Index DES, date: 02.12.2011.

Bloomberg [ed.] (2011cz): SXOE Index DES, date: 02.12.2011.

Bloomberg [ed.] (2011da): SXME Index DES, date: 02.12.2011.

Bloomberg [ed.] (2011db): SXPE Index DES, date: 02.12.2011.

Bloomberg [ed.] (2011dc): SX86E Index DES, date: 02.12.2011.

Bloomberg [ed.] (2011dd): SXFE Index DES, date: 02.12.2011.

Bloomberg [ed.] (2011de): SXTE Index DES, date: 02.12.2011.

Bloomberg [ed.] (2012df): Austria 10yr govt CRPR, date: 15.08.2012.

Bloomberg [ed.] (2012dg): Belgium 10yr govt CRPR, date: 15.08.2012.

Bloomberg [ed.] (2012dh): Cyprus 10yr govt CRPR, date: 15.08.2012.

Bloomberg [ed.] (2012di): Estonia 10yr govt CRPR, date: 15.08.2012.

Bloomberg [ed.] (2012dj): Finnland 10yr govt CRPR, date: 15.08.2012.

Bloomberg [ed.] (2012dk): France 10yr govt CRPR, date: 15.08.2012.

Bloomberg [ed.] (2012dl): Germany 10yr govt CRPR, date: 15.08.2012.

Bloomberg [ed.] (2012dm): Greece 10yr govt CRPR, date: 15.08.2012.

Bloomberg [ed.] (2012dn): Ireland 10yr govt CRPR, date: 15.08.2012.

Bloomberg [ed.] (2012do): Italy 10yr govt CRPR, date: 15.08.2012.

Bloomberg [ed.] (2012dp): Luxembourg 10yr govt CRPR, date: 15.08.2012.

Bloomberg [ed.] (2012dq): Malta 10yr govt CRPR, date: 15.08.2012.

Bloomberg [ed.] (2012dr): Netherlands 10yr govt CRPR, date: 15.08.2012.

Bloomberg [ed.] (20112s): Portugal 10yr govt CRPR, date: 15.08.2012.

Bloomberg [ed.] (20112t): Slovakia 10yr govt CRPR, date: 15.08.2012.

Bloomberg [ed.] (20112u): Slovenia 10yr govt CRPR, date: 15.08.2012.

Bloomberg [ed.] (2012dv): Spain 10yr govt CRPR, date: 15.08.2012.

Blümel, Rainer (1995): Aktienindizes als Basisinstrumente für das passive Portfolio-Management, Stuttgart 1995.

Bodie, Zvi; Kane, Alex; Marcus, Alan J. (2005): Investments, Vol. 6, Boston 2005.

Boemle, Max (1998): Praxis der Jahresabschlussanalyse, Zurich 1998.

Bogle, John C. (2005): The Uncanny Ability to Recognize the Obvious, in: Journal of Applied Finance, Vol. 15, No. 2, pp. 114-118.

Bogle, John C.; Malkiel, Burton G. (2006): Turn on a Paradigm?, in: Wall Street Journal, June 2006, pp. 14.

Bohdalová, Mária; Greguš, Michael (2010): Fractal Analysis of Forward Exchange Rates, in: Acta Polytechnica Hungarica, Vol. 7, No. 4, pp. 57-69.

Boido, Claudio; Fulci, Giovanni (2010): A Risk Contribution Approach to Asset Allocation, in: Journal of Financial Risk Management, Vol. 7, No. 1/2, pp. 58-77.

Boivie, Steven; Lange, Donald; McDonald, Michael L.; Westphal, James D. (2011): Me or we: The Effects of CEO Organizational Identification on Agency Costs, in: Academy of Management Journal, Vol. 54, No. 3, pp. 551-576.

Booth, G. Geoffrey; So, Raymond W. (2003): Intraday volatility spillovers in the German equity index derivatives market, in: Applied Financial Economics, Vol. 13, No. 7, pp. 487-494.

Borys, Magdalena; Zemcik, Petr (2011): Size and Value Effects in the Visegrad Countries, in: Emerging Markets Finance & Trade, Vol. 47, No. 3, pp. 50-68.

Boscaljon, Brian; Filbeck, Greg; Zhao, Xin (2011): Market timing using the VIX for style rotation, in: Financial Services Review, Vol. 20, No. 1, pp. 35-44.

Bosch, Karl (1992): Elementare Einführung in die angewandte Statistik, Vol. 4, Braunschweig/Wiesbaden, 1992.

Botha, Marius (2007): A Comparison of South African Hedge Fund Risk Measures, in: South African Journal of Economics, Vol. 75, No. 3, pp. 459-477.

Bouleau, Nicolas; Thomas, Alan (2004): Financial markets and martingales, Berlin 2004.

Boutahar, Mohamed (2009): Behaviour of skewness, kurtosis and normality test in long memory data, in: Econometrics Journal, Vol. 12, No. 2, pp. 232-247.

Branch, Ben; Cai, Li (2011): Fundamental Weighting, in: Journal of Applied Finance, Vol. 20, No. 1, pp. 64-77.

Brealey, Richard A.; Myers, Stewart C. (2006): Principles of Corporate Finance, New York, Vol. 8, 2006.

Brealey, Richard A.; Myers, Stewart C.; Marcus, Alan J. (2007): Fundamentals of Corporate Finance, Vol. 5, New York 2007.

Breuer, Wolfgang; Gürtler, Marc; Schuhmacher, Frank (2004): Portfoliomanagement I, Wiesbaden 2004.

Briand, Remy; Owyong, David T. (2009): How to kill a black swan, in: Journal of Indexes, Vol. 12, No. 4, pp. 10-17.

Brigham, N. H.; Kiesel, Rüdiger (2002): Semi-parametric modelling in finance: theoretical foundations, in: Quantitative Finance, Vol. 2, No. 4, pp. 241-250.

Brochet, Francois (2010): Information Content of Insider Traders before and after the Sarbanes-Oxley Act, in: Accounting Review, Vol. 85, No. 2, pp. 419-446.

Brooks, George (2009): Oil and the Dollar: Which is the Tail Which is the Dog?, in: Equities, Vol. 58, No. 3, pp. 38-39.

Brooks, Nicholas; Langerup, Michael (2011): How To Choose A Commodity Index, in: Journal of Indexes Europe, July/August 2011, pp. 30-35.

Brown, Jack; Jones, Travis (2011): An Application of Asset-Liability Management for Financial Planners, in: Journal of Financial Planning, Vol. 24, No. 5, pp. 62-69.

Bruce, Alistair; Buck, Trevor; Main, Brian G. M. (2005): Top Executive Remuneration: A View form Europe, in: Journal of Management Studies, Vol. 42, No. 7, pp. 1493-1506.

Brüggelambert, Gregor (2004): Information and efficiency in political markets: using computerized markets to predict electronic results, in: Applied Economics, Vol. 36, No. 7, pp. 753-768.

Bruns, Christoph; Meyer-Bullerdiek, Frieder (2008): Professionelles Portfoliomanagement, Vol. 4, Stuttgart 2008.

Budinsky, Ralf (2002): Aktienindexfonds - Produktidee und Umsetzung, Frankfurt a. M. 2002.

Büning, Herbert; Trenkler, Götz (1994): Nichtparametrische statistische Methoden, Vol. 2, Berlin/New York 1994

Bulti, Marco; van den Noord, Paul (2004): Fiscal Discretion and Elections in the Early Years of EMU, in: Journal of Common Market Studies, Vol. 24, No. 4, pp. 737-756.

Buraschi, Andrea; Porchia, Paolo; Trojani, Fabio (2010): Correlation Risk and Optimal Portfolio Choice, in: Journal of Finance, Vol. 65, No. 1, pp. 393-420.

Burke, Walter (2003): The CRB: A top-down and bottom-up look, in: Futures; News, Analysis & Strategies for Futures, Options & Derivatives Traders, Vol. 32, No. 6, p. 34.

Buttell, Amy E. (2010): Harry M. Markowitz on Modern Portfolio Theory, the Efficient Frontier, and His Life's Work, in: Journal of Financial Planning, Vol. 23, No. 5, pp. 18-23.

Caers, Ralf; Du Bois, Cindy; Jegers, Marc; De Gieter, Sara; Schepers, Catherine; Pepermans, Roland (2006): Principal-agent relationships on the stewardship-agency axis, in : Nonprofit Management & Leadership, Vol. 17, No. 1, pp. 25-47.

Cai, Charlie X.; Keasey, Kevin; Short, Helen (2006): Corporate Governance and Information Efficiency in Security Markets, in: European Financial Management, Vol. 12, No. 5, pp. 763-787.

Cai, Jie (2007): What's in the News? Information Content of S&P 500 Additions, in: Financial Management, Vol. 36, No. 3, pp. 113-124.

Cain, Brianna; Zurbruegg, Ralf (2010): Can switching between risk measures lead to better portfolio optimization?, in: Journal of Asset Management, Vol. 10, No. 6, pp. 358-369.

Camarero, Miriam; Esteve, Vicente; Tamarit, Cecilio (2000): Price convergence of peripheral European countries on the way to the EMU: A time series approach, in: Empirical Economics, Vol. 25, No. 3, pp. 149-168.

Camerer, Colin F. (2003): Behavioural Game Theory: Experiments in Strategic Integration, in: Princeton: Princeton University Press, Princeton 2003.

Campbell, Scott (2006): Risk and the Subjectivity of Preference, in: Journal of Risk Research, Vol. 9, No. 3, pp. 225-242.

Casarin, Roberto; Lazzarin, Marco; Pelizzon, Loriana; Sartore, Domenico (2005): Relative Benchmark Rating and Persistence Analysis: Evidence from Italian Equity Funds, in: The European Journal of Finance, Vol. 11, No. 4, pp. 297-308.

Cassar, Gavin; Gerakos, Joseph (2010): Determinants of Hedge Fund Internal Controls and Fees, in: Accounting Review, Vol. 85, No. 6, pp. 1887-1919.

Cavaglia, Stefano; Brightman, Christopher; Aked, Michael (2000): The Increasing Importance of Industry Factors, in: Financial Analysts Journal, September 2000, pp. 41-54.

Cavaglia, Stefano; Moroz, Vadim (2001): Cross-Industry, Cross-Country Allocation, in: Financial Analysts Journal, Vol. 58, No. 6, pp. 78-97.

Cecchetti, Stephen G.; Wynne, Mark A. (2003): Inflation measurement and the ECB's pursuit of price stability: a first assessment, in: Economic Policy, Vol. 18, No. 37, pp. 395-434.

Cespa, Giovanni (2008): Information Sales and Insider Trading with Long-Lived Information, in: Journal of Finance, Vol. 63, No. 2, pp. 639-672.

Chae, Joon; Wang, Albert (2009): Determinants of Trading Profits: The Liquidity Provision Decision, in: Emerging Markets Finance & Trade, Vol. 45, No. 6, pp. 33-56.

Chamberlain, Laurie (2011): Does Your Performance Management Need a Tune-Up?, in: Strategic Finance, Vol. 93, No. 5, pp. 18-61.

Chan, Kalok; Yue-Cheong Chan, Betty-J.; Fong, Wai-Ming (2004): Free Float and Market Liquidity: A Study of Hong Kong Government Intervention, in: Journal of Financial Research, Vol. 27, No. 2, pp. 179-197.

Chan, Kam; Lo, Yung (2011): Credit ratings and long-term IPO performance, in: Journal of Economics & Finance, Vol. 35, No. 4, pp. 473-483.

Chandra, Ramesh; Sandilands, Roger (2006): The role of pecuniary external economies and economies of scale in the theory of increasing returns, in: Review of Political Economy, Vol. 18, No. 2, pp. 193-208.

Chang, Chun-Hao; DuPoyet, Brice; Prakash, Arun (2008): Optimum allocation of weights to assets in a portfolio: the case of normalized annualization versus effective annualization of returns, in: Applied Financial Economics, Vol. 18, No. 20, pp. 1635-1646.

Chaudhry, Ashraf; Johnson, Helen (2008): The Efficacy of the Sortino Ratio and Other Benchmark Performance Measures Under Skewed Return Distributions, in: Australian Journal of Management, Vol. 32, No. 3, pp. 485-502.

Chauvin, Kyle; Laibson, David; Mollerstrom, Johanna (2011): Asset Bubbles and the Cost of Economic Fluctuation, in: Journal of Money, Credit & Banking, Vol. 43, pp. 233-260.

Chazal, Frédéric; Cohen-Steiner, David; Lieutier, André; Thibert, Boris (2009): Stability of Curvature Measures, in: Computer Graphics Forum, Vol. 28, No. 5, pp. 1485-1496.

Chen, Haiwei; Estes, Jim (2010): A Monte Carlo study of the strategies for 401(k) plans: dollar-cost-averaging, value-averaging, and proportional rebalancing, in: Financial Services Review, Vol. 19, No. 2, pp. 95-109.

Chen, Ho-Chyuan; Wu, Juping (2009): Volatility, Depth, and Order Composition: Evidence from a Pure Limit Order Futures Market, in: Emerging Markets Finance & Trade, Vol. 45, No. 5, pp. 72-85.

Chen, Honghui; Noronha, Gregory, Singal, Vjay (2004): The Price Response to S&P 500 Index Additions and Deletions: Evidence of Asymmetry and a New Explanation, in: Journal of Finance, Vol. 59, No. 4, pp. 1901-1929.

Chen, Hsiu-Lang (2006): On Russell index reconstruction, in: Review of Quantitative Finance & Accounting, Vol. 26, No. 4, pp. 409-430.

Chen, Jo-Hui; Huang, Chya-Yuan (2010): An Analysis of the Spillover Effects of Exchange-Traded Funds, in: Applied Economics, Vol. 42, No. 9, pp. 1155-1168.

Chen, Nan; Glasserman, Paul (2007): Additive and multiplicative duals for American option pricing, in: Finance & Stochastics, Vol. 11, No. 2, pp. 153-179.

Chhabra, Ashvin B. (2005): Beyond Markowitz: A Comprehensive Wealth Allocation Framework for Individual Investors, in: Journal of Wealth Management, Vol. 7, No. 4, pp. 8-34.

Christensen, Morten M.; Platen, Eckhard (2007): Sharpe Ratio Maximization and expected Utility when Asset Prices have Jumps, in: International Journal of Theoretical & Applied Finance, Vol. 10, No. 8, pp. 1339-1364.

Christopherson, Jon (1998): Normal Portfolios: Construction of Customized Benchmarks, in: Fabozzi, Frank [ed.], Active Equity Portfolio Management, New Hope/Pennsylvania 1998.

Chua, Choong Tze; Goh, Jeremy; Zhang, Zhe (2010): Expected Volatility, Unexpected Volatility, and the Cross-Section of Stock Returns, in: Journal of Financial Research, Vol. 33, No. 2, pp. 103-123.

Chun, Chang; Xiaojun, Yu (2010): Informational Efficiency and Liquidity Premium as the Determinants of Capital Structure, in: Journal of Financial and Quantitative Analysis, Vol. 45, No. 2, pp. 401-440.

Chye, Kob Hian; Meng, Chan Seet; Gupta, Pranjal; Ramakrishna, Sujata (2000): 'Blue Chip' Characteristics: A Study of Manager's Perceptions, in: Singapore Management Review, Vol. 22, No. 1, pp. 19-33.

Cini, Michelle (2001): The soft law approach: Commissions rule-making in the EU's stat aid regime, in: Journal of European Public Policy, Vol. 8, No. 2, pp. 192-207.

Cipriani, Marco; Guarino, Antonio (2005): Noise Trading in a Labatory Financial Market: A Maximum Likelihood Approach, in: Journal of the European Association, Vol. 3, No. 2/3, pp. 315-321.

Clark, Tom S. (2009): A Principal-Agent Theory of En Bac Review, in: Journal of Law, Economics & Organization, Vol. 25, No. 1, pp. 55-79.

Clarke, Roger; de Silva, Harindra; Thorley, Steven (2002): Portfolio Constraints and the Fundamental Law of Active Management, in: Financial Analysts Journal, Vol. 58, No. 5, pp. 48-66.

Cloyd, Pamela; Siegel, Larry; Schoenfelder, Stefen A. (2004): The Vital Importance and Fundamental Uses of Benchmarks, in: Schoenfelder, Steven A. [ed.], Active Index Investing, pp. 63-80, New Jersey 2004.

Cohen, Benjamin J. (2003): Global Currency Rivalry: Can the Euro Ever Challenge the Dollar?, in: Journal of Common Market Studies, Vol. 41, No. 4, pp. 575-595.

Cohen, D. Allen (2011): Slow-Timing the Market, an Alternative Portfolio-Allocation Approach, in: Journal of Financial Planning, Vol. 24, No. 2, pp. 45-53.

Cohen, David I. (2003): Equal weighting could add to indexing strategy, in: Pensions & Investments, Vol. 31, No. 6, p. 40.

Coldiron, Kevin; Kroner, Kenneth F. (1999): EMU and the asset allocation decision, in: Journal of Investing, Vol. 8, p. 39.

Collins, Cary M.; Wansley, James W.; Robinson, Breck (1995): Price and Volume Effects Associated with the Creation of Standard and Poor's Midcap Index, in: Journal of Financial Research, Vol. 18, pp. 329-350.

Colomer, Nora (2011): Europe on the Precipice, in: Asset Securitization Report, Vol. 11, No. 8, pp. 8-13.

Comerton-Forde, Carole; Gallagher, David R.; Nahhas, Jumana; Walter, Terry S. (2010): Transaction costs and institutional trading in small-cap equity funds, in: Australian Journal of Management, Vol. 35, No. 3, pp. 313-327.

Commerzbank AG [ed.] (2008): Handbuch der Indizes, Berlin 2008.

Conyon, Martin J. (2006): Executive Compensation and Incentives, in: Academy of Management Perspectives, Vol. 20, No. 1, pp. 25-44.

Conyon, Martin J.; Florou, Annita (2002): Top executive dismissal, ownership and corporate performance, in: Accounting & Business Research, Vol. 32, No. 4, pp. 209-225.

Cooper, Daniel; Woglom, Geoffrey (2003): The S&P 500 Effect: Not So Good in the Long Run, in: Journal of Investing, Vol. 12, No. 4, pp. 62-73.

Cootner, Paul H. (1978): Stock Market Indexes: Fallacies and Illusions, in: Lorie, James H.; Brealey, Richard [ed.]: Modern Developments in Investment Management, pp. 94-100, New York 1978.

Cornand, Camille; Heinemann, Frank (2009): Speculative Attacks with Multiple Sources of Public Information, in: Journal of Economics, Vol. 111, No. 1, pp. 73-102.

Cortez, Annetta; Ke, Wei (2010): The Portfolio Approach to Asset Allocation, in: Bank Accounting & Finance, Vol. 23, No. 6, pp. 28-34.

Costa, Bruce A.; Jakob, Keith (2010): Enhanced Performance Measurement of Mutual Funds: Running the Benchmark Index through the Hurdles, in: Journal of Applied Finance, Vol. 20, No. 1, pp. 95-102.

Cronqvist, Henrik; Nilsson, Mattias (2003): Agency Costs of Controlling Minority Shareholders, in: Journal of Financial & Quantitative Analysis, Vol. 38, No. 4, pp. 695-719.

Cummins, J. David; Rubio-Misas, Maria (2006): Deregulation, Consolidation, and Efficiency: Evidence from the Spanish Insurance Industry, in: Journal of Money, Credit & Banking, Vol. 38, No. 2, pp. 323-355.

Cumming, Douglas; Dai, Na (2010): Hedge Fund Regulation and Misreported Returns, in: European Financial Management, Vol. 16, No. 5, pp. 829-857.

Cumming, Douglas; Johan, Sofia (2008): Hedge Fund Strategies and Regulation, in: Banking & Financial Services Policy Report, Vol. 27, No. 7, pp. 1-15.

Currier, Kevin M. (2009): Price Cap regulation of a dominant firm facing competition, in: Journal of Economics, Vol. 98, No. 3, pp. 221-233.

Curtillet, Jean-Christophe; Dieudonné, Mathieu (2007): Sector-specific optimum asset allocation - An example for non-life insurers, in: Journal of Asset Management, Vol. 7, No. 6, pp. 404-411.

Curtis, Gregory (2004): Modern Portfolio Theory and Behavioural Finance, in: Journal of Wealth Management, Vol. 7, No. 2, pp. 16-22.

Cvitanic, Jakša; Wan, Xuhu; Zhang, Jianfeng (2009): Optimal Compensation with Hidden Action and Lump-Sum Payment in a Continuous-Time Model, in: Applied Mathematics & Optimization, Vol. 59, No. 1, pp. 99-146.

da Fonseca, Jose Soares (2010): The performance of the European stock markets: a time-varying the Sharpe ratio approach, in: European Journal of Finance, Vol. 16, No. 7, pp. 727-741.

Damodaran, Aswath (2002): Investment Valuation, Vol. 2, New York 2002.

D'Antonio, Louis; Johnsen, Tommi (2011): Equity Collars as an Alternative to Debt in Traditional Asset Allocation, in: Journal of Financial Service Professionals, Vol. 65, No. 4, pp. 37-42.

Darkiewicz, Grzegorz; Deelstra, Griselda; Dhaene, Jan; Hoedemakers, Tom; Vanmaele, Michèle (2009): Bounds For Right Tails of Deterministic and Stochastic Sums of Random Variables, in: Journal of Risk and Insurance, Vol. 76, No. 4, pp. 847-866.

Darnell, Max; Maramot, Marmi; Vaughn, David (1998): Investment implications of the EMU, in: Journal of Investing, Vol. 7, p. 19.

Das, Sanjiv Ranjan; Uppal, Raman (2004): Systematic Risk and International Portfolio Choice, in: Journal of Finance, Vol. 59, No. 6, pp. 2809-2834.

Dash, Srikant; S&P [ed.] (2005): Unveiling the Next Generation of Style Indexing, September 2005, pp. 1-26.

DeFusco, Richard; Ivanov, Stoyu; Karels, Gordon (2011): The exchange traded funds' pricing deviation: analysis and forecasts, in: Journal of Economics & Finance, Vol. 35, No. 2, pp. 181-197.

DeFusco, Richard; Mishra, Suchi; Raghunandan, Kannan (2010): Changes in the Information Efficiency of Stock Prices: Additional Evidence, in: Financial Review, Vol. 45, No. 1, pp. 153-165.

De Giorgi, Enrico; Post, Thierry (2008): Second-Order Stochastic Dominance, Reward-Risk Portfolio Selection, and the CAPM, in: Journal of Financial & Quantitative Analysis, Vol. 43, No. 2, pp. 525-546.

de Groot, Wilma; Swinkels, Laurens (2008): Incorporating uncertainty about alternative assets in strategic pension fund asset allocation, in: Pensions. An International Journal, Vol. 13, No. 1/2, pp. 71-77.

Deininger, Claus (2005): Indexeffekte am deutschen Kapitalmarkt und deren Ursachen, diss., Würzburg 2005.

Deininger, Claus; Kaserer, Christoph; Roos, Stephanie (2005): Der Indexeffekt am deutschen Aktienmarkt und seine Ursachen, in: Zeitschrift für Bankrecht und Bankwirtschaft, Vol. 4, pp. 262-279.

De La Grandville, Olivier; Pakes, Anthony U.; Tricot, Claude (2002): Random rates of growth and return: introducing the expo-normal distribution, in: Applied Stochastic Models in Business & Industry, Vol. 18, No. 1, pp. 23-51.

Del Brio, Esther D.; de Miguel, Alberto (2010): Dividends and Market Signalling: an Analysis of Corporate Insider Trading, in: European Financial Management, Vol. 16, No. 3, pp. 480-497.

Delquié, Philippe (2008): Interpretation of the Risk Tolerance Coefficient in Terms of Maximum Acceptable Loss, in: Decision Analysis, Vol. 5, No. 1, pp. 5-9.

Demchuk, Andriy; Gibson, Rajna (2006): Stock Market Performance and the Term Structure of Credit Spreads, in: Journal of Financial and Quantitative Analysis, Vol. 41, No. 4, pp. 863-887.

De Melo Mendes, Beatriz Vaz (2006): A Bayesian analysis of clusters of extreme losses, in: Applied Stochastic Models in Business & Industry, Vol. 22, No. 2, pp. 155-167.

Dempsey, Mike (2009): Rankings for Australian managed funds: Contrariness and performance index failure, in: Journal of Asset Management, Vol. 10, No. 3, pp. 138-157.

Denis, Diane K.; McConnell, John J.; Ovtchinnikov, Alexei V.; Yu, Yun (2003): S&P Index Additions and Earnings Expectations, in: Journal of Finance, Vol. 58, pp. 1821-1840.

Deroose, Servaas; Hodson, Dermot; Kuhlmann, Joost (2007): The legitimation of EMU: Lessons from the early years of the euro, in: Review of International Political Economy, Vol. 14, No. 5, pp. 800-819.

De Souza, Clifford; Gokcan, Soueyman (2004): Hedge Fund Investing: A Quantitative Approach to Hedge fund Manager Selection and De-Selection, in: Journal of Wealth Management, Vol. 6, No. 4, pp. 52-73.

Deutsche Börse AG [ed.] (2004): REX und REXP – Kuzinformation, Frankfurt a. M. 2004.

Deutsche Börse AG [ed.] (2008): Leitfaden zu den Aktienindizes der Deutschen Börse, Frankfurt a. M. 2008.

Devereux, Michael B.; Yetman, James (2010): Leverage Constraints and the International Transmission of Shocks, in: Journal of Money, Credit & Banking, Vol. 42, pp. 71-105.

Dichtl, Hubert; Drobetz, Wolfgang (2009): Does tactical asset allocation work? Another look at the fundamental law of active management, in: Journal of Asset Management, Vol. 10, No. 4, pp. 235-252.

Dichtl, Hubert; Petersmeier, Kerstin; Schlenger, Christian (2003): Dynamische Asset Allocation im Lichte der Präferenzen institutioneller Anleger, in: Dichtl, Hubert; Kleeberg, Jochen; Schlenger, Christian [ed.] Handbuch Asset Management, Bad Soden 2003.

Diesinger, Peter; Kraft, Holger; Seifried, Frank (2010): Asset allocation and liquidity breakdowns: what if your broker does not answer the phone?, in: Finance & Stochastics, Vol. 14, No. 3 2010, pp. 343-374.

Dietrich, J. Richard; Kachelmeier, Steven J.; Kleinmuntz, Don N.; Linsmeier, Thomas J. (2001): Market Efficiency, Bounded Rationality, and Supplemental Business Reporting Disclosures, in: Journal of Accounting Research, Vol. 39, No. 2, pp. 243-268.

Dietze, Leif Holger; Entrop, Oliver; Wilkens, Marco (2009): The performance of investment grade corporate bond funds: evidence from the European market, in: European Journal of Finance, Vol. 15, No. 2, pp. 191-209.

Ding, Yuangyao; Jia, Rangcheng; Tang, Shaoxiang (2003): Dynamic principal agent model based on CMDP, in: Mathematical Methods of Operations Research, Vol. 58, No. 1, pp. 149-157.

Docking, Diane Scott; Dowen, Richard J. (2006): Evidence on Stock Price Effects Associated with Changes in the S&P 600 SmallCap Index, in: Quarterly Journal of Business & Economics, Vol. 45, No. 1/2, pp. 89-114.

Döhnert, Karsten; Kunz, Roger M.; Wälchli, Urs (2000): Diversifikation: Länder oder Branchen?, Zürich 2000.

Dolde, Walter; Giaccotto, Carmelo; Mishra, Dev R.; O'Brien, Thomas (2011): Foreign Exchange Exposure and Cost of Equity for US Companies: Local versus Global CAPM, in: Journal of Applied Finance, Vol. 21, No. 1, pp. 78-86.

Dolvin, Steven D.; Templeton, Willian K.; Riebe, William J. (2010): Asset Allocation for Retirement: Simple Heuristic and Target-Date Funds, in: Journal of Financial Planning, Vol. 23, No. 3, pp. 60-71.

Domowitz, Ian; Glen, Jack; Madhavan, Ananth (2001): Liquidity, Volatility and Equity Trading Costs Across Countries and Over Time, in: International Finance, Vol. 4, No. 2, pp. 221-255.

Donnelly, Shawn (2004): Reshaping Economic and Monetary Union: membership rules and budget policies in Germany, France and Spain, in: Manchester University Press, Manchester 2004.

Donnelly, Shawn (2005): Explaining EMU Reform, in: Journal of Common Market Studies, Vol. 43, No. 5 2005, pp. 947-967.

Dorenkamp, Axel (2002): Kombination aus Diversifikation- und Wachstumsstrategien im Lichte von Rendite, Risiko und Unternehmensgröße, diss., Osnabrück 2002.

Dorfleitner, Gregor (2002): Stetige versus diskrete Renditen: Überlegungen zur richtigen Verwendung beider Begriffe in Theorie und Praxis, in: Kredit und Kapital, Vol. 35, Nr. 2, pp. 216-241.

Dow, James R. Jr. (2009): Age, investing horizon and asset allocation, in: Journal of Economics & Finance, Vol. 33, No. 4, pp. 422-436.

Downing, Chris; Underwood, Shane; Xing, Yuhang (2009): The Relative Information Efficiency of Stocks and Bonds: An Intraday Analysis, in: Journal of Financial and Quantitative Analysis, Vol. 44, No. 5, pp. 1081-1102.

Dreman, David N.; Lufkin, Eric A. (2000): Investor Overreaction: Evidence that its Basics is Psychological, in: Journal of Psychology and Financial Markets, Vol. 1, No. 1, pp. 61-75.

Dridi, Ramdan; Germain, Laurent (2004): Bullish/Bearish Strategies of Trading: A Nonlinear Equilibrium, in: Journal of Financial & Quantitative Analysis, Vol. 39, No. 4, pp. 873-886.

Drobetz, Wolfgang (2001): How to Avoid the Pitfalls in Portfolio Optimization? Putting the BLACK-LITTERMAN Approach at Work, in: Swiss Society for Financial Market Research, Vol. 15, No. 1, pp. 59-75.

Drummen, Martin; Lips, Thomas; Zimmermann, Heinz (1992): Portfolioeffekte des Währungsrisikos, in: Finanzmarkt und Portfolio Management, Vol. 6, No. 1, pp. 80-102.

Duan, Ying; Hu, Gang; McLean, R. David (2009): When is stock picking likely to be successful? Evidence from mutual funds, in: Financial Analysts Journal, Vol. 65, No. 2, pp. 55-66.

Duchin, Ran; Haim, Levy (2009): Markowitz versus the Talmudic Portfolio Diversification Strategies, in: Journal of Portfolio Management, Vol. 35, No. 2, pp. 71-74.

Duchin, Ran; Levy, Moshe (2010): Friend of Foe? The Role of State and Mutual Fund Ownership in the Split Share Structure Reform in China, in: Journal of Financial & Quantitative Analysis, Vol. 45, No. 3, pp. 623-640.

Dueker, Michael; Assenmacher-Wesche, Katrin (2010): Forecasting macro variables with a Qual VAR business cycle turning point index, in: Applied Economics, Vol. 42, No. 23, pp. 2909-2920.

Dufour, Jean-Marie; Farhat, Abdeljelil; Gardiol, Lucien; Khalaf, Lynda (1998): Simulation-based finite sample normality test in linear regressions, in: Economics Journal, Vol. 1, No. 1, pp. 154-173.

Dunham, Lee M.; Simpson, Thuy H. (2008): Do Index Fund Managers Trade Opportunistically around Index Changes? An Empirical Examination of S&P 500 Index Funds, in: Journal of Index Investing, Vol. 1, No. 3, pp. 58-64.

Dunis, Christian L.; Laws, Jason; Sermpinis, Georgios (2009): The robustness of neural networks for modelling and trading the EUR/USD exchange rate at the ECB fixing, in: Journal of Derivatives & Hedge Funds, Vol. 15, No. 3, pp. 186-205.

Dunn, Robert Jr. (2008): EMU Convergence: Reasons for Encouragement, in: Challenge, Vol. 51, No. 2, pp. 85-96.

Durand, Robert B.; Jafarpour, Hedieh; Klüppelberg, Claudia; Maller, Ross (2010): Maximize the Sharpe Ration and Minimize a VaR, in: Journal of Wealth Management, Vol. 13, No. 1, pp. 91-102.

Duvall, Richard M.; Quinn, Judith L. (2001): Skewness preference in stable markets, Journal of Financial Research, Vol. 4, No. 3, pp. 248-263.

Eberlein, Ernst; Madan, Dilip B. (2009): Hedge Fund Performance: Sources and Measures, in: International Journal of Theoretical & Applied Finance, Vol. 12, No. 3, pp. 267-282.

Eberly, Janice; Wang, Neng (2009): Capital Reallocation and Growth, in: American Economic Review, Vol. 99, No. 2, pp. 560-566.

EBF [ed.] (2011): Euribor Code of Conduct, http://www.euribor-ebf.eu/assets/files/Euribor _code_condust.pdf, date: 06.12.2011.

ECB [ed.] (2001): The Evolution of the ECB and the Euro, in: The Region, Vol. 14, No. 4, p. 36.

ECB [ed.] (2007): Die Geschichte des Euro: Ein Überblick über die Entstehung der Euro-Banknoten und –Münzen, Frankfurt a. M. 2007.

ECB [ed.] (2011): Measuring Inflation in the Euro Area, http://www.ecb.int/stats/prices/hicp/html/inflation.en.html, date: 31.12.2011.

ECB [ed.] (2012): Key ECB interest rates, http://www.ecb.int/stats/monetary/rates/html/index.en.html, date: 15.082012.

Eckey-Hans-Friedrich; Kosfeld, Reinhold; Türck, Matthias (2008): Streuung und Schiefe, in: Deskriptive Statistik, Vol. 5, Wiesbaden 2005.

Egert, Balzazs; Kierzenkowski, Rafal; Reininger, Thomas (2005): Asymmetric Fluctuation Bands in the ERM and ERM II, in: Eastern European Economics, Vol. 43, No. 1, pp. 82-115.

Ehling, Paul; Ramos, Sofia Brito; ECB [ed.] (2005): Geographic versus industry diversification, constraints matter, Frankfurt a. M. 2005.

Ehmer, Philipp (2009): Krise 2009 trifft die Industrie hart, in: DB Research, July 2009, pp. 1-2.

Eisenhardt, Kathleen (1989): Agency Theory. An Assessment and Review, in: Academy of Management Review, Vol. 14, pp. 57-74.

Ekelund, Robert B. Jr.; Hébert, Robert F. (2002): The Origins of Neoclassical Microeconomics, in: Journal of Economic Perspectives, Vol. 16, No. 3, pp. 197-215.

Eling, Martin (2006): Autocorrelation, bias and fat tails: Are hedge funds really attractive investments?, in: Derivatives Use, Trading & Regulation, Vol. 12, No. 1/2, pp. 28-47.

Eling, Martin; Farinelli, Simone; Rossello, Damiano; Tibiletti, Luisa (2011): One-size or tailor-made performance ratios for ranking hedge funds?, in: Journal of Derivatives & Hedge Funds, Vol. 16, No. 4, pp. 267-277.

Elschen, Rainer (1991): Gegenstand und Anwendungsmöglichkeiten der Agency-Theorie, in: Zeitschrift für betriebswirtschaftliche Forschung, Vol. 43, pp. 1002-1012.

Elton, Edwin J.; Gruber, Martin J. (1997): Modern portfolio theory, 1950 to date, in: Journal of Banking & Finance, Vol. 21, pp. 1743-1759.

Elton, Edwin J.; Gruber, Martin J.; Busse, Jefferey A. (2004): Are Investors Rational? Choice among Index Funds, in: Journal of Finance, Vol. 58, No. 1, pp. 261-288.

Elton, Edwin J.; Gruber, Martin J.; Brown, Stephan J.; Goetzmann, William N. (2007): Modern Portfolio Theory and Investment Analysis, Vol. 7, New York 2007.

Enderlein, Henrik; Verdun, Amy (2009): EMU's teenage challenge: what have we learned and can we predict from political science?, in: Journal of European Policy, Vol. 16, No. 4, pp. 490-507.

Ennis, Richard M.; Sebastian, Michael D. (2005): Asset Allocation with Private Equity, in: Journal of Private Equity, Vol. 8, No. 3, pp. 81-87.

Entzian, Till (2008): Institutionelles Asset Management zum Umgang mit neuen Freiheiten, in: Zeitschrift für das Kreditwesen, Vol. 16, pp. 754-760.

Erhardt, Michael C.; Tucker, Alan L. (1990): Pricing CRB Futures Contracts, in: Journal of Financial Research, Vol. 13, No. 1, pp. 7-14.

Ernst, Edgar; Vater, Hendrik (2005): DivDAX: Motivation, Konzeption und Konstruktion, in: Finanzbetrieb, Vol. 6, pp. 427-431.

Erwin, Danny M.; Faulk, Gregory K.; Smolira, Joseph C. (2009): The impact of asset allocation, savings, and retirement horizons, savings rates, and social security income in retirement planning: A Monte Carlo analysis, in: Financial Services Review, Vol. 18, No. 4, pp. 313-331.

Erwin, Gayle R.; Miller, James M. (1998): The liquidity effects associated with additions of a stock to the S&P 500 index: Evidence from bid/ask spread, in: Financial Review, Vol. 33, No. 1, pp. 131-146.

Estrada, Javier (2008): Fundamental Indexation and International Diversification, in: Journal of Portfolio Management, Spring 2008, pp. 93-109.

Etterer, Alexander; Beer, Robert; Fleischer, Klaus (2003): Indexing - Wie Sie zukünftig mit Indexanlagen erfolgreich investieren, Augsburg 2003.

European Commission [ed.] (2011): Public finances in EMU 2011, in: European Economy, Vol. 3, pp. 1-212.

Evans, Richard B. (2010): Mutual Fund Incubation, in: Journal of Finance, Vol. 65, No. 5, pp. 1581-1611.

Evensky, Harold; Clark, John; Boscaljon, Brian (2010): Asset Allocation – New and Improved?, in: Journal of Financial Planning, Vol. 23, No. 9, pp. 32-35.

Fama, Eugene F. (1970): Efficient Capital Markets: A Review of Theory and Empirical Work, in: Journal of Finance, Vol. 25, pp. 383-423.

Fama, Eugene F. (1991): Efficient Capital Markets: II, in: Journal of Finance, Vol. 46, No. 5, pp. 1575-1617.

Fama, Eugene F. (2006): The Value Premium and the CAPM, in: Journal of Finance, Vol. 61, No. 5, pp. 2163-2185.

Fama, Eugene; Blume, Marshall E. (1970): Filter rules and stock market trading returns, in: Journal of Finance, Vol. 25, pp. 226-241.

Fang, Hsing; Lai, Tsong-Yue (1997): Co-Kurtosis and Capital Asset Pricing, in: Financial Review, Vol. 32, No. 2, May 1997, pp. 293-307.

Farzard, Roben (2006): Blue Chip Blues, in: BusinessWeek, 17.04.2006, pp. 66-75.

Farzard, Roben (2011): Why Apple isn't in the Dow, in: Bloomberg Businessweek, 20.06.2011, pp. 49-50.

Fava, Vera Lucia (2010): Price dispersion and price indexes, in: Applied Economics, Vol. 42, No. 1, pp. 23-36.

Feathersone, Kevin (2003): Greece and EMU: between external empowerment and domestic vulnerability, in: Journal of Common Market Studies, Vol. 41, No. 5, pp. 923-940.

Feldman, David; Reisman, Haim (2003): Simple Construction of the Efficient Frontier, in: European Financial Management, Vol. 9, No. 2, pp. 251-259.

Ferguson, Robert; Leistikow, Dean; Rentzler, Joel; Yu, Susana (2009): The Effect of Value Estimation Errors on Portfolio Growth Rates, in: Journal of Investing, Vol. 18, No. 2, pp. 69-75.

Fernandez, Viviana P. (2005): The International CAPM and a Wavelet-Based Decomposition of Value at Risk, in: Studies in Dynamics & Econometrics, Vol. 9, No. 4, pp. 1-35.

Fernholz, Robert E. (2000): Stochastic Portfolio Theory, New York 2000.

Ferreira, Miguel A.; Gama, Paulo M. (2005): Have World, Country, and Industry Risks changed over Time? An Investigation of the Volatility of Developed Stock Markets?, in: Journal of Financial & Quantitative Analysis, Vol. 40, No. 1, pp. 195-222.

Ferris, Stephen, R.; Sen, Nilanjan; Nguyen, Thi Anh Thu (2010): Firm value and the diversification choice: international evidence from global and industrial diversification, in: Applied Economics, Vol. 17, No. 11, pp. 1027-1031.

Ferris, Stephen R.; Yan, Yuemin (2007): Agency Conflicts in Delegated Portfolio Management: Evidence from Namesake Mutual Funds, in: Journal of Financial Research, Vol. 30, No.4, pp. 473-494.

Ferruz, Luis; Munoz, Fernando; Vargas, Maria (2010): Stock picking, market timing and style differences between socially responsible and conventional pension funds: evidence from the United Kingdom, in: Business Ethics: A European Review, Vol. 19, No. 4, pp. 408-422.

Festré, Agnès (2010): Incentives and Social Norms: A Motivation-Based Economic Analysis of Social Norms, in: Journal of Economic Surveys, Vol. 24, No. 3, pp. 511-528.

Field, Arthur (2010): Moving average envelopes in the S&P, in: Futures; News, Analysis & Strategies for Futures, Options & Derivatives Traders, Vol. 39, No. 8, pp. 34-36.

Fieldings Zoe (2006): Active returns more luck than judgement, in: Money Management, Vol. 20, No. 11, p. 8.

Fildes, Toby (2010): Braced for impact, in: Euroweek, May 2010, pp. 6-10.

Fingland, Lisa; Bailey, Stephan J. (2008): The EU's Stability and Growth Pact: Its Credibility and Sustainability, in: Public Money & Management, Vol. 28, No. 4, pp. 223-230.

Fiori, Anna Maria (2008): Measuring Kurtosis by Right and Left Inequality Orders, in: Communications in Statistics – Theory and Methods, Vol. 37, pp. 2665-2680.

Fischer, Bernd R. (2010): Performanceanalyse in der Praxis, Vol. 3, Oldenburg 2010.

Fischer, Edwin O.; Glawischnig, Markus (2007): Branchendiversifikation in der Eurozone: Eine empirische Untersuchung, in: Finanzbetrieb, Vol. 9, No. 3, pp. 180-188.

Fletcher, Jonathan (2009): Risk Reduction and Mean-Variance Analysis: An Empirical Investigation, in: Journal of Business Finance & Accounting, Vol. 36, No. 7/8, pp. 951-971.

Focardi, Sergio M.; Fabozzi, Frank J. (2003): Fat Tails, Scaling, and Stable Laws: A Critical Look at Modeling Extremal Events in Financial Phenomena, in: Journal of Rsik Finance, Vol. 5, No. 1, pp. 5-26.

Fogler, H. Russel (2008): Sharpe's State-Preference Approach and Beyond: A Practitioner Overview, in: Journal of Portfolio Management, Vol. 34, No. 3, pp. 120-131.

Fong, Kingsley; Gallagher, David R.; Lee, Adrian D. (2008): Benchmarking Benchmarks: measuring characteristic selectivity using portfolio holdings data, in: Accounting & Finance, Vol. 48, No. 5, pp. 761-781.

Fontana, Claudio; Runggaldier, Wolfgang J. (2010): Credit Risk and Incomplete Information: Filtering and EM Parameter Estimation, in: International Journal of Theoretical and Applied Finance, Vol. 13, No. 5, pp. 683-715.

Fourcans, Andre; Warin, Thierry (2007): Stability and Growth Pact II: Incentives and Moral Hazard, in: Journal of Economic Policy Reform, Vol. 10, No. 1, pp. 51-62.

Franke, Gunter (1987): Costless signalling in financial markets, in: Journal of Finance, Vol. 42, pp. 809-822.

Freeman, Glenn (2006): Commodities not a standalone asset, in: Super Review, Vol. 20, No. 8, p. 3.

Freimann, Eckhard (1998): Economic integration and country allocation in Europe, in: Financial Analysts Journal, Vol. 54, No. 5, pp. 32-41.

Frère, Eric; Rojahn, Joachim; Schyra, Andreas (2010): Risikomanagement von Bond-Portfolios, in: Handelsblatt Business Briefing, No. 1, pp. 7-9.

Frino, Alex; Gallagher, David R.; Neubert, Albert S.; Oetomo, Teddy N. (2004): Index Design and Implications for Index Tracking, in: Journal of Portfolio Management, Vol. 30, No. 2, pp. 89-95.

Frino, Alex; Gallagher, David R.; Oetomo, Teddy N. (2005): Chapter 2: The Index Tracking Strategies of Passive and Enhanced Index Equity Funds, in: Australian Journal of Management, Vol. 30, No. 1, pp. 23-55.

FTSE [ed.] (1996): Guide to Calculation Methods, London 1996.

FTSE [ed.] (1999): Setting a Global Standard for Indices: A Consultation Paper from FTSE International, London 1999.

Furrer, Bernhard; Herger, Beat (1999): Struktur europäischer Aktienrenditen: Bedeutung und Veränderung internationaler, nationaler und sektoraler Faktoren, in: Finanzmarkt und Portfolio Management, Vol. 13, No. 2, pp. 194-206.

Füss, Roland; Rehkugler, Heinz; Disch, Wolfgang (2005): Hegde Funds als Anlagealternative: Chancen und Risiken, in: Finanzbetrieb, Vol. 1, pp. 40-56.

Gahn, Roland (1994): Delegiertes Portfolio Management deutscher institutioneller Anleger aus dem Nichtbanken-Bereich, München 1994.

Galagedera, Don U. A. (2009): An Analytical Framework for Explaining Relative Performance of CAPM Beta and Downside Risk, in: International Journal of Theoretical & Applied Finance, Vol. 12, No. 3, pp. 341-358.

Galariotis, Emilios C.; Giouvris, Evangelos (2007): Liquidity Commonality in the London Stock Exchange, in: Journal of Business Finance & Accounting, Vol. 34, No. 1/2, pp. 374-388.

Galati, Gabriele; Tsatsaronis, Kostas (2003): The Impact of the Euro on Europe's Financial Markets, in: Financial Markets, Institutions and Instruments, Vol. 12, pp. 165-221.

Gannon, Niall J.; Blum, Michael J. (2006): After-Tax Returns on Stocks versus Bonds for the High Tax Bracket Investor, in: Journal of Wealth Management, Vol. 9, No. 2, pp. 35-45.

Ganser, Florian (2008): Korrelationen von Aktienindizes, Stuttgart 2008.

Garbade, Kenneth D. (1982): Securities Markets, New York 1982.

Garcia-Solanes, Jos; Maria-Dolores, Ramon (2008): The New Member States and the Process towards EMU, in: Review of Development Economics, Vol. 12, No. 3, pp. 655-667.

Garobbio, Roberto C. (1995): Risikoeigenschaften der internationalen Aktienindizes, Aachen 1995.

Gärtner, Manfred; Griesbach, Björn; Jung, Florian (2011): PIGS or Lambs? The European Sovereign Debt Crisis and the Role of Rating Agencies, in: International Advances in Economic Research, Vol. 17, No. 3, pp. 288-299.

Garz, Hendrik; Günther, Stefan; Moriabadi, Cyrus (2006): Portfolio-Management Theorie und Anwendung, Frankfurt a. M. 2006.

Gastineau, Gary L. (2008): The Short Side of 130/30 Investing for the Conservative Portfolio Manager, in: Journal of Portfolio Management, Vol. 34, No. 2, pp. 39-52.

Gauld, Robin (2007): Principal-Agent Theory and Organisational Change, in: Policy Studies, Vol. 28, No. 1, pp. 17-34.

Gemmill, Gordon; Soosung, Hwang; Salmon, Mark (2006): Performance measurement with loss aversion, in: Journal of Asset Management, Vol. 7, No. 3, pp. 56-59.

Georgiev, Iliyan (2007): A mixture-distribution factor model for multivariate outliers, in: Econometrics Journal, Vol. 10, No. 3, pp. 605-636.

Gerard, Bruno; Guojun, Wu (2006): How Important Is Intertemporal Risk for Asset Allocation?, in: Journal of Business, Vol. 79, No. 4, pp. 2203-2241.

Gerber, Anke; Hens, Thorsten; Woehrmann, Peter (2010): Dynamic General Equilibrium and T-Period Fund Separation, in: Journal of Financial & Quantitative Analysis, Vol. 45, No. 2, pp. 369-400.

Gerke, Wolfgang; Arneth, Stefan; Fleischer, Jörg (2001): Kursgewinne bei Aufnahmen in den DAX 100, Verluste bei Entnahmen am deutschen Kapitalmarkt, in: Zeitschrift für Betriebswirtschaft, Vol. 71, pp. 45-66.

Gerke, Wolfgang; Röhrs, Alexander; Mager, Ferdinand (2005): Twenty Years of International Diversification from a German Perspective, in: Schmalenbach Business Review, Vol. 57, pp. 86-102.

German Bundestag [ed.] (2011): Aktueller Begriff – Europa: Etablierung eines dauerhaften Europäischen Stabilitätsmechanismus im vereinfachten Vertragsänderungsverfahren, in: Wissenschaftliche Dienste, Vol. 4, pp. 1-2.

Gerrans, Paul; Clark-Murphy, Marilyn; Speelman, Craig (2010): Asset allocation and age effects in retirement savings choices, in: Accounting & Finance, Vol. 50, No. 2, pp. 301-319.

Giannellis, Nikolaus; Papadopoulos, Athanasios (2011): What causes exchange rate volatility? Evidence from selected EMU members and candidates for EMU membership countries, in: Journal of international Money & Finance, Vol. 30, No. 1, pp. 39-61.

Gintschel, Andreas; Scherer, Bernd (2008): Optimal asset allocation for sovereign wealth funds, in: Journal of Asset Management, Vol. 9, No. 3, pp. 215-238.

Giofré, Maela M. (2008): EMU Effects on Stock Markets: From Home Bias to Euro Bias, Munich Personal RePEc Archive, May 2008.

Gleißner, Werner; Wolfrum, Marco (2008): Eigenkapitalkosten und die Bewertung nicht börsennotierter Unternehmen: Relevanz von Diversifikationsgrad und Risikomaß, in: Coprorate Finance, Vol. 9, pp. 602-614.

Goetzmann, William N.; Kumar, Alok (2008): Equity Portfolio Diversification, in: Review of Finance, Vol. 12, pp. 433-463.

Goetzmann, William N.; Massa, Massimo (1999): Heterogeneity of Trade and Stock Returns. Evidence from Index Fund Investors, in: Yale ICF Working Paper, Nr. 00-29, March 2001.

Goldberg, Steven T. (2009): Why the Dow Is a Dumb Index, in: Kiplinger's Personal Finance, Vol. 63, No. 10, p. 31.

Goldberg, Victor P. (1976): Regulation and administered contracts, in: The Bell Journal of Economics and Management Science, Vol. 7, pp. 439-441.

Gorman, Stephan A. (1998): The international equity commitment, in: The Research Foundation of the Institute of Chartered Financial Analysts 1998.

Grauer, Robert R. (2008): Benchmarking Measures of Investment Performance with Perfect-Foresight and Bankrupt Asset Allocation Strategies, in: Journal of Portfolio Management, Vol. 34, No. 4, pp. 43-57.

Greeley, Brendan; Czuczka, Tony; Cullen, Angela; Frye, Andrew (2011): The Good Germany, in: Bloomberg Businessweek, Vol. 4247, pp. 10-12.

Gregoriou, Greg N. (2004): Performance of Canadian hedge funds using a modified Sharpe ratio, in: Derivatives Use, Trading & Regulation, Vol. 10, No. 2, pp. 149-155.

Gregoriou, Greg N.; Pascalau, Razvan (2010): An empirical analysis of short-biased hedge funds' risk-adjusted performance: A panel approach, in: Journal of Derivatives & Hedge Funds, Vol. 16, No. 3, pp. 176-190.

Gregory-Allen, Rusell B.; Shawky, Hany A.; Stangl, Jeffrey (2009): Quantitative vs. Fundamental Analysis in Institutional Money Management: Where's the Beef?, in: Journal of Investing, Vol. 18, No. 4, pp. 42-52.

Greiner, Alfred; Semmler, Willi (2001): The Maastricht Criteria and Sustainability of German Fiscal Policy, in: Annals of Public & Cooperative Economics, Vol. 72, No. 2, pp. 271-284.

Griese, Knut; Kempf, Alexander (2003): Lohnt aktives Fondsmanagement aus Anlegersicht?, in: Zeitschrift für Betriebswirtschaft, Vol. 73, No. 2, pp. 201-224.

Grill, Wolfgang; Perczynski, Hans (2001): Wirtschaftslehre des Kreditwesens, Bad Homburg von der Höhe 2001.

Grinold, Richard C.; Kahn, Ronald N. (2000): Active Portfolio Management a Quantitative Approach for Producing Superior Returns and Controlling Risk, Vol. 2, New York 2000.

Grobys, Klaus (2009): Portfoliomanagement Index-Tracking Strategies, Norderstedt 2009.

Gülpinar, Nalan; Katata, Kabir; Pachamanova, Dessislava A. (2011): Robust portfolio allocation under discrete asset choice constraints, in: Journal of Asset Management, Vol. 12, No. 1, pp. 67-83.

Guido, Ron; Walsh, Kathleen (2005): Bond Term Premium Analysis in the Presence of Multiple Regimes, in: International Review of Finance, Vol. 5, No. 1/2, pp. 31- 54.

Guo, Zhaohui (2002): Behavioral Finance: Die empirische Überprüfbarkeit behavioraler Modelle, diss., St. Gallen 2002.

Guojin, Gong; Li, Laura Yue; Shin, Jae Yong (2011): Relative Performance Evaluation and Related Peer Groups in Executive Compensation Contracts, in: Accounting Review, Vol. 86, No. 3, pp. 1007-1043.

Gupta, Francis (2011): Inflation and Inflation Hedges, in: Journal of Indexes Europe, September/Oktober 2011, pp. 14-20.

Guse, Frank; Rudolf, Markus (2006): Schiefe in der Portfolioselektion, Vallendar 2006.

Gwilym, Owain; Buckle, Mike (2001): The lead-lag relationship between the FTSE100 stock index and its derivative contracts, in: Applied Financial Economics, Vol. 11, No. 4, pp. 385-393.

Gygax, André F.; Otchere, Isaac (2010): Index composition changes and the cost of incumbency, in: Journal of Banking & Finance, Vol. 34, No. 10, pp. 2500-2509.

Haas, Markus (2009): Modelling skewness and kurtosis with the skewed Gauss-.Laplace sum distribution, in: Applied Economics Letters, Vol. 16, pp. 1277-1283.

Haas, Markus; Mittnik, Stefan; Paolella, Marc S. (2006): Modelling and predicting market risk with Laplace-Gaussian mixture distribution, in: Applied Financial Economics, Vol. 16, No. 15, pp. 1145-1162.

Hagdtvedt, Reidar (2009): Stock return dynamics and the CAPM anomalies, in: Applied Economics Letter, Vol. 16, No. 16, pp. 1593-1596.

Hakenes, Hendrik; Wilkens, Sascha (2003): Der Value-at-Risk auf Basis der Extremwerttheorie, in: Finanzbetrieb, Vol. 12, pp. 821-829.

Hamada, Mahmoud; Valdez, Emiliano A. (2008): CAPM and Option Pricing With Elliptically Contoured Distribution, in: Journal of Risk & Insurance, Vol. 75, No. 2, pp. 387-409.

Hamza, Olfa; Kortas, Mohamed, L'Her, Jean-Francois; Roberge, Mathieu (2007): International Equity Indices: Exploring Alternatives to Market Cap-Weighting, in: Journal of Investing, Vol. 16, No. 2, pp. 103-118.

Hand, Graham (2011): Exploiting inefficient markets, in: Money Management, Vol. 25, No. 9, pp.19-21.

Hansen, Jorgen Drud; Nielsen, Ulff-Moller (2010): Market Integration, Choice of Technology, and Welfare, in: Review of International Economics, Vol. 18, No. 2, pp. 229-242.

Hardouvelis, Gikas A.; Malliaropulos, Dimitrios; Priestley, Richard (2006): EMU and European Stock Market Integration, in: Journal of Business, Vol. 79, No. 1, pp. 365-392.

Hargis, Kent; Jianping, Mei (2006): Is Country Diversification better than Industry Diversification, in: European Financial Management, Vol. 12, No. 3, pp. 319-340.

Harris, Daniel L. (2010): Seasonal patterns are open for options, in: Futures; News, Analysis & Strategies for Futures, Options & Derivatives Traders, Vol. 39, No. 10, pp. 36-38.

Harris, Lawrence; Gurel, Eitan (1986): Price and volume effects associated with changes in the S&P 500 list: New Evidence for the existence of price pressure, in: Journal of Finance, Vol. 41, pp. 815-829.

Hartmann-Wendels, Thomas (1989): Principal-Agent-Theorie und asymmetrische Informationsverteilung, in: Zeitschrift für Betriebswirtschaft, Vol. 59, pp. 713-735.

Harvey, Campbell R.; Liechty, John C.; Liechty, Merrill W.; Müller, Peter (2004): Portfolio Selection with Higher Moments, Houston 2004.

Hasebrouck, Joel (2009): Trading Costs and Returns for U.S. Equities: Estimating Effective Costs from Daily Data, in: Journal of Finance, Vol. 64, No. 3, pp. 1445-1477.

Haslem, John A. (2009): Mutual Fund Arbitrage and Transaction Costs, in: Journal of Investing, Vol. 18, No. 2, pp. 57-61.

Hatherley, Anthony; Alcock, Jamie (2007): Portfolio construction incorporating asymmetric dependence structures: a user's guide, in: Accounting & Finance, Vol. 47, No. 3, pp. 447-472.

Hau, Harald; Rey, Hélène (2008): Home Bias at the Fund Level, in: American Economic Review, Vol. 98, No. 2, pp. 333-338.

Hau, Harald; Thum, Marcel (2009): Subprime Crisis and board (in-) competence: private versus public banks in Germany, in: Economic Policy, Vol. 24, No. 60, pp. 701-752.

Hayes, Brian (2006): Maximum Drawdowns of Hedge Funds with Serial Correlation, in: Journal of Alternative Investments, Vol. 8, No. 4, pp. 26-38.

Heath, Joseph (2009): The Uses and Abuses of Agency Theory, in: Business Ethics Quarterly, Vol. 19, No. 4, pp. 497-528.

Heckman, Leila; Narayanan, Singanallur R.; Patel, Sandeep A. (1999): Country and Industry Importance in European Returns, SSRN working paper series 1999.

Hedesström, Ted Martin; Svedsäter, Henrik; Gärling, Tommy (2009): Naïve Diversification in the Swedish Premium Pension Scheme: Experimental Evidence, in: Applied Psychology: An International Review, Vol. 58, No. 3, pp. 403-417.

Heidorn, Thomas; Hoppe, Christian; Kaiser, Dieter G. (2006): Implikationen der Heterogenität auf das Benchmarking mit Hedgefondsindizes, in: Finanzbetrieb, Vol. 9, pp. 557-571.

Heidorn, Thomas; Kaiser, Dieter G.; Roder, Christoph (2009): The Risk of Funds of Hedge Funds: An Empirical Analysis of the Maximum Drawdown, in: Journal of Wealth Management, Vol. 12, No. 2 pp. 89-100.

Heinen, Nicolaus; Böttcher, Barbara [ed.] (2009): Schuldenspirale oder Exit-Strategie: Was kann der Stabilitäts- und Wachstumspakt leisten?, in: DB Research, Vol. 71, pp. 1-24.

Heinen, Nicolaus; Böttcher, Barbara [ed.] (2010): Schuldenbremse für Euroland: Mit nationalen Schuldenregeln den Stabilitätspakt stärken, in: DB Research, Vol. 74, pp. 1-20.

Heinen, Nicolaus; Theiss, Alessandro (2011): EFSF – Where do national parliaments have a say in the EMU?, in DB Research, Frankfurt a. M. 2011.

Herold, Ulf; Maurer, Raimond (2004): Tactical Asset Allocation and Estimation Risk, in: Financial Markets and Portfolio Management, Vol. 18, No. 1, pp. 39-57.

Herold, Ulf; Maurer, Raimond (2008): Structural positions and risk budgeting: Quantifying the impact of structural positions and deriving implications for active portfolio management, in: Journal of Asset Management, Vol. 9, No. 2, pp 149-157.

Herrmann, Ralf (1997): Indexierung und Preisbildung - Eine empirische Studie am Beispiel des Deutschen Aktienindex (DAX), Karlsruhe 1997.

Herzog, Sebastian; Koziol, Christian; Thabe, Tim (2008): Optimal Credit Ratings, in: International Journal of Theoretical & Applied Finance, Vol. 11, No. 2, pp. 225-247.

Heston, Steven L.; Rouwenhorst, K. Geert (1994): Does Industrial Structure Explain the Benefits of International Diversifikation?, in: Journal of Financial Economics, Vol. 36, pp. 3-27.

Hielscher, Udo (1988): Ursprünge und Grundgedanken der modernen Portfolio-Theorie, in: Beiträge zur Aktienanalyse, Vol. 25, pp. 19-43.

Hildebrand, Philip M. (1996): Maastricht fudge factor, in: International Economy, Vol. 10, No. 5, pp. 50-52.

Hodgkinson, Lynn; Holland, Kevin; Jackson, Richard H. G. (2006): Dividend valuation, trading and transactions costs: the 1997 partial abolition of dividend tax credit repayments, in: Accounting & Business Research, Vol. 36, No. 4, pp. 253-270.

Hodgson, Allan; van Praag, Bart (2006): Information trading by corporate insiders based on accounting accruals: forecasting economic performance, in: Accounting & Finance, Vol. 46, No. 5, pp. 819-842.

Hodson, Dermot (2009): EMU and political union: what, in anything, have we learned from the euro's first decade?, in: Journal of European Public Policy, Vol. 16, No. 4, pp. 508-526.

Hodson, Dermot; Maher, Imelda (2004): Soft law and sanctions: economic policy co-ordination and reform of the Stability and Growth Pact, in: Journal of Public Policy, Vol. 11, No. 5, pp. 798-813.

Hörth, Ellen (1998): €uro Watch – New reference rates in EMU, in: DB Research, Frankfurt a. M. 1998.

Hoje, Jo; Yongtae, Kim; Park, Myung (2008): The impact of surprise offer-share adjustments on offer-day returns: evidence from seasoned equity offers, in: Review of Quantitative Finance & Accounting, Vol. 31, No. 3, pp. 261-286.

Holmén, Martin; Knopf, John D. (2004): Minority Shareholder Protections and the Private Benefits of Control for Swedish Mergers, in: Journal of Financial & Quantitative Analysis, Vol. 39, No. 1, pp. 167-191.

Holmes, Millicant (2007): Improved Study Finds Index Management Usually Outperforms Acitve Management, in: Journal of Financial Planning, Vol. 20, No. 1, pp. 48-58.

Holton, Lisa (2009): Is Markowitz Wrong? Market Turmoil Fuels Nontraditional Approaches to Managing Investment Risk, in: Journal of Financial Planning, Vol. 22, No. 1, pp. 20-26.

Hooper, Peter; Mayer, Thomas; Spencer, Michael; Slok, Torsten (2011): Global Economic Perspective – Currency War Games, in: DB Research, Frankfurt a. M. 2011.

Horasanli, Mehmet; Fidan, Neslihan (2007): Portfolio Selection by Using Time Varying Covarince Matrices, in: Journal of Economics & Social Research, Vol. 9, No. 2, pp. 1-22.

Horvitz, Jeffrey E.; Wilcox, Jarrod (2007): Back to Markowitz: The Problems of Portfolio Compartmentalization, in: Journal of Wealth Management, Vol. 10, No. 1, pp. 43-53.

Hossain, Mahmud; Mitra, Santanu; Rezaee, Zabihllah, Sarath, Bharat (2011): Corporate Governance and Earnings Management in the Pre- and Post-Sarbanes-Oxley Act Regimes: Evidence from Implicated Option Backdating Firms, in: Journal of Accounting, Auditing & Finance, Vol. 26, No. 2, pp. 279-315.

Howard, Scott (2010): Thoughts on the euro: Where to from here?, in: PPI; Pulp & Paper International, Vol. 52, No. 6, p. 48.

HSBC Bank plc. [ed.] (2008): HSBC Optimised Indices, London 2008.

Hseu, Mei-Maun; Chung, Huimin; Sun, Erh-Yin (2007): Price Discovery across the Stock Index Futures and the ETF Markets: Intra-Day Evidence from the S&P 500, Nasdaq-100and DJIA Indices, in: Review of Pacific Basin Financial Markets & Policies, Vol. 10, No. 2, pp. 215-236.

Hsia, Chi-Cheng; Fuller, Beverly R.; Chen, Brian Y. J. (2000): Is Beta Dead or Alive, in: Journal of Business Finance & Accounting, Vol. 27, No. 3/4, pp. 283-311.

Hsu, Jason C. (2006): Cap-Weighted Portfolios are Sub-Optimal Portfolios, in: Journal of Investment Management, Vol. 4, No. 3, pp. 1-10.

Hsu, Jason C.; Campollo, Carmen (2006): New Frontiers in Index Investing, in: Journal of Indexes, January/February 2006, pp. 32-58.

Hsu, Jason C.; Kalesnik, Vitali; Myers, Brett W. (2010): Performance Attribution: Measuring Dynamic Allocation Skill, in: Financial Analysts Journal, Vol. 66, No. 6, pp. 1-10.

Hu, Wenbo; Kercheval, Alec N. (2010): Portfolio optimization for student t and skewed returns, in: Quantitative Finance, Vol. 10, No. 1, pp. 91-105.

Huang, Hong-Chih (2010): Optimal Multiperiod Asset Allocation: Matching Assets to Liabilities in a Discrete Model, in: Journal of Risk & Insurance, Vol. 77, No. 2, pp. 451-472.

Huang, Lixing; Liu, Hong (2007): Rational Inattention and Portfolio Selection, in: Journal of Finance, Vol. 62, No. 4, pp. 1999-2040.

Huber, Jürgen; Rieger, Andreas (2004): The EMU and changes in optimal diversification strategies in Europe: The importance of industry vs. country effects, Innsbrück 2004.

Hung, Chi-Hsiou (2008): Return Predictability of Higher-Moment CAPM Market Models, in: Journal of Business Finance & Accounting, Vol. 35, No. 7/8, pp. 998-1022.

Hung, Daniel Chi-Hsiou; Shackleton, Mark; Xu, Xinzhong (2004): CAPM, Higher Comoment and Factor Models of UK Stock Returns, in: Journal of Business Finance & Accounting, Vol. 31, No. 1, pp. 87-112.

Hung, Mao-Wei; Jan, Yin-Ching (2005): Sharpe Timing Ratio, in: Journal of Investing, Vol. 14, No. 4, pp. 75-79.

Hur, Jungshik; Pritamani, Mahesh; Sharma, Vivek (2010): Momentum and the Disposition Effect: The Role of Individual Investors, in: Financial Management, Vol. 39, No. 3, pp. 1155-1176.

Hwang, Soosung; Satchell, Stephen E. (2002): Calculating the misspecification in beta from using a proxy for the market portfolio, in: Applied Financial Economics, Vol. 12, No. 11, pp. 771-781.

Hyland, David C.; Swidler, Steve (2002): Trading behaviour of stocks added to New Zealand's NZSE40 index, in: Applied Economics Letter, Vol. 9, No. 5, pp. 301-304.

Ibbotson, Roger G. (2010): The Importance of Asset Allocation, in: Financial Analysts Journal, Vol. 66, No. 2, pp. 18-20.

Ibbotson, Roger G.; Kaplan, Paul D. (2000): Does asset allocation policy explain 40, 90 or 100 per cent of performance, in: Financial Analysts Journal, Vol. 56, No. 1, pp. 26-33.

Islam, Ifty; DB Research [ed.] (1998): Die EWU - Umbruch an den europäischen Finanzmärkten, in: DB Research, London 1998.

Israelsen, Craig L. (2001): Sharpe and to the Point, in: Financial Planning, Vol. 31, No. 10, pp. 51-54.

Israelsen, Craig L. (2004): A refinement to the Sharpe ratio and information ratio, in: Journal of Asset Management, Vol. 5, No. 6, pp. 423-427.

Israelsen, Craig L. (2010): Alpha and Beta, in: Financial Planning, Vol. 40, No. 7, pp. 79-82.

Itoh, Hideshi (2004): Moral Hazard and Other-Regarding Preferences, in: Japanese Economic Review, Vol. 55, No. 1, pp. 18-45.

Iyer, Ananth V.; Schwarz, Leroy B.; Zenios, Stefanos A. (2005): A Principal-Agent Model for Product Specification and Production, in: Management Science, Vol. 51, No. 1, pp. 106-119.

Jackson, Matthew O. (2003): Efficiency and information aggregation in auctions with costly information, in: Review of Economic Design, Vol. 8, No. 2, pp. 121-141.

Jacobsen, Brian J. (2010): Consistent Asset Allocation, in: Journal of Financial Planning, Vol. 23, No. 11, pp. 50-56.

Jacquet, Pierre (1998): EMU: a worthwile gamble, in: International Affairs, Vol. 74, No. 1, pp. 55-72.

Jaemin, Kim (2005): Cross-Sectional Differences in the Liquidity Effects of Open Market Share Repurchases, in: Journal of Economics & Finance, Vol. 29, No. 1, pp. 1-31.

Jagannathan, Ravi; Ma, Tongshu (2003): Risk Reduction in Large Portfolios: Why Imposing the Wrong Constraints Helps, in: Journal of Finance, Vol. 58, No. 4, pp. 1651-1684.

Jagannathan, Ravi; McGrattan, Ellen R. (1995): The CAPM Debate, in: Federal Reserve Bank of Minneapolis Quarterly Review, Vol. 19, No. 4, pp. 2-17.

Jagd, Philip; Madsen, Jakob B. (2009): Myopic loss aversion, bond returns and the equity premium puzzle, in: Applied Financial Economics, Vol. 18, No. 17, pp. 1383-1390.

Jaggi, Andreas; Jeanneret, Pierre; Scholz, Stefan (2011): Boost your traditional portfolio: Activate traditional asset classes with alternative investments, in: Journal of Derivatives & Hedge Funds, Vol. 17, No. 2, pp. 133-150.

Jaisfeld, Manfred; National-Bank AG [ed.] (2008): Veränderungen im STOXX 50 und im Euro STOXX 50, in: Research Aktuell, Vol. 15, Essen 2008.

James, Jessica; Yang, Lois (2010): Stop-losses, maximum drawdown-at-risk and replicating financial time series with the stationary bootstrap, in: Quantitative Finance, Vol. 10, No. 1, pp. 1-12.

James, Thomas; Mohideen, Mohamed M. (2011): Dividend Payment Versus Ploughing Back Profits: An Exploration with reference to Information Technology Industries, in: Advances in Management, Vol. 4, No. 4, pp. 45-49.

Janackova, Stanislava (1998): Convergence for European Union Accession, in: Eastern European Economics, Vol. 36, No. 3, pp. 80-95.

Janakiraman, Surya; Radhakrishnan, Suresh; Tsang, Albert (2010): Institutional investors, Managerial Ownership, and Executive Compensation, in: Journal of Accounting, Vol. 25, No. 4, pp. 673-707.

Jang, Bong-Gyu; Koo, Hyeng Keun; Liu, Hong; Loewenstein, Mark (2007): Liquidity Premia and Transaction Costs, in: Journal of Finance, Vol. 62, No. 5, pp. 2329-2366.

Jansen, David-Jan; De Haan, Jakob (2009): Has ECB communication been helpful in predicting interest rate decisions? An evaluation of the early years of the Economic and Monetary Union, in: Applied Economics, Vol. 41, No. 16, pp. 1995-2003.

Jennings, William W.; Martin, Gregory W. (2007): Socially Enhanced Indexing: Applying Enhanced Indexing Techniques to Socially Responsible Investment, in: Journal of Investing, Vol. 16, No. 2, pp. 18-51.

Jensen, Michael C.; Meckling William H. (1976): Theory of the Firm: Managerial Behaviour, Agency Costs and Ownership Structure, in: Journal of Financial Economics, Vol. 3, pp. 305-360.

Jobson, J. Dave; Korkie, Bob (1981): Performance Hypothesis Testing with the Sharpe and Treynor Measures, in: Journal of Finance, Vol. 36, No. 4, pp. 889-908.

Jobst, Peter (1997): Keine Angst vor Aktien, Stuttgart 1997.

Johnson, Robert; Soenen, Luc (2009): European Economic Integration and Stock Market Co-Movement with Germany, in: Multinational Business Review, Vol. 17, No. 3, pp. 205-227.

Johnson, William F. (2009): Tracking Error of exchange traded funds, in: Journal of Asset Management, Vol. 10, No. 4, pp. 253-262.

Jondeau, Eric; Rockinger, Michael (2003): Conditional volatility, skewness, and kurtosis: Existence and persistence, in: Journal of Dynamics and Control, Vol. 27, pp. 1699-1737.

Jones, Samuel Kyle; Stine, Joe Bert (2010): Expected utility and the non-normal returns of common portfolio rebalancing strategies, in: Journal of Asset Management, Vol. 10, No. 6, pp. 406-419.

Jonung, Lars; Larch, Martin; Fischer, Jonas (2008): 101 Proposals to Reform the Stability and Growth Pact. Why so many? A Survey, in: Public Finance & Management, Vol. 8, No. 3, pp. 502-560.

Jorion, Philippe; Goetzmann, William N. (2000): A century of global stock markets, Cambridge 2000.

Jost, Peter-J. (2001): Die Prinzipal-Agenten-Theorie in der Betriebswirtschaftslehre, Stuttgart 2001.

Jung, Maximilian; Spremann, Klaus (1989): Transaktionsrisiken, in: Zeitschrift für Betriebswirtschaft, Vol. 59, pp. 94-112.

Kahn, Ronald D. (2010): Quantitative Equity Investing: Out of Style?, in: Journal of Portfolio Management, Vol. 36, No. 2, pp. 5-6.

Kaiser, Dieter; Thießen, Friedrich (2007): Implikationen der Renditedispersion von Hedgefonds bei der Berechnung von Performancekennzahlen auf Basis von Hedgefondsindizes, in: Finanzbetrieb, Vol. 6, pp. 425-432.

Kan, Raymond; Zhou, Guofu (2007): Optimal Portfolio Choice with Parameter Uncertainty, in: Journal of Financial and Quantitative Analysis, Vol. 42, No. 3, pp. 621-656.

Kang, Jun-Koo; Stulz, R. (1997): Why is there a Home Bias? An Analysis of Foreign Portfolio Equity Ownership in Japan, in: Journal of Financial Economics, Vol. 46, pp. 3-28.

Kaplanski, Guy; Kroll, Yoram (2002): VaR risk measures versus traditional risk measures: An analysis and survey, in: Journal of Risk, Vol. 4, No. 3, pp. 1-27.

Karamjeet, Kaur; Balwinder, Singh (2010): Bonus Share Announcements and Market Efficiency: A Study of BSE Listed Companies, in: Advances in Management, Vol. 3, No. 11, pp. 49-58.

Kaserer, Christoph; Achleitner, Ann-Kristin; Moldenhauer, Benjamin (2005): German Entrepreneurial Index (GEX), in: Finanzbetrieb, Vol. 2, pp. 118-126.

Kaserer, Christoph; Achleitner, Ann-Kristin; Moldenhauer, Benjamin; Ampenberger, Markus (2006): Ein Jahr „German Entrepreneurial Index (GEX) – Bestandsaufnahme und Analyse, in: Finanz Betrieb, Vol. 8, pp. 10-17.

Kat, Harry M. (2002): Indexation Doesn't Make Sense, ISMA Discussion Papers in Finance, Vol. 29.

Kawaller, Ira G. (2007): Interest Rate Swaps: Accounting vs. Economics, in: Financial Analysts Journal, Vol. 63, No. 2, pp. 15-18.

Kelly, Michael; Clark, Steven (2011): Returns in trading versus non-trading hours: The difference is day and night, in: Journal of Asset Management, Vol. 12, No. 2, pp. 132-145.

Kenjegalieva, Karligash A,; Simper, Richard, Weyman-Jones, Thomas G. (2009): Efficiency of transition banks: inter-country banking industry trends, in: Applied Financial Economics, Vol. 19, No. 19, pp. 1531-1546.

Kercheval, Alec; Goldberg, Lisa; Breger, Kudovic (2003): Modeling Credit Risk, in: Journal of Portfolio Management, Vol. 29, No. 2, pp. 90-110.

Kerling, Matthias (1998): Moderne Konzepte der Finanzanalyse: Markthypothese, Renditegenerierungsprozesse und Modellierungswerkzeuge, Bad Soden 1998.

Khademian, Anne M. (2011): The Financial Crisis: A Retroperspective, in: Public Administration Review, Vol. 71, No. 6, pp. 841-849.

Kida, Thomas; Moreno, Kimberly K.; Smith, James F. (2010): Investment Decision Making: Do Experienced Decision Makers Fall Prey to the Paradox of Choice?, in: Journal of Behavioural Finance, Vol. 11, No. 1, pp. 21-30.

Kim, Heeho (2011): Market Instability and Revision Error in Risk Premium, in: International Advances in Economic Research, Vol. 17, No. 2, pp. 169-180.

Kim, Kenneth A.; Park, Jungsoo (2010): Why Do Price Limits Exist in Stock Markets? A Manipulation-Based Explanation, in: European Financial Management, Vol. 16, No. 2, pp. 296-318.

Kim, Kyung-Joong; Cho, Sung-Bae; Mandziuk, Jacek; Jaruszewicz, Marcin (2011): Neuro-genetric system for stock index prediction, in: Journal of Intelligent & Fuzzy Systems, Vol. 22, No. 2/3, pp. 93-123.

Kim, Sei-Wan; Lee, Bong-Soo (2008): Stock Returns, Asymmetric Volatility, Risk Aversion, and Business Cycle: Some New Evidence, in: Economic Inquiry, Vol. 46, No. 2, pp. 131-148.

King, David (2007): Portfolio optimisation and diversification, in: Journal of Asset Management, Vol. 8, No. 5, pp. 296-307.

Klein, Benjamin; Crawford, Robert G.; Alchian, Armen A. (1978): Vertical integration, appropriable rents, and the competitive contracting process, in: Journal of Law and Economics, Vol. 22, pp. 297-326.

Klein, Marc; Grimm, Martin; Röhl, Christian W. [ed.]; Heussinger, Werner H. [ed.] (2006): Der große Index-Guide die 100 wichtigsten Investment-Märkte im Profil, München 2006.

Klein, Matthias (2009): Aktives versus passives Portfoliomanagement - neue Überlegungen in der Krise, in: Zeitschrift für das gesamte Kreditwesen, Vol. 19, p. 760.

Klement, Joachim (2011): Earnings Stability as a Source of Alpha, in: Journal of Financial Planning, Vol. 24, No. 10, pp. 46-50.

Klos, Alexander (2003): Descriptive Aspects of Asset Allocation Decisions, Mannheim 2003.

Knight, John; Lizieri, Colin; Satchell, Stephen (2005): Diversification when It Hurts? The joint Distributions of Real Estate and Equity Markets, in: Journal of Property Research, Vol. 22, No. 4, pp. 309-323.

Knight, John; Satchell, Stephan (2005): A Re-Examination of Sharpe's Ratio for Log-Normal Prices, in: Applied Mathematical Finance, Vol. 12, No. 1, pp. 87-100.

Kobelt, Helmut; Steinhausen, Detlef (2000): Wirtschaftsstatistik für Studium und Praxis, Vol. 6, Stuttgart 2000.

Kocabiyikoglu, Ayse; Popescu, Ioana (2007): Managerial Motivation Dynamics and Incentives, in: Management Science, Vol. 53, No. 5, pp. 834-848.

Kochman, Ladd; Badarinathi, Ravij (1996): A Better Beta?, in: Atlantic Economic Journal, Vol. 24, No. 4, p. 381.

Kochman, Ladd; Cenac, Cecilia (1992): Rating Mutual Funds From a Downside –Deviation Perspective, in: American Business Review, Vol. 10, No. 2, pp. 1-4.

Kogan, Leonid; Ross, Stephan A.; Wan, Jiang; Westerfield, Mark M. (2006): The Price Impact and Survival of Irrational Traders, in: Journal of Finance, Vol. 61, No. 1, pp. 195-229.

Kohn, Robert V.; Papazoglu-Statescu, Oana M. (2006): On the equivalence of the static and dynamic asset allocation problems, in: Quantitative Finance, Vol. 6, No. 2, pp. 173-183.

Konzelmann, Sue; Wilkinson, Frank; Fovargue-Davies, Marc; Sankey, Duncan (2010): Governance, regulation and financial market instability: the implications for policy, in: Journal of Economics, Vol. 34, No. 5, pp. 929-954.

Korn, Donald Jay (2007): ETF Mania, in: Financial Planning, Vol. 37, No. 3, pp. 72-75.

Krein, David (2010): Through A Glass, Darkly, in: Journal of Indexes, September/October 2010, pp. 20-25.

Krishnan, Jayanth K. (2010): The Joint Law Venture: A Pilot Study, in: Berkeley Journal of International Law, Vol. 28, No. 2, pp. 431-461.

Kritzman, Mark; Page, Sebastian; Turkington, David (2010): In defense of optimization: the fallacy of 1/N, in: Financial Analysts Journal, Vol. 66, No. 2, pp. 31-39.

Kryzanowski, Lawrence; Rahman, Abdul (2008): Portfolio performance ambiguity and benchmark inefficiency revisited, in: Journal of Asset Management, Vol. 9, No. 5, pp. 321-332.

Kugler, Peter; Henn-Overbeck, Jacqueline; Zimmermann, Heinz (2010): Style consistency of hedge fund indexes across providers, in: Applied Financial Economics, Vol. 20, No. 5, pp. 355-369.

Kuhnen, Camelia M. (2009): Business Networks, Corporate Governance, and Contracting in the Mutual Fund Industry, in: Journal of Finance, Vol. 64, No. 5, pp. 2185-2220.

Kumbhakar, Subal C.; Lozano-Vivas, Ana (2004): Does deregulation make markets more competitive? Evidence of mark-ups in Spanish savings banks, in: Applied Financial Economics, Vol. 14, No. 7, pp. 507-515.

Kurz, Heinz D. (2010): Technical progress, capital accumulation and income distribution in Classical economics: Adam Smith, David Ricardo and Karl Marx, in: European Journal of the History of Economic Thought, Vol. 17, No. 5, pp. 1183-1222.

Kyrychenko, Vladyslav (2008): Optimal asset allocation in the presence of nonfinancial assets, in: Financial Services Review, Vol. 17, No. 1, pp. 69-86.

Lai, Hung-Wei; Chen, Cheng-Wei; Huang, Chin-Sheng (2010): Technical Analysis, Investment Psychology, and Liquidity Provision: Evidence from the Taiwan Stock Market, in: Emerging Markets Finance & Trade, Vol. 46, No. 5, pp. 18-38.

Lam, David; Lin, Bing-Xuan; Michayluk, David (2011): Demand and Supply and Their Relationship to Liquidity: Evidence from the S&P 500 Chang to Free Float, in: Financial Analysts Journal, Vol. 67, No. 1, pp. 55-71.

Lamont, Owen A.; Thaler, Richard H. (2001): Can the Market Add and Subtract? Mispricing in Tech Stock Carve-Outs, Cambridge 2001.

Lander, Gerald; Barker, Katherine; Zabelina, Margarita; Williams, Tiffany (2009): Subprime Mortgage Tremors: An International Issue, in: International Advances in Economic Research, Vol. 15, No. 1, pp. 1-16.

Landis, David (2006): Reinvesting the index, in: Kiplinger's Personal Finance, Vol. 60, No. 10, pp. 44-47.

Landis, David (2008): Own the market with index funds and ETFs, in: Kiplinger's Personal Finance, Fall 2008 Retirement Planning, pp. 50-53.

Landsberg, Richard D. (2012): The Procedural Prudence Pipeline: Investment Fiduciaries in the Crosshairs of ERIS 3(21), in: Journal of Pension & Compliance, Vol. 37, No. 4, pp. 33-52.

Lang, Scott; Gupta, Francis; Prestbo, John A. (2004): Hedge Fund Drawdowns: An Empirical Analysis, Working Paper Dow Jones Indexes, New York 2004.

Lang, Stephanie E.; Röder, Klaus (2008): Die Kosten des Indextrackings - Eine Fallstudie über den Exchange Traded Fund DAX, in: Zeitschrift für betriebswirtschaftliche Forschung, Vol. 60, pp. 298-321.

Laopodis, Nikiforos (2008): Noise trading and autocorrelation interactions in the foreign exchange market: Evidence from developed and emerging economies, in: Journal of Economics & Finance, Vol. 32, No. 3, pp. 271-293.

Laspeyers, Étienne (1971): Die Berechnung einer mittleren Warenpreissteigerung, in: Jahrbücher für Nationalökonomie und Statistik, Vol. 16, pp. 296-314.

Lau, Hon-Shiang; Martin G. E. (1987): The effects of skewness and kurtosis of processing time in unpaced lines, in: International Journal of Production Research, Vol. 25, No. 10, pp. 1483-1493.

Lawford, Steve (2005): Finite-Sample Quantiles of the Jarque-Bera Test, in: Applied Economics Letters, Vol. 12, No. 6, pp. 351-354.

Leblond, Patrick (2006): The Political Stability and Growth Pact is Dead: Long Live the Economic Stability and Growth Pact, in: Journal of Common Market Studies, Vol. 44, No. 5, pp. 969-990.

Lee, Hsiu-Chuan; Chien, Cheng-Yi; Liao, Tzu-Hsiang (2009): Determination of stock closing prices and hedging performance with stock indices futures, in: Accounting and Finance, Vol. 49, No. 4, pp. 827-847.

Lee, Huai-I; Hsu, Hsinan; Chiang, Min-Hsien (2010): Portfolio insurance with a dynamic floor, in: Journal of Derivatives & Hedge Funds, Vol. 16, No. 3, pp. 219-230.

Leggio, Karyl B.; Lien, Donald (2003): Comparing Alternative Investment Strategies Using Risk-Adjusted Performance Measures, in: Journal of Financial Planning, Vol. 16, No. 1, pp. 82-86.

Leggio, Karyl B.; Lien, Donald (2003a): An Empirical Examination of the Effectiveness of Dollar-Cost Averaging Using Downside Risk Performance Measures, in: Journal of Economics & Finance, Vol. 27, No. 2, pp. 211-223.

Lehman Brothers [ed.] (2011): General Information, http://chapter11.epiqsystems.com/LBH/Project/default.aspx, date: 12.11.2011.

Lei, Adam Y. C.; Li, Huihua (2009): The value of stop loss strategies, in: Financial Services Review, Vol. 18, No. 1, pp. 23-51.

Lescourret, Laurence; Robert, Christian Y. (2006): Extreme dependence of multivariate catastrophic losses, in: Scandinavian Actuarial Journal, Vol. 2006, No. 4, pp. 203-225.

Lessard, Donald R. (1974): World, national, and industry factors in equity returns, in: Journal of Finance, Vol. 29, No. 2, pp. 379-391.

Lessard, Donald R. (1976): International diversification, in: Financial Analysts Journal, Vol. 32, January 1976, pp. 32-38.

Lettau, Martin; Wachter, Jessica A.: Why Is Long-Horizon Equity Less Risky? A Duration-Based Explanation of the Value Premium, in: Journal of Finance, Vol. 62, No. 1, pp. 55-92.

Levesque, Terrence J.; Libby, Theresa; Mathieu, Robert; Robb, Sean W. G. (2010): The Effect of Director Monitoring on Bid and Ask Spreads, in: Journal of International Accounting Research, Vol. 9, No. 2, pp. 45-65.

Levy, Haim (2010): The CAPM is Alive and Well: A Review and Synthesis, in: European Financial Management, Vol. 16, No. 1, pp. 43-71.

Levy, Haim; Levy, Moshe; Benita, Golan (2006): Capital Asset Prices with Heterogeneous Beliefs, in: Journal of Business, Vol. 79, No. 3, pp. 1317-1353.

Levy, Moshe (2010): Loss aversion and the price of risk, in: Quantitative Finance, Vol. 10, No. 9, pp. 1009-1022.

Lewis, Karen (1999): Trying to Explain the Home Bias in Equities and Consumption, in: Journal of Economic Literature, Vol. 37, pp. 571-608.

Lewis, Nigel D. (2009): Using hedge funds to enhance asset allocation in life cycle pension funds, in: Pension: An International Journal, Vol. 14, No.1, pp. 47-52.

Li, C. Wei; Xue, Hui (2009): A Bayesian's Bubble, in: Journal of Finance, Vol. 64, No. 6, pp. 2665-2701.

Liau, Pen-Hwang (2009): Confidence Interval Estimation in Ultrastructural Model, in: Communications in Statistics: Theory & Methods, Vol. 38, No. 5, pp. 675-681.

Lidén, Erik R. (2007): Swedish Stock Recommendations: Information Content or Price Pressure?, in: Multinational Finance Journal, Vol. 11, No. 3/4, pp. 253-285.

Liebscher, Klaus (2009): The stability architecture of the EMU, in: Progress in Development Studies, Vol. 9, No. 4, pp. 377-383.

Liedtke, Rüdiger (1999): Wer beherrscht den DAX, Frankfurt a. M. 1999.

Lim, Kian-Ping (2009): Efficiency test of the UK financial futures markets and the impacts of electronic trading systems: a note on relative market efficiency, in: Applied Economics Letters, Vol. 16, No. 11, pp. 1129-1132.

Lima, Eduardo Jose Araújo; Tabak, Benjamin Miranda (2007): Tests of the random walk hypothesis for equity markets: evidence from China, Hong Kong and Singapore, in: Applied Economics Letter, Vol. 11, No. 4, pp. 255-258.

Lin, Chin-Tsai; Yeh, Hsin-Yi (2009): Empirical of the Taiwan stock index option price forecasting model – applied artificial neural network, in: Applied Economics, Vol. 41, No. 15, pp. 1965-1972.

Linsmeier, Thomas J. (2011): Financial Reporting and Financial Crises: The Case for Measuring Financial Instruments at Fair Value in the Financial Statements, in: Accounting Horizons, Vol. 25, No. 2, pp. 409-417.

Lintner, John (1965): Security Prices, Risk and maximal Gains from Diversification, in: Journal of Finance, Vol. 20, No. 4, pp. 587 – 615.

Liow, Kim Hiang; Chan, Lanz C. W. J. (2005): Co-skewness and Co-kurtosis in Global Real Estate Securities, Vol. 22, No. 2-3, pp. 163-203.

Liu, Jun; Peleg, Ehud; Subrahmanyam, Avanidhar (2010): Information, Expected Utility, and Portfolio Choice, in: Journal of Financial and Quantitative Analysis, Vol. 45, No. 5, pp. 1221-1251.

Lo, Andrew W. (2002): The Statistics of Sharpe Ratios, in: Financial Analysts Journal, Vol. 58, No. 18, pp. 36-52.

Longhofer, Stanley D.; Peters, Stephan R. (2005): Self-Selection and Discrimination in Credit Markets, in: Real Estate Economics, Vol. 33, No. 2, pp. 237-268.

Lorie, James H.; Hamilton, Mary T. (1978): Stock Market Indexes, in: Lorie, James H.; Brealey, Richard [ed.] Modern Developments in Investment Management, pp. 78-93, New York 1978.

Lovell, Robert M. Jr.; Arnott, Robert D. (1989): Monitoring and Rebalancing the Portfolio, in: Investment Management Reflections, Vol. 3, pp. 1-12.

Loy, Benedikt; Jostarndt, Philipp (2006): Capital structure arbitrage - Can investors set up profitable trading strategies?, in: Corporate Finance, Vol. 7-8, pp. 487-499.

Lützel, Heinrich; Jung, Wolfram (1984): Neuberechnung des Index der Aktienkurse, in: Wirtschaft und Statistik, Vol. 1, pp. 43-56.

Lusk, Edward J.; Halperin, Michael; Bern, Manuel (2008): Towards Reformulation of the Capital Asset Pricing Model (CAPM) Focussing on Idiosyncratic Risk and Roll's Meta-Analysis: Methodological Approach, in: Journal of Management & Analysis, Vol. 21, No. 1 pp. 1-23.

Lynch, Anthony W.; Mendenhall, Richard R. (1997): New Evidence on Stock Price Effects Associated with Changes in the S&P 500, in: Journal of Business, Vol. 70, pp. 351-384.

Lynch, Anthony W.; Tan, Sinan (2010): Multiple Risky Assets, Transaction Costs, and Return Predictability: Allocation Rules and Implications for U.S. Investors, in: Journal of Financial and Quantitative Analysis, Vol. 45, No. 4, pp. 1015-1053.

Madhavan, Ananth; Ming, Kewei (2003): The Hidden Costs of Index Rebalancing, in: Journal of Investing, Vol. 12, No. 3, pp. 29-35.

Madura, Jeff; Richie, Nivine (2004): Overreaction of Exchange-Traded Funds During the Bubble of 1998-2002, in: Journal of Behavioural Finance, Vol. 5, No. 2, pp. 91-104.

Magdon-Ismail, Malik; Atiya, Amir F. (2004): Maximum drawdown, in: Risk Magazine, Vol. 17, No. 10, pp. 99-102.

Maguire, Guy; Karaban, Simon; S&P [ed.] (2009): Introducing a New Index versus Active Funds Scorecard for Australia, July 2009, pp. 1-12.

Majumdar, Satya N.; Bouchaud, Jean-Philippe (2008): Optimal time to sell a stock in the Black-Scholes model: comment on 'Thou shalt buy and hold', in: Quantitative Finance, Vol. 8, No. 8, pp. 753-760.

Mahdavi, Mahnaz (2004): Risk-Adjusted Return When Returns Are Not Normally Distributed: Adjusted Sharpe Ratio, in: Journal of Alternative Investments, Vol. 6, No. 4, pp. 47-57.

Mainik, Georg; Rüschendorf, Ludger (2010): On optimal portfolio diversification with respect to extreme risks, in: Finance & Stochastics, Vol. 14, No. 4, pp. 593-623.

Malevergne, Yannick; Sornette, Didier (2005): Extreme Financial Risk, Berlin, 2005.

Malhotra, Madhuri; Thenmozhi, M.; Kumar, G. Arun (2007): Announcement Effect of Rights Issue on Stock Returns: A Study of Selected Indian Manufacturing Companies, in: Journal of Service Research, Vol. 7, No. 1, pp. 215-231.

Malkiel, Burton G. (2003): Passive Investment Strategies and Efficient Markets, in: European Financial Management, Vol. 9, No. 1, pp. 1-10.

Mallick, Soumitra K. (2010): Asset-based economy and management in emerging capital markets, in: Journal of Asset Management, Vol. 11, No. 5, pp. 309-313.

Mamoghli, Chokri; Dabousi, Sami (2009): Performance Measurement of Hedge Funds Portfolios in a Downside Risk Framework, in: Journal of Wealth Management, Vol. 12, No. 2, pp. 101-112.

Mandal, Nivedita; Rao, N. Krishna (2010): Semi-Strong Form of Indian Stock Market Efficiency: An Empirical Study, in: Journal of Management, Vol. 7, No. 1, pp. 1-16.

Mankiw, Gregory N. (2004): Grundzüge der Volkswirtschaftslehre, Vol. 3, Stuttgart 2004.

Mardas, Dimitri; Nikas, Christos (2008): European Integration, Intra-industry Trade in Vertically Differentiated Products and the Balkan Countries, in: International Advances in Economic Research, Vol. 14, No. 4, pp. 355-368.

Markowitz, Harry M. (1952): Portfolio Selection, in: Journal of Finance, Vol. 7, No. 1, pp. 77-91.

Markowitz, Harry M. (1959): Portfolio Selection: Efficient Diversification of Investments, London 1959.

Markowitz, Harry M. (1970): Portfolio Selection: Efficient Diversification of Investments, Vol. 2, London 1970.

Markowitz, Harry M. (1978): Markowitz Revisited, in: Financial Analysts Journal, September/October 1978, pp. 47-52.

Markowitz, Harry M. (1991): Portfolio Selection: Efficient Diversification of Investments, Vol. 2, Cambridge 1991.

Markowitz, Harry M. (2002): Efficient Portfolios, Sparse Matrices, and Entities: A Retrospective, in: Operations Research, Vol. 50, No. 1, pp. 154-160.

Markowitz, Harry M. (2008a): CAPM Investors Do Not Get Paid for Bearing Risk: A Linear Relation Does Not Imply Payment for Risk, in: Journal of Portfolio Management, Vol. 34, No. 2, pp. 91-94.

Markowitz, Harry M. (2008b): Portfolio Selection: Die Grundlagen der optimalen Portfolio-Auswahl, Vol. 2, München 2008.

Marks, Peter; Stuart, Andrew (1971): An Arithmetic Version of the Financial Times Industrial Ordinary Share Index, in: Journal of the Institute of Actuaries, Vol. 9, pp. 397-324.

Marquering, Wessel; Verbeek, Marno (2004): The Economic Value of Predicting Stock Index Returns and Volatility, in: Journal of Financial & Quantitative Analysis, Vol. 39, No. 2, pp. 407-429.

Martin, Marcus R. W.; Reitz, Stefan; When, Carsten S. (2006): Kreditderivate und Kreditrisikomodelle, eine mathematische Einführung, Wiesbaden 2006.

Martins, António Miguel; Serra, Ana Paula (2007): Market impact of international sporting and cultural events, in: Journal of Economics and Finance, Vol. 35, No. 4, pp. 382-416.

Martins-da-Rocha, V. Filipe; Vailakis, Yiannis (2010): Financial markets with endogenous transaction costs, in: Economic Theory, Vol. 45, No. 1/2, pp. 65-97.

Masse, Isidore; Hanrahan, Robert; Kushner, Joseph; Martinello, Felice (2000): The effect of additions to or deletions from the TSE 300 Index on Canadian share prices, in: Canadian Journal of Economics, Vol. 33, No. 2, pp. 341-359.

Matthes, Jürgen (2009): The years EMU – Reality test for the OCA endogeneity hypothsis, economic divergences and future challenges, in: Intereconomics, Vol. 44, No. 2, pp. 114-128.

Mayer, Thomas (2006): Euroland: Südeuropäische Länder und die "EWU-Falle", in: DB Research, Vol. 23, pp. 1-3.

Mayer, Thomas (2011): Der Euro aus politökonomischer Perspektive, in: DB Research, Vol. 82, pp. 1-12.

Mayhew, Stewart (1995): Implied Volatility, in: Financial Analysts Journal, Vol. 51, Mai-Juni 1995, pp. 8-20.

Mazouz, Khelifa; Saadouni, Brahim (2007): The price effects of FTSE 100 index revision: what drives the long-term abnormal return reversal?, in: Applied Financial Economics, Vol. 17, No. 6, pp. 501-510.

McAllister, Patrick; Hughes, Catherine; Gallimore, Paul (2008): Principal-agent Issues in Asset Acquisition: UK Institutions and their Investment Agents, in: Journal of Property Research, Vol. 25, No. 4, pp. 269-283.

McCormick, Dominic (2011): Multi-asset revolution, in: Money Management, Vol. 25, No. 45, pp. 20-21.

McFall Lamm, Robert Jr. (2000): Economic Foundations and Risk Analysis in Investment Management, in: Business Economics, Vol. 35, No. 1, pp. 26-32.

McFarlin, Michael (2011): Are stock indexes experiencing Déjà vu?, in: Futures; News, Analysis & Strategies for Futures, Options & Derivatives Traders, Vol. 40, No. 8, pp. 24-27.

McLeod, Warren; van Vuuren, Gary (2004): Interpreting the Sharpe Ratio When Excess Returns are Negative, in: Investment Analysts Journal, Vol. 59, pp. 15-20.

McQuarrie, Edward F. (2008): Fundamentally Indexed or Fundamentally Misconceived: Locating the Source of RAFI Outperformance, in: Journal of Investing, Vol. 17, No. 4, pp. 29-37.

Meijun, Qian (2011): Stale Prices and the Performance Evaluation of Mutual Funds, in: Journal of Financial & Quantitative Analysis, Vol. 46, No. 2, pp. 369-394.

Meinhövel, Harald (1998): Defizite der Principal-Agent-Theorie, Cologne 1998.

Melas, Dimitris; Kang, Xiaowei (2010): Applications of Systematic Indexes in the Investment Process, in: Journal of Indexes, September/October 2010, pp. 10-19.

Melas, Dimitris; Suryanarayanan, Raghu; Cavaglia, Stefano (2010): Efficient Replication of Factor Returns: Theory and Applications, in: Journal of Portfolio Management, Vol. 36, No. 2, pp. 39-51.

Menchero, Jose; Morozov, Andrei (2011): Decomposing Global Equity Cross-Sectional Volatility, in: Financial Analysts Journal, Vol. 67, No. 5, pp. 58-68.

Merchant, Kenneth A. (2010): Performance-Dependent Incentives: Some Puzzles to Ponder, in: Journal of Accounting, Auditing & Finance, Vol. 25, No. 4, pp. 559-567.

Meric, Ilhan; Meric, Gulser (1997): Co-Movements of European Equity Markets Before and After the 1987 Crash, in: Multinational Finance Journal, Vol. 1, No. 2, pp. 137-152.

Mertens, Karel; Raven, Morten O. (2011): Leverage and the Financial Accelerator in the Liquidity Trap, in: American Economic Review, Vol. 101, No. 3, pp. 413-416.

Miller, Kent D.; Leiblein, Michael J. (1996): Corporate Risk-Return Relations: Returns Variability versus Downside Risk, in: Academy of Management Journal, Vol. 39, No. 1, pp. 91-122.

Miller, Todd; Meckel, Timothy S. (1999): Beating Index Funds with Derivatives, in: Journal of Portfolio Management, Vol. 25, No. 5, 75-88.

Milonas, Nikolaos T.; Rompotis, Gerasimos G. (2010): Dual Offerings of ETFs on the Same Stock Index: U.S. vs. Swiss ETFs, in: Journal of Alternative Investments, Vol. 12, No. 4, pp. 97-113.

Mitchell, Donna (2010): The Big Bang, in: Financial Planning, Vol. 40, No. 8, pp. 41-42.

Mitra, Leela; Mitra, Gautam; Di Bartolomeo, Dan (2009): Equity portfolio risk estimation using market information and sentiment, in: Quantitative Finance, Vol. 9, No. 8, pp. 887-895.

Mittal, Manish; Vyas, Rameshbhai K. (2009): Does Irrationality in Investment Decisions Vary with Income?, in: Journal of Behavioural Finance, Vol. 6, No. 1, pp. 26-42.

Moerman, Gerard A. (2004): Diversification in Euro Area Stock Markets: Country versus Industry, in: ECB Working Paper Series, No. 327, Frankfurt a. M. 2004.

Moosa, Imad A. (2007): Operational Risk: A Survey, in: Financial Markets, Institutions & Instruments, Vol. 16, No. 4, pp. 167-200.

Moreney, Richard J.; Sweet, Robert A.; Carlson, Charles B.; Wright, David A.; Walle, David B. (2011): Seeking safety with fund picks, in: Dow Theory Forecasts, Vol. 67, No. 33, pp. 1-2.

Mossin, Jan (1966): Equilibrium in Capital Asset Market, in: Econometrica, 1966, pp. 768–783.

Mosser, Mike (1999): Commodities come off the canvas, in: Futures; News, Analysis & Strategies for Futures, Options & Derivatives Traders, Vol. 28, No. 15, pp. 36-71.

Müller-Stewens, Günter; Lechner, Christoph (2001): Strategisches Management, Stuttgart 2001.

Muga, Luis; Santamaria, Rafael (2007): The momentum effect: omitted risk factors of investor behaviour? Evidence from the Spanish stock market, in: Quantitative Finance, Vol. 7, No. 6, pp. 637-650.

Mukherji, Sandip (2003): Optimal Portfolios for Different Holding Periods and Target Returns, in: Financial Services Review, Vol. 12, No. 1, pp. 61-71.

Mulvey, John M.; Kim, Woo Chang (2008): Active Equity Managers in the U.S.: Do the Best Follow Momentum Strategies?, in: Journal of Portfolio Management, Vol. 34, No. 2, pp. 126-134.

Mura, Roberto (2007): Firm Performance: Do Non-Executive Directors Have Minds of their Own? Evidence from UK Panel Data, in: Financial Management, Vol. 36, No. 3, pp. 81-112.

Murdock, Kevin (2002): Intrinsic motivation and optimal incentive contracts, in: Journal of Economics, Vol. 33, No. 4, pp. 650-671.

Murguia, Alejandro; Umemoto, Dean T. (2006): An Active Approach to Indexing, in: Journal of Financial Services Professionals, Vol. 60, No. 1, pp. 73-80.

Murthy, R. Venkatesha (2010): Information Sourcing Through Traditional and Electronic Resources for Strategy Formulation: A Case of Small-Scale Manufacturing Firms in Udupi, Karnataka, in: Journal of Management Economics, Vol. 8, No. 4, pp. 35-53.

Najand, Mohammad; Lin, Crystal Yan; Fitzgerald, Elizabeth (2006): The Conditional CAPM and Time Varying Risk Premium for Equity REITS, in: Journal of Real Estate Portfolio Management, Vol. 12, No. 2, pp. 167-175.

Nawrocki, David; Carter, William (2010): Industry competitiveness using Herfindahl and entropy concentration indices with firm market capitalization data, in: Applied Economics, Vol. 42, No. 22, pp. 2855-2863.

Nelles, Michael; Uzik, Martin; Holtfort, Thomas (2007): Rollierende Momentum-Strategie am deutschen Aktienmarkt, in: Finanzbetrieb, Vol. 7-8, pp. 444-449.

Nguyen, Duong; Mishra, Suchismita, Prakash, Arun; Ghosh, Dilip K. (2007): Liquidity and Asset Pricing under the Three-Moment CAPM Paradigm, in: Journal of Financial Research, Vol. 30, No. 3, pp. 379-398.

Ng, Siu-Ah (2005): An Infinitesimal Analysis of the Stop-Loss-Start-Gain Strategy, in: International Journal of Theoretical and Applied Finance, Vol. 8, No. 5, pp. 623-633.

Nielsen, Lars Tyge; Vassalou, Maria (2004): Sharpe Ratios and Alphas in Continuous Time, in: Journal of Financial and Quantitative Analysis, Vol. 39, No. 1, pp. 103-114.

Nielsen, Lars Tyge; Vassalou, Maria (2006): The instantaneous capital market line, in: Economic Theory, Vol. 28, No. 3, pp. 651-664.

Nieto, Maia J.; Penalosa, Juan M. (2004): The European architecture of regulation, supervision and financial stability: A central bank perspective, in: Journal of International Banking Regulation, Vol. 5, No. 3, pp. 228-242.

Nöth, Markus; Weber, Martin (2003): Information Aggregation with Random Ordering: Cascades and Overconfidence, in: Economic Journal, Vol. 113, No. 1, pp. 166-189.

Nyberg, Anthony J.; Fulmer, Ingrid Smithey; Gerhart, Barry; Carpenter, Mason A. (2010): Agency Theory Revisited: CEO Return and Shareholder interest Alignment, in: Academy of Management Journal, Vol. 53, No. 5, pp. 1029-1049.

Nygaard, Arne; Myrtveit, Ingunn (2000): Moral hazard, competition and contract design: empirical evidence from managerial, franchised and entrepreneurial business in Norway, in: Applied Economics, Vol. 32, No. 3, pp. 349-356.

O'Brien, John (2006): Rebalancing: A Tool for Managing Portfolio Risk, in: Journal of Financial Service Professionals, Vol. 60, No. 3, pp. 62-68.

Oesterhelweg, Olaf; Schiereck, Dirk (1993): Messkonzepte für die Liquidität von Finanzmärkten, in: Die Bank, Vol. 7, pp. 390-397.

Offerman, Theo; Sonnemans, Joep (2004): What's Causing Overreaction? An Experimental Investigation of Recency and the Hot-hand Effect, in: Scandinavian Journal of Economics, Vol. 106, No. 3, pp. 533-553.

Okunev, John (2010): What Should Your Asset Allocation Be When You Retire?, in: Journal of Wealth Management, Vol. 12, No. 4, pp. 60-67.

Ollier, Sandrine (2007): On the generalized principal-agent problem: a comment, in: Review of Economic Design, Vol. 11, No. 1, pp. 1-11.

Opdyke, John Douglas (2007): Comparing Sharpe ratios: So where are the p-values?, in: Journal of Asset Management, Vol. 8, No. 5, pp. 308-336.

Orgland, Magne; Leveau, Daniel (2008): Revolution der Indexierungsmethoden, in: Finanz und Wirtschaft, Nr. 64, p. 24.

Osler, Carol L. (2003): Currency Orders and Exchange Rate Dynamics: An Explanation for the Predictive Success of Technical Analysis, in: Journal of Finance, Vol. 58, No. 5, pp. 1791-1820.

Ozkan, F. Gulcin; Sibert, Anne; Sutherland, Anne (2004): Monetary union and the Maastricht inflation criterion: The accession countries, in: Economics of Transition, Vol. 12, No. 4, pp. 635-652.

Paasche, Hermann (1974): Über die Preisentwicklung der letzten Jahre nach den Hamburger Börsennotierungen, in: Jahrbücher für Nationalökonomie und Statistik, Vol. 23, pp. 168-178.

Pang, Gaobo; Warshawsky, Mark (2010): Asset Allocation and Risk-Return Tradeoffs of Target-Date Funds, in: Journal of Pension Benefits: Issues in Administration, Vol. 17, No. 3, pp. 24-25.

Paolo Natale, Francesco (2008): Optimisation in the presence of tail-dependence ana tail risk: A heuristic approach for strategic asset allocation, in: Journal of Asset Management, Vol. 8, No. 6, pp. 374-400.

Parker, Gareth (2011): Pan-European Tradable Indices: The State of Play, in: Journal of Indexes Europe, July/August 2011, pp. 8-11.

Parson, Christopher (2003): Moral Hazard in Liability Insurance, in: Geneva Papers on Risk & Insurance – Issues & Practice, Vol. 28, No. 3, pp. 448-471.

Patchett, Edward; Horgan, Jonathan (2011): A Contemporary View of Portfolio Risk and Diversification, in: Benefits Magazine, Vol. 48, No. 1, pp. 30-37.

Patra, Theophano; Poshakwale, Sunil S. (2008): Long-run and short-run relationship between the main stock indexes: evidence from the Athens stock exchange, in: Applied Financial Economics, Vol. 18, No. 7, pp. 1401-1410.

Pedersen, Christian S.; Satchell, Stephen E. (2002): On the foundation of performance measures under asymmetric returns, in: Quantitative Finance, Vol. 2, No. 3, pp. 217-223.

Penman, Stephen H.; Richardson, Scott A.; Tuna, Irem (2007): The Book-to-Price Effect in Stock Returns: Accounting for Leverage, in: Journal of Accounting Research, Vol. 45, No. 2, pp. 427-467.

Pereira, Camara Leal; Vaz de Melo Mendes, Beatriz (2005): Journal of Alternative Investments, Vol. 7, No. 4, pp. 83-91.

Perold, André F.; Sharpe, William F. (1995): Dynamic Strategies for Asset Allocation, in: Financial Analysts Journal, January-February 1995, pp. 149-160.

Perridon, Louis; Steiner, Manfred (2004): Finanzwirtschaft der Unternehmung, Vol. 13, Munich 2004.

Pfau, Wade D. (2010): Lifecycle funds and wealth accumulation for retirement: evidence for a more conservative asset allocation as retirement approaches, in: Financial Services Review, Vol. 19, No, 1, pp. 59-74.

Phillips, Peter J.; Cathcart, Alex; Teale, John (2007): The Diversification and Performance of Self-Managed Superannuation Funds, in: Australian Economic Review, Vol. 40, No. 4, pp. 339-352.

Phylaktis, Kate; Xia, Lichuan (2006): The Changing Roles of Industry and Country Effects in the Global Equity Markets, in: European Journal of Finance, Vol. 12, No. 8, pp. 627-648.

Pilinkus, Donatas (2010): Macroeconomic Indicators and their Impact on Stock Market Performance in the short and long run: The Case of the Baltic States, in: Technological & Economic Development of Economy, Vol. 16, No. 2, pp. 291-304.

Pilotte, Eugene A.; Sterbenz, Frederic P. (2006): Sharpe and Treynor Ratio on Treasury Bonds, in: Journal of Business, Vol. 79, No. 1, pp. 149-180.

Piplack, Jan; Straetmans, Stefan (2010): Comovements of Different Asset Classes During Market Stress, in: Pacific Economic Review, Vol. 15, No. 3, pp. 385-400.

Pisani-Ferry, Jean (2006): Only One Bed for Two Dreams: A Critical Retrospective on the Debate over the Economic Governance of the Euro Area, in: Journal of Common Market Studies, Vol. 44, No. 4, pp. 823-844.

Platt, Gardner; Pope, Brad; Rakvin, Chad (2004): U.S. Equity Benchmarks - Broad-Cap, Size, and Style Indexes, in: Schoenfeld, Steven A. [ed.], Active Index Investing, New Jersey 2004.

Poddig, Thorsten; Brinkmann, Ulf; Seiler, Katharina (2009): Portfolio Management Konzepte und Strategien, Vol. 2, Bad Soden 2009.

Pospisil, Libor; Vecer, Jan (2010): Portfolio sensitivity to changes in the maximum and the maximum drawdown, in: Quantitative Finance, Vol. 10, No. 6, pp. 617-627.

Postert, Andreas (2007): Der Anlagestil deutscher Aktienfonds – Eine portfoliobasierte Analyse mittels style-identifizierender Fundamentalfaktoren, Wiesbaden 2007.

Puttonen, Vesa; Seppä, Tatu (2006): Do style benchmarks differ?, in: Journal of Asset Management, Vol. 7, No. 6, pp. 425-428.

Qi, Min; Zhao, Xinlei (2008): Market Breadth, Trin Statistic, and Market Returns, in: Journal of Investing, Vol. 17, No. 1, pp. 65-73.

Qi, Yue; Hirschberger, Markus; Steuer, Ralph E. (2009): Dotted Representations of Mean-Variance Efficient Frontiers and their Computation, in: INFOR, Vol. 47, No. 1, pp. 15-21.

Rakowski, David (2010): Fund Flow Volatility and Performance, in: Journal of Financial & Quantitative Analysis, Vol. 45, No. 1, pp. 223-237.

Ranyard, Rob (2007): Euro Stories: The Irish Experience of Currency Change, in: Journal of Consumer Policy, Vol. 30, No.4, pp. 313-322.

Rayhorn, Charles; Hasssan, Kabir M.; Yu, Jung-Suk; Janson, Kenneth R. (2007): Emerging Market Efficiency: New Zealand's Maturation Experience in the Presence of Non-Linerarity, Thin Trading and Asymmetric Information, in: International Review of Finance, Vol. 7, No. 1/2, pp. 21-34.

Rehkugler, Heinz (2002): Grundlagen des Portfoliomanagements, in: Kleeberg, Jochen M. [ed.]; Rehkugler, Heinz [ed.]: Handbuch Portfoliomanagement, Strukturierte Ansätze für ein modernes Wertpapiermanagement, Vol. 4, Bad Soden 2008.

Reichenstein, William (2007): Calculating After-Tax Asset Allocation is Key to Determining Risk, Return, and Asset Location, in: Journal of Financial Planning, Vol. 20, No. 7, pp. 44-53.

Reilly, Frank K.; Brown, Keith C. (2006): Investment Analysis and Portfolio Management, Vol. 8, Mason 2006.

Resmini, Laura (2007): Regional Patterns of Industry Location in Transition Countries: Does Economic Integration with the European Union Matter?, in: Regional Studies, Vol. 41, No. 6, pp. 747-764.

Resnik, Bruce L. (2010): Did Modern Portfolio Theory Fail Investors in the Credit Crisis, in: CPA Journal, Vol. 80, No. 10, pp. 10-12.

Reuse, Svend (2010): Comparing Variance/Covariance and Historical Simulation in the Context of the Financial Crisis – Do extreme movements have an influence onto Portfoliolio Selection?, in: FAI – Finanical Assets and Investing, September 2010, pp. 15-30.

Reuse, Svend (2011a): Korrelationen in Extremsituationen, diss., Wiesbaden 2011.

Reuse, Svend (2011b): Korrelationen in der Gesamtbanksteuerung, in: BankPraktiker, Vol. 07/08, pp. 270-275.

Richard, Hermann-Josef (1992): Aktienindizes, Bergisch-Gladbach 1992.

Richman, Vincent; Santos, Michael R.; Barkoulas, John T. (2005): Short- and Long-Term Effects of the 9/11 Event: The International Evidence, in: International Journal of Theoretical & Applied Finance, Vol. 8, No. 7, pp. 947-958.

Riepe, Mark W.; Iachini, Michael (2011): Volume and Assets as Determinants of ETF Bid-Ask Spreads, in: Journal of Financial Planning, Vol. 24, No. 5, pp. 32-40.

Rinne, Horst (1994): Wirtschafts- und Bevölkerungsstatistik, München 1994.

Ripley, Duncan M. (1973): Systematic elements in the linkage of national stock market indices, in: Review of Economics and Statistics, Vol. 55, pp. 356-361.

Risk, Hamish (2010): Greece gets junked and calls the EU and IMF, in: Euromoney, Vol. 42, No. 493, pp. 33-38.

Robinson, Chris; Bingyong, Zheng (2010): Moral hazard, insurance claim, and repeated insurance contracts, in: Canadian Journal of Economics, Vol. 43, No. 3, pp. 967-993.

Rockel, Nick (2010): Evolutionary Road, in: Institutional Investor – International Edition, Vol. 35, No. 4, pp. 66-82.

Rodriguez-Fuentes, Carlos; Dow, Sheila (2003): EMU and the Regional Impact of Monetary Policy, in: Regional Studies, Vol. 37, No. 9, pp. 969-980.

Rohweder, Herold (1992): Bestimmung anlagespezifischer Benchmark-Portfolios, in: Die Bank, Vol. 1, pp. 23-29.

Rojahn, Joachim; Röhl, Christian W.; Frère, Eric (2010): Optimum Portfolio ETF Indices Benchmarking für multidimensional diversifizierte Wertpapierportfolios, Essen 2010.

Rojahn, Joachim; Schyra, Andreas (2010): Underpricing Deutscher Corporate Bond Emissionen, in: Corporate Finance, Vol. 2, pp. 123-128.

Roll, Richard (1977): A Critique of the Asset Pricing Theory's Test, in: Journal of Financial Economics, March 1997, pp. 129-176.

Roll, Richard (1978): Ambiguity when Performance is Measured by the Securities Market Line, in: Journal of Finance, Vol. 33, No. 4, pp. 1051-1069.

Rollo, Jim (2006): EMU: Three challenges, in: Public Policy Research, Vol. 13, No.2, pp. 102-108.

Rompolis, Leonidas S.; Tzavalis, Elias (2010): Risk Premium Effects on Implied Volatility Regression, in: Journal of Financial Research, Vol. 33, No. 2, pp. 125-151.

Rompotis, Gerasimos G. (2009): Interfamily competition of index tracking: The case of the vanguard ETFs and index funds, in: Journal of Asset Management, Vol. 10, No. 4, pp. 263-278.

Rompotis, Gerasimos G. (2010): Active versus Passive ETFs: An Investigation of Bid-Ask Spread, in: Journal of Applied Finance, Vol. 16, No. 3, pp. 5-25.

Roßbach, Peter (2001): Behavioural Finance – Eine Alternative zur vorherrschenden Kapitalmarkttheorie?, in: Working Paper No. 31, HfB Hochschule für Bankwirtschaft, Frankfurt a. M. 2001.

Rose, Jane (2005): UCITS III: Mutual Fund Regulation in Europe with a Focus on Luxembourg, in: Investment Lawyer, Vol. 12, No. 9, pp. 20-25.

Rostowski, Jacek (2003): When should the Central Europeans Join EMU?, in: International Affairs, Vol. 79, No. 5, pp. 993-1008.

Roth, Allan S. (2009): Bear Markets Compared, in: Financial Planning, Vol. 39, No. 1, pp. 77-79.

Rouwenhorst, K. Geert (1999): European Equity Markets and the EMU, in: Financial Analysts Journal, Vol. 55, No. 3, pp. 57-64.

Rubinstein, Mark; Stephens, Paul (2001): Rational Markets: Yes or No? The Affirmative Case, in: Financial Analysts Journal, Vol. 57, No. 3, pp. 15-29.

Rubinstein, Mark (2002): Markowitz's "Portfolio Selection": A Fifty-Year Retroperspective, in: Journal of Finance, Vol. 57, No. 3, pp. 1041-1045.

Rühle, Alf-Sibrand (1991): Aktienindizes in Deutschland, Wiesbaden 1991.

Ruggiero, Murray A. Jr. (2009): Buy and hold, R.I.P. 1900-2007, in: Futures; News, Analysis & Strategies for Futures, Options & Derivatives Traders, Vol. 38, No. 2, pp. 42-45.

Rutledge, Emilie (2008): Is EMU a viable model for monetary integration in the Arabian Gulf?, in: Journal of Economic Policy Reform, Vol. 11, No. 2, pp. 123-134.

Saam, Nicole J. (2002): Prinzipale, Agenten und Macht, Tübingen 2002.

Sadeh, Tal (2009): EMU's diverging micro foundations: a study of governments' preferences and the sustainability of EMU, in: Journal of European Public Policy, Vol. 16, No. 4, pp. 545-563.

Saitta, Alex (1999): Relating to inflation, in: Futures; News, Analysis & Strategies for Futures, Options & Derivatives Traders, Vol. 28, No. 11, pp. 36-37.

Salter, Malcolm S.; Weinhold, Wolf A. (1978): Diversification via acquisition: creating value, in: Harvard Business Review, Vol. 57, pp. 166-176.

Sangbae, Kim; In, Francis (2005): Multihorizon Sharpe Ratios, in: Journal of Portfolio Management, Vol. 31, No. 2, pp. 105-111.

Santillan, Javier; Bayle, Marc; Thygesen, Christian (2000): The Impact of the Euro on Money and Bond Markets, ECB Occasional Paper, July 2000.

Saritas, Hakan; Aygoren, Hakan (2005): International indexing as a means of portfolio diversification, in: Applied Financial Economics, Vol. 15, No. 18, pp. 1299-1304.

Scherer, Bernd (2004): An alternative route to performance hypothesis testing, in: Journal of Asset Management, Vol. 5, No. 1, pp. 5-12.

Schleifer, Andrei (1986): Do Demand Curves for Stocks Slope Down?, in: Journal of Finance, Vol. 41, pp. 579-590.

Schlienkamp, Christoph; Frei, Norbert (1997): Aktie im Aufwind, Cologne 1997.

Schlittgen, Rainer (2004): Statistische Auswertungen: Standardmethoden und Alternativen mit ihrer Durchführung in R, München 2004.

Schlumpf, Philipp M.; Schmid, Markus M.; Zimmermann, Heinz (2008): The First- and Second-Hand Effect of Analysts' Stock Recommendations: Evidence from the Swiss Stock Market, in: European Financial Management, Vol. 14, No. 5, pp. 962-988.

Schmidt-Tank, Stephan (2005): Indexeffekte am europäischen Kapitalmarkt, Wiesbaden, 2005.

Schmidt-von Rhein, Andreas (1996): Die moderne Portfoliotheorie im praktischen Wertpapiermanagement, Bad Soden 1996.

Schmies, Claudia (2001): Der Benchmarkansatz im Portfoliomanagement, Hamburg 2001.

Schmitz-Esser, Valerio (2000): Aktienindizes: Funktionen, Konstruktionen, Indexeffekte, diss., Freiburg 2000.

Schmitz-Esser, Valerio (2001): Aktienindizes im Portfoliomanagement, Bad Soden, 2001.

Schnatterly, Karen; Shaw, Kenneth W.; Jennings, William W. (2008): Information advantages of large institutional owners, in: Strategic Management Journal, Vol. 29, No. 2, pp. 219-227.

Schoenfelder, Steven A. (2004): Active Index Investing, New Jersey 2004.

Schoenfeld, Stefen A.; Ginis, Robert (2006): Worth the Weight?, in: Journal of Indexes, April 2006, pp. 1-9.

Scholz, Hendrik (2006): Refinements to the Sharpe ratio: Comparing alternatives for bear markets, in: Journal of Asset Management, Vol. 7, No. 5, pp. 347-357.

Scholz, Hendrik; Wilkens, Marco (2006): Die Marktphasenabhängigkeit der Sharpe-Ratio - eine empirische Untersuchung für deutsche Aktienfonds, in: Zeitschrift für Betriebswirtschaft, Vol. 76, No. 12, pp. 1275-1302.

Schopf, Michael (2009): Aktives und passives Portfoliomanagement für Asset Manager, Hamburg 2009.

Schotter, James (2011): Commentary: The euro zone has taken drastic steps to shore up its currency, in: European Policy Analyst, Vol. 7, pp. 3-5.

Schröder, Michael, ZEW [ed.] (2005): Is there a Difference? The Performance Characteristics of SRI Equity Indexes, Mannheim 2005.

Schröder, Ulrich (2003): €uro Watch – Four years of the euro: more light than darkenss, in: DB Research, Frankfurt a. M. 2003.

Schüle, Fritz M. (1992): Diversifikation und Unternehmenserfolg - Eine Analyse empirischer Forschungsergebnisse, Wiesbaden 1992.

Schusteritsch, Michael; Niederl, David (2007): Aktienindizes, Graz 2007.

Schwarzer, Daniela (2007): Spannung im Club der 13 – Reformbedarf der Eurozone, Bonn 2007.

Schyra, Andreas; Rojahn, Joachim (2010): Portfolioallokation mit Anleihen, in: Handelsblatt Business Briefing, Vol. 5, pp. 11-12.

Sebastião, Helder M. C. V. (2010): The informational impact of electronic trading systems of the FTSE 100 stock index and its future contracts, in: The European Journal of Finance, Vol. 16, No. 7, pp. 611-640.

Seifert, Bruce; Gonenc, Halit (2010): Pecking Order Behaviour and Emerging Markets, in: Journal of International Financial Management, Vol. 21, No. 1, pp. 1-31.

Serfaty, Simon (2010): The EU's Future, in: International Economy, Vol. 24, No. 4, pp. 54-71.

Sharpe, William F. (1964): Capital Asset Prices: A Theory of Market Equilibrium Under Conditions of Risk, in: Journal of Finance, Vol. 19, pp. 425 – 442.

Sharpe, William F. (1966): Mutual Fund Performance, in: Journal of Portfolio Management, Vol. 39, pp. 573-599.

Sharpe, William F. (1975): Adjusting for risk in portfolio performance measurement, in: Journal of Portfolio Management, Vol. 1, pp. 29-34.

Sharpe, William F. (1987): Integrated Asset Allocation, in: Financial Analysts Journal, Vol. 43, No. 5, pp. 25-32.

Sharpe, William F. (1992): Asset Allocation: Management Style and performance measurement, in: Journal of Portfolio Management, winter 1992, pp. 7-19.

Sharpe, William F. (2007): Expected Utility Asset Allocation, in: Financial Analysts Journal, Vol. 18, No. 5, pp. 18-30.

Sharpe, William F. (2010): Adaptive Asset Allocation Policies, in: Financial Analysts Journal, Vol. 66, No. 3, pp. 45-59.

Sharpe, William F.; Alexander, Gordon J.; Bailey, Jeffery V. (1999): Investments, Vol. 6, Upper Saddle River 1999.

Shefrin, Hersh (2000): Benchmarks and indexing: A behavioural perspective, in: Journal of Asset Management, Vol. 1, pp. 19-38.

Sheikh, Abdullah Z.; Qiao, Hongtao (2010): Non-Normality of Market Returns: A Framework for Asset Allocation Decision Making, in: Journal of Alternative Investments, Vol. 12, No. 3, pp. 8-35.

Sheu, Her-Jiun; Wei, Yu-Chen (2011): Options Trading Based on the Forecasting of Volatility Direction with the Incorporation of Investor Sentiment, in: Emerging Markets Finance & Trade, Vol. 47, No. 2, pp. 31-47.

Shum, Wai Cheong; Tang, Gordon Y. N. (2010): Risk-Return Characteristics, in: Chinese Economy, Vol. 43, No. 5, pp. 15-31.

Siegel, Andrew F.; Woodgate, Artemiza (2007): Performance of Portfolios Optimized with Estimation Error, in: Management Science, Vol. 53, No. 6, pp. 1005-1015.

Siegel, Jeremy J. (2006): The 'Noisy Market' Hypothesis, in: Wall Street Journal, Juni 2006, p. 14.

Singh, Ranjit (2010): Behavioural Finance Studies: Emergence and Developments, in: Journal of Contemporary Management Research, Vol. 4, No. 2, pp. 1-9.

Sinha, Nishi; Watts, John (2001): Economic Consequences of the Declining Relevance of Financial Reports, in: Journal of Accounting Research, Vol. 39, No. 3, pp. 663-681.

Smith, Graham (2007): Random walks in Middle Eastern stock markets, in: Applied Financial Economics, Vol. 17, No. 7, pp. 587-596.

Smith, Julie K. (2004): Weighted Median Inflation: Is This Core Inflation?, in: Journal of Money, Credit & Banking, Vol. 36, No. 2, pp. 253-263.

Snigaroff, Robert; Wroblewski, David (2009): The End of the Boutique: Concentration in the Institutional Asset Management Industry, in: Journal of Investing, Vol. 18, No. 1, pp. 126-134.

Soe, Aye M.; Dash, Srikant; S&P [ed.] (2008): The Shrinking Index Effect, in: Standard & Poor's Working Paper Series, November 2008.

Sokulsky, David; Brooks, Robert; Davidson, Sinclair (2008): Untangling demand curves from information effects: evidence from Australian index adjustments, in: Applied Financial Economics, Vol. 18, No. 8, pp. 605-616.

Solow, Kenneth R. (2009): Buy and Hold Is Dead (AGAIN): The Trouble with Quant Model, in: Journal of Financial Planning, Vol. 22, No. 9, pp. 58-70.

Sortino, Frank A.; Price, Lee N. (1994): Performance Measurement in a Downside Risk Framework, in: Journal of Investing, Vol. 3, No. 3, pp. 59-64.

Sortino, Frank A.; van der Meer, Robert (1991): Downside risk, in: Journal of Portfolio Management, Vol. 17, No. 4, pp. 27-31.

Sosvilla-Rivero, Simon; Rodriguez, Pedro N. (2010): Linkages in international stock markets: evidence from a classification procedure, in: Applied Economics, Vol. 42, No. 16, pp. 2081-2089.

Specht, Katja; Gohout, Wolfgang (2009): Grundlagen der Kapitalmarkttheorie und des Portfoliomanagements, Oldenburg 2009.

Speyer, Bernhard (2011): Financial supervision in the EU, in: DB Research, Vol. 84, pp. 1-16.

Spremann, Klaus (2008): Portfoliomanagement, Vol. 4, Oldenburg 2008.

Spremann, Klaus; Gantenbein, Pascal (2005): Kapitalmärkte, Stuttgart 2005.

S&P [ed.] (2011a): Standard & Poor's Puts Ratings Of Eurozone Sovereigns On Credit-Watch With Negative Implications, http://standardandpoors.com/ratings/articles/en/eu/?article Type =HTML&assetID=1245325249443, date: 05.12.2011.

S&P [ed.] (2011b): Germany's Unsolicited Long-Term 'AAA' Rating Placed on Credit Watch Negative, http://standardandpoors.com/ratings/articles/en/eu/?articleType=HTML&assetID=1245325253951, date: 05.12.2011.

S&P [ed.] (2012): Standard & Poor's Takes Various Rating Actions On 16 Eurozone Sovereign Governments, http://www.standardandpoors.com/ratings/articles/en/us/?articleType=HTML&assetID=1245327294763, date: 13.01.2012.

Statman, Meir; Scheid, Jonathan (2008): Correlation, Return Gaps, and the Benefits of Diversification, in: Journal of Portfolio Management, Vol. 34, No. 3, pp. 132-139.

Stavárek, Daniel (2010): Exchange rate volatility and the asymmetric fluctuation band on the way to the Eurozone, in: Applied Economics Letters, Vol. 17, No. 1, pp. 81-86.

Stehle, Richard (1999): Renditevergleich von Aktien und festverzinslichen Wertpapieren auf Basis des DAX und des REXP, Working Paper Humboldt-Universität Berlin, Berlin 1999.

Stehle, Richard; Hartmond, Annette (1991): Durchschnittsrenditen Deutscher Aktien 1954-1988, in: Kredit und Kapital, Vol. 24, pp. 371-411.

Stein, David M. (2004): Active and Passive Arguments: In Search of an Optimal Investment Experience, in: Senior Consultant, Vol. 7, No. 6, June, pp. 1-7.

Stein, Jeremy C. (2001): Agency, Information and Corporate Investment, Cambridge 2001.

Steinbach, Marc C. (2001): Markowitz Revisited: Mean-Variance Models in Financial Portfolio Analysis, in: SIAM Review, Vol. 43, No. 1, pp. 31-56.

Steiner, Manfred; Bruns, Christoph (2007): Wertpapiermanagement, Vol. 9, Stuttgart 2007.

Stock, Detlev (2002): Zur Relevanz von CAPM-Anomalien für den deutschen Aktienmarkt, Berlin 2002.

STOXX Ltd. [ed.] (2011a): Access to STOXX Data, http://www.stoxx.com/data/data.html, date: 07.02.2011.

STOXX Ltd. [ed.] (2011b): Index Rulebook, http://www. stoxx.com/indices/index_ information.html?symbol=SXXE, date: 07.02.2011.

STOXX Ltd. [ed.] (20011c): Find Industry Index by Region, http://www.stoxx.com/indices /byregion.html?superRegion=Europe&subRegion=Eurozone&superType=Sector%20Indices &subType=Industries, date: 07.02.2011.

STOXX Ltd. [ed.] (2011d): Dow Jones Euro STOXX 50, http://www.stoxx.com/indices/in-dex_information. html?symbol=SX5E, date: 07.02.2011.

STOXX Ltd. [ed.] (2011e): Find Supersector Index by Region http://www.stoxx.com/indices /byregion.html?superRegion=Europe&subRegion=Eurozone&superType=Sector_Indces&sub Type=Supersectors, date: 15.11.2011.

STOXX Ltd. [ed.] (2011f): Dow Jones Euro STOXX TMI Financial Services, http://www. stoxx.com/indices/index_information.html?symbol=BFST, date: 15.11.2011.

STOXX Ltd. [ed.] (2011g): Dow Jones Euro STOXX TMI Insurance, http://www.stoxx .com/indices/index_information.html?symbol=BINT, date: 15.11.2011.

STOXX Ltd. [ed.] (2011h): Dow Jones Euro STOXX TMI Banks, http://www.stoxx.com/ indices/index_information.html?symbol=BBAT, date: 15.11.2011.

STOXX Ltd. [ed.] (2011i): STOXX Equity Methodology Guide, http://www.stoxx.com/ download/indices/rulebooks/stoxx:_indexguide.pdf, date: 15.11.2011.

STOXX Ltd. [ed.] (2011j): STOXX Changes Composition of Blue-Chip Indices, http://www.stoxx.com/download/news/2010/stoxxnews_20100831.pdf, date: 28.11.2011.

STOXX Ltd. [ed.] (2011k): STOXX Announces Changes to its Blue-Chip Indexes, http://www.stoxx.com/download/news/2009/stoxxnews_20090831.pdf, date: 28.11.2011.

STOXX Ltd. [ed.] (2011l): STOXX Announces Changes to its Blue-Chip and Style Indexes, http://www.stoxx.com/download/news/2008/stoxxnews_20080901.pdf, date: 28.11.2011.

STOXX Ltd. [ed.] (2011m): STOXX Announces Changes to its Blue-Chip and Style In-dexes, http://www.stoxx.com/download/news/2007/stoxxnews_20070903a.pdf, date: 28.11.2011.

STOXX Ltd. [ed.] (2011n): STOXX Announces Changes to its Blue-Chip and Style Indexes, http://www.stoxx.com/download/news/2006/stoxxnews_20060901.pdf, date: 28.11.2011.

STOXX Ltd. [ed.] (2011o): STOXX Limited Announces Changes to its Blue-Chip Index Series, http://www.stoxx.com/download/news/2005/stoxxnews_20050901.pdf, date: 28.11.2011.

STOXX Ltd. [ed.] (2011p): STOXX Limited Announces Changes to its Blue-Chip Index Series, http://www.stoxx.com/download/news/2004/stoxxnews_20040901.pdf, date: 28.11.2011.

STOXX Ltd. [ed.] (2011q): STOXX Limited Announces Changes to its Blue-Chip Index Series, http://www.stoxx.com/download/news/2003/stoxxnews_20030901.pdf, date: 28.11.2011.

STOXX Ltd. [ed.] (2011r): STOXX Limited Announces Changes to its Blue-Chip Index Series, http://www.stoxx.com/download/news/2002/stoxxnews_20020902.pdf, date: 28.11.2011.

STOXX Ltd. [ed.] (2011s): 2001 Annual Blue Chip Index Reviews, http://www.stoxx.com /download/news/2001/stoxxnews_20010903.pdf, date: 28.11.2011.

STOXX Ltd. [ed.] (2011t): STOXX Company Profile, http://www.stoxx.com/corporate /company/stoxx.html, date: 02.12.2011.

STOXX Ltd. [ed.] (2011u): Euro STOXX Supersector Indices, http://www.stoxx.com/indices/byregion.html?superRegion=Europe&subRegion=Eurozone&superType=Sector%20Indices&subType=Supersectors, date: 02.12.2011.

STOXX LTD. [ed.] (2011v): Euro STOXX index information, http://www.stoxx.com/indices/index_information.html?symbol=SXXE, date: 31.12.2011.

STOXX LTD. [ed.] (2011w): Euro STOXX Factsheet, http://www.stoxx.com/download/indices/factsheets/sxxe_fs.pdf , date: 02.12.2011.

STOXX Ltd. [ed.] (2011x): Euro STOXX Supersector Indices: http://www.stoxx.com/ indices/byregion.html?superRegion=Europe&subRegion=Eurozone&superType=SectorIndices& subType=Supersectors, date: 02.12.2011.

STOXX LTD. [ed.] (2011y): Euro STOXX 50 Factsheet, http://www.stoxx.com/ download/indices/factsheets/sx5e_fs.pdf , date: 02.12.2011.

Stracca, Livio (2006): Delegated Portfolio Management: A Survey of the Theoretical Literature, in: Journal of Economic Surveys, Vol. 20, No. 5, pp. 823-848.

Strobel, Frank (2005): Leaving EMU: a real options perspective, in: Applied Economics, Vol. 37, No. 13, pp. 1449-1453.

Strong, Norman; Walker, Martin (1987): Information and Capital Markets, New York 1987.

Stucki, Thomas (1996): Die Rolle der Benchmarks im Portfolio Management, in: Finanzmarkt und Portfolio Management, Vol. 2, pp. 181-196.

Sultan, Jahangir; Hasan, Mohammad S. (2008): The effectiveness of dynamic hedging: evidence from selected European stock index futures, in: European Journal of Finance, Vol. 14, No. 6, pp. 469-488.

Sumnicht, Vern (2009): MPT Principles Valid After 5 Decades, in: Journal of Financial Planning, Trends in Investing, June 2009, pp. 16-18.

Sutherland, Peter (1997): The Case for EMU, in: Foreign Affairs, Vol. 76, No. 1, pp. 9-14.

Svendrup, Ulf (2002): An institutional perspective on treaty reform: contextualizing the Amsterdam and Nice Treaties, in: Journal of European Public Policy, Vol. 9, No. 1, pp. 120-140.

Swedroe, Larry (2010): Wise Investing Made Simpler, in: Journal of Indexes, November/December 2010, pp. 46-51.

Swedroe, Larry (2011): Foolish Ideas, in: Financial Planning, Vol. 41, No. 5, p. 148.

Swensen, David (2010): Calvins Kapitalanlage, in: Portfolio Institutional, No. 12, pp. 29-35.

Switzer, Lorne N.; Omelchak, Andrey (2009): Time-varying asset allocation across hedge fund indices, in: Journal of Derivatives & Hedge Funds, Vol. 15, No. 1, pp. 70-85.

Sydsaeter, Knut; Hammond, Peter (2006): Mathematik für Wirtschaftswissenschaftler: Basiswissen mit Praxisbezug, Munich 2006.

Szado, Edward (2009): VIX Futures and Options: A Case Study of Portfolio Diversification during the 2008 Financial Crisis, in: Journal of Alternative Investments, Vol. 12, No. 2, pp. 68-85.

Tarasi, Crina O.; Bolton, Ruth N.; Hutt, Michael D.; Walker, Beth A. (2011): Balancing Risk and Return in a Customer Portfolio, in: Journal of Marketing, Vol. 75, No. 3, pp. 1-17.

Tavlas, George S. (2009): Optimum-Currency-Area Paradoxes, in: Review of International Economics, Vol. 17, No. 3, pp. 536-551.

Thadewald, Thorsten; Büning, Herbert (2007): Jarque-Bera Test and its Competitors for Testing Normality – A Power Comparison, in: Journal of Applied Statistics, Vol. 34, No. 1/2, pp. 87-102.

Thomson Reuters [ed.] (2010): CRB Thomson Reuters/Jefferies Index Summary 2010, London 2010.

Thygesen, Niels (1989): The Delors Report and European economic and monetary union, in: International Affairs, Vol. 65, No. 4, pp. 637-652.

Timmreck, Christian (2002): ß-Faktoren - Anwendungsprobleme und Lösungsansätze, in: Finanzbetrieb, Vol. 5, pp. 300-306.

Tobin, James (1958): Liquidity Preference as Behaviour Towards Risk, in: Review of Economic Studies, Vol. 25, No. 1, pp. 65-86.

Topp, Rebekka; Perl, Robert (2010): Through-the-Cycle Ratings versus Point-in-Time Ratings and Implications of the Mapping between Both Rating Types, in: Financial Markets, Institutions & Instruments, Vol. 19, No. 1, pp. 47-61.

Toutenburg, Helge; Heumann, Christian (2008): Deskriptive Statistik, Vol. 6, Munich 2008.

Trachtenberg, Andrea (2001): Risk Reconsidered, in: Financial Planning, Vol. 31, No. 1, pp. 74-75.

Trivellato, Barbara (2009): Replication and shortfall risk in a binomial model with transaction costs, in: Mathematical Methods of Operation Research, Vol. 69, No. 1, pp. 1-26.

Tropeano, Domenica (2011): Financial Regulation after the Crisis, in: International Journal of Political Economy, Vol. 40, No. 2, pp. 45-60.

Trotignon, Jérome (2005): EMU Enlargement to Include CEE Countries: Risks of Sector-based and Geographical Asymmetric Shocks, in: Post-Communist Economics, Vol. 17, No. 1, pp. 3-20.

Tsai, Shih-Chuan (2008): Information Asymmetry and Corporate Investment Decisions: A Dynamic Approach, in: Financial Review, Vol. 43, No. 2, pp. 241-271.

Tsoukalis, Loukas (2005): What Kind of Europe?, Oxford University Press, Oxford 2005.

Urwyler, Antje; Homberger, Andreas (2001): International Comparison of Stock Market Behaviour - The European Case, Zurich 2001.

Van Aarle, Bas; Di Bartolomeo, Giovanni; Engerda, Jacob, Plasmans, Joseph (2004): Journal of Economics, Vol. 82, No. 1, pp. 1-21.

Van de Locht, Nicole (2009): Informationsgewinnung aus Optionspreisen, Wiesbaden 2009.

Van der Spek, Maarten R.; Hoorenman, Chris (2011): Leverage: Please Use Responsibly, in: Journal of Real Estate Portfolio Management, Vol. 17, No. 2, pp. 75-88.

Van Poeck, André; Borghijs, Alain (2001): EMU and Labour Market Reform: Needs, Incentives and Realisations, in: World Economy, Vol. 24, No. 10, pp. 1327-1352.

Van Long, Ngo; Sorger, Gerhard (2010): A dynamic principal-agent problem as a feedback Stackelberg differential game, in: Central European Journal of Operations Research, Vol. 18, No. 4, pp. 491-509.

Van Poeck, André; Borghijs, Alain (2001): EMU and Labour Market Reform: Needs, Incentives and Realisations, in: World Economy, Vol. 24, No. 10, pp. 1327-1352.

Vareman, Niklas; Persson, Johannes (2010): Why separate risk assessors and risk managers? Further external value affecting the risk assessor qua risk assessor, in: Journal of Risk Research, Vol. 13, No. 5, pp. 687-700.

Velvadapu, Pradeep (2011): The Evolution of Equal Weighting, in: Journal of Indexes, January/February 2011, pp. 20-29.

Verdun, Amy (1999): The Delors Report and European economic and monetary union, in: International Affairs, Vol. 65, No. 4, pp. 308-328.

Verdun, Amy (2005): Economic and Monetary Union, in: Memo prepared for the State of the European Union Vol. 8 meetings, Princeton University 2005.

Vermorken, Maximilian A. M. (2011): GICS or ICB, how different is similar?, in: Journal of Asset Management, Vol. 12, No. 1, pp. 30-44.

Vespro, Cristina (2006): Stock Price and Volume Effects Associated with Compositional Changes in European Stock Indices, in: European Financial Management, Vol. 12, No. 1, pp. 103-127.

Vo, Xuan Vinh; Daly, Kevin (2008): Volatility amongst firms in the Dow Jones Eurostoxx 50 Index, in: Applied Financial Economics, Vol. 18, No. 7, pp. 569-582.

Voigt, Kai-Ingo (1993): Strategische Unternehmensplanung, Wiesbaden 1993.

Wagner, Niklas; Diller, Christian; Brück, Bernhard (2005): Optimale Nachbildungs- und Umschichtungsstrategien im Management europäischer Akientportfolios, in: Finanzbetrieb, Vol. 1, pp. 56-67.

Wallick, Daniel W.; Bhatia, Neeraj; Clarke, Andrew S.; Stern, Raphael A. (2011): Shopping For Alpha, in: Journal of Indexes Europe, September/October 2011, pp. 28-33.

Wallmeier, Martin (2000): Determinanten erwarteter Renditen am deutschen Aktienmarkt - Eine empirische Untersuchung anhand ausgewählter Kennzahlen, in: Zeitschrift für betriebswirtschaftliche Forschung, Vol. 52, pp. 27-57.

Walter, Norbert (2005): The Euro: Well established as a reserve currency, in: DB Research, Frankfurt a. M. 2005.

Wang, Shouyang; Xia, Yusen (2002): Portfolio Selection and Asset Pricing, Heidelberg 2002.

Watanabe, Toshiaki (2000): Excess kurtosis of conditional distribution for daily stock returns: the case of Japan, in: Applied Economics Letters, Vol. 7, pp. 353-355.

Weber, Steven; Posner, Elliot (2001): Creating a Pan-European Equity Market, in: Weber, Steven [ed.]: Globalization and the European Political Economy, New York, 2001, pp. 140-196.

Wegmann, Patrick (2001): Time-Varying Comovements across International Equity Markets, Bamberg 2001.

Weißbach, Rafael; Tschiersch, Patrick; Lawrenz, Claudia (2009): Testing time-homogeneity of rating transition after origination of debt, in: Empirical Economics, Vol. 36, No. 3, pp. 575-596.

Wenzelburger, Jan (2010): The two-fund separation theorem revisited, in: Annals of Finance, Vol. 6, No. 2, pp. 221-239.

Wetzel, André (2000): Aktienindizes, Studien des Deutschen Aktieninstituts, Vol. 12, Frankfurt a. M. 2000.

Wiandt, Jim (2011): Considering Alternatives, in: Journal of Indexes, January/ February 2011, p. 8.

Wilcox, Jarrod (2003): Harry Markowitz and the Discretionary Wealth Hypothesis, in: Journal of Portfolio Management, Vol. 29, No. 3, pp. 58-65.

Wilcox, Rand (2006): Confidence intervals for prediction intervals, in: Journal of Applied Statistics, Vol. 33, No. 3, pp. 317-326.

Willenbrock, Scott (2011): Diversification Return, Portfolio Rebalancing, and the Commodity Return Puzzle, in: Financial Analysts Journal, Vol. 67, No. 4, pp. 42-49.

Williams, Darren (2009): EMU and the Credit Crunch: Can the Euro Survive?, in: Alliance Bernstein Global Investment Research, March 2009, pp. 1-10.

Williams, Richard H.; Zumbo, Broun D.; Ross, Donald; Zimmermann, Donald W. (2003): On the Intellectual Versatility of Karl Pearson, in: Human Nature Review, Vol. 3, pp. 296-301.

Willman, Paul; Fenton-O'Creevy, Mark; Nicholson, Nigel; Soane, Emma (2006): Noise Trading and the Management of Operational Risk; Firms, Traders and Irrationality in Financial Markets, in: Journal of Management Studies, Vol. 43, No. 6, pp. 1357-1374.

Wimmer, Bradley S.; Chezum, Brian (2006): Adverse Selection, Seller Effort, and Selection Bias, in: Southern Economic Journal, Vol. 73, No. 1, pp. 201-218.

Winchester, Danielle D.; Huston, Sandra J.; Finke, Michael S. (2011): Investors Prudence and the Role of Financial Advice, in: Journal of Financial Service Professionals, Vol. 65, No. 4, pp. 43-51.

Witte, Björn-Christopher (2010): Temporal information gaps and market efficiency: a dynamic behaviour analysis, in: Applied Financial Economics, Vol. 20, No. 13, pp. 1057-1070.

Wohlenberg, Holger; Brockmann, Malte; Grass, Gunnar (2006): Funktionen von Strategieindizes - Das Beispiel des DAXplus Export Strategy Index, in: Finanzbetrieb, Vol. 11, pp. 730-736.

Wolf, Britta (1995): Organisation durch Verträge, Wiesbaden 1995.

Wong, Karen H. Y.; Shum, Wai Cheong (2010): Exchange-traded funds in bullish and bearish markets, in: Applied Economics Letters, Vol. 17, No. 16, pp. 1615-1624.

Woods, Paul; Richard, Evans (2003): Fundamental Profit Based Equity Indexation, in: Journal of Indexes, 2nd quarter 2003, pp. 1-10.

Woolf, Emile (2008): Has The Lesson Been Learned?, in: Accountancy, Vol. 142, No. 1383, p. 16.

Wray, L. Randall (2004): Loanable funds, liquidity preference, and endogenous money: do credit cards make a difference?, in: Journal of Post Keynesian Economics, Vol. 26, No. 2, pp. 309-323.

Wu, Liang-Chuan; Chou, Seng-Cho; Yang, Chau-Chen; Ong, Chomg-Shyong (2007): Enhanced Index Investing Based on Goal Programming, in: Journal of Portfolio Management, Vol. 33, No. 3, pp. 49-56.

Wüthrich, Elena (2010): Portfolio versus Benchmark, Wien 2010.

Wulf, Torsten (2007): Diversifikation eine top-management-orientierte Perspektive, Wiesbaden 2007.

Wynne, Mark A.; Rodriguez-Palenzuela, Diego (2004): Measurement Bias in the HICP: What do we know and What do we need to know?, in: Journal of Economics, Vol. 18, No. 1, pp. 79-112.

Xiong, James X.; Ibbotson, Roger G.; Idzorek, Thomas M; Chen, Peng (2010): The Equal Importance of Asset Allocation and Active Management, in: Financial Analysts Journal, Vol. 66, No. 2, pp. 1-9.

Xiong, James X.; Idzorek, Thomas M. (2011): The Impact of Skewness and Fat Tails on the Asset Allocation Decision, in: Financial Analysts Journal, Vol. 67, No. 2, pp. 23-35.

Xu, Yongquing; Song, Liping (2008): Gaussian copula under multiscale volatility, in: Applied Stochastic Models in Business and Industry, Vol. 24, No. 6, pp. 569-589.

Yalcin, Atakan; Ersahin, Nuri (2011): Does the Conditional CAPM Work? Evidence from the Istanbul Stock Exchange, in: Emerging Markets Finance & Trade, Vol. 47, No. 4, pp. 28-48.

Yang, Ming Jing; Lai, Yi-Chuan (2009): An out-of-sample comparative analysis of hedging performance of stock index futures: dynamic versus static hedging, in: Applied Financial Economics, Vol. 19, No. 3, pp. 282-306.

Yang, Minxian (2008): Normal log-normal mixture, leptokurtosis and skewness, in: Applied Economics Letters, Vol. 15, No. 9, pp. 737-742.

Yang, Xi; Gondzio, Jacek (2010): Asset Liability Management Modelling with risk control by stochastic dominance, in: Journal of Asset Management, Vol. 11, No. 2/3, pp. 73-93.

Yang, Xiakai; Yeh, Yeaong-nan (2002): Endogenous Specialisation and Endogenous Principal-agent Relationship, in: Australian Economic Papers, Vol. 41, No. 1, pp. 15-36.

Yazici, Berna; Yolacan, Senay (2007): A comparison of various tests of normality, in: Journal of Statistical Computation & Simulation, Vol. 77, No. 2, pp. 175-183.

Yeh, Kuo-Chun (2007): Prospects for EMU Enlargement: What Will Be the Consequences of a Fiscal Union, in: Eastern European Economics, Vol. 45, No. 6, pp. 80-103.

Yeung, P. Eric (2009): Uncertainty and Expectation Revisions after Earnings Announcements, in: Contemporary Accounting Research, Vol. 26, No. 1, pp. 273-301.

Yilmaz, Mustafa Kemal; Gulay, Guhzan (2006): Dividend Policies and Price-Volume Reactions to Cash Dividends on the Stock Market, in: Emerging Markets Finance & Trade, Vol. 42, No. 4, pp. 19-49.

Yiu, Matthew S.; Ho, Wai-Yip Alex; Choi, Daniel F. (2011): Dynamic correlation analysis of financial contagion in Asian markets in global financial turmoil, in: Applied Financial Economics, Vol. 20, No. 4, pp. 345-354.

Yong, Chen (2011): Derivatives Use and Risk Taking: Evidence from the Hedge Fund Industry, in: Journal of Financial & Quantitative Analysis, Vol. 46, No. 4, pp. 1973-1106.

Yoon, Sun-Joong; Byun, Suk Joon (2012): Implied risk aversion and volatility risk premiums, in: Applied Financial Economics, Vol. 22, No. 1, pp. 59-70.

Yoshida, Yushi; Carlos Leitao, Nuno; Faustino, Horacio (2009): Vertical Intra-Industry Trade and Foreign Direct Investment between Japan and European Countries, in: Atlantic Economic Journal, Vol. 37, No. 4, pp. 351-365.

Young, Michael N.; Peng, Mike W.; Ahlstrom, David; Bruton, Garry D.; Jiang, Yi (2008): Corporate Governance in Emerging Economies: A Review of the Principal-Principal Perspective, in: Journal of Management Studies, Vol. 45, No. 2, pp. 196-220.

Youngjun, Yoon (2010): Glide path dynamic asset allocation of target date funds, in: Journal of Asset Management, Vol. 11, No. 5, pp. 346-360.

Yu, Kwok Wai; Yang, Xiao Qi; Wong, Heung (2007): Asst allocation by using the Sharpe rule: How to improve an existing portfolio by adding some new assets?, in: Journal of Asset Management, Vol. 8, No. 2, pp. 133-145.

Yu, Ming-Miin (2011): Performance Evaluation, in: Advances in Management, Vol. 4, No. 11, pp. 5-6.

Yu, Susana; Rentzler, Joel; Wolf, Avner (2004): Long-Short Strategies May Not Be Factor-Neutral, in: Journal of Investing, Vol. 13, No. 3, pp. 44-53.

Zakamouline, Valeri; Koekebakker, Steen (2009): A Generalisation of the Mean-Variance Analysis, in: European Financial Management, Vol. 15, No. 5, pp. 934-970.

Zhang, Chu (2009): Testing the APT with the Maximum Sharpe Ratio of Extracted Factors, in: Management Science, Vol. 55, No. 7, pp. 1255-1266.

Zhang, Hao; Stefanos, Zenios (2008): A Dynamic Principal-Agent Model with Hidden Information: Sequential Optimality through Truthful State Revelation, in: Operations Research, Vol. 56, No. 3, pp. 681-696.

Zheng, Yudan (2010): Heterogeneous institutional investors and CEO compensation, in: Review of Quantitative Finance & Accounting, Vol. 35, No. 1, pp. 21-46.

Zhou, Haigang (2007): Asymmetric Changes in Stock Prices and Investor Recognition around Revisions to the S&P 500 Index, in: Financial Analysts Journal, Vol. 67, No. 1, pp. 72-81.

Ziemba, William T. (2005): The Symmetric Downside-Risk Sharpe Ratio, in: CFA Digest, Vol. 36, No. 2, pp. 83-85.

Zimmerer, Thomas (2008): Mythos Absolute Return: Was bestimmt die Partizipationsquote von statischen und dynamischen Konzepten? in: Finanzbetrieb, Vol. 3, pp. 129-139.

Zimmermann, Heinz; Bill, Markus; Dubacher, René (1989): Finanzmarkt Schweiz: Sturkturen im Wandel, Zürich 1989.

Zwick, Steve (2003): Battle for a benchmark, in: Analysis & Strategies for Futures, Options & Derivatives Traders, Vol. 32, No. 4, p. 19.

Zwick, Steve; Collins, Daniel P. (2002): Narrow-based and sector indexes step up to the plate, in: Futures: News, Analysis & Strategies for Futures, Options & Derivatives Traders, Vol. 31, No. 10, pp. 66-69.

MIX
Papier aus verantwortungsvollen Quellen
Paper from responsible sources
FSC® C105338

If you have any concerns about our products,
you can contact us on
ProductSafety@springernature.com

In case Publisher is established outside the EU,
the EU authorized representative is:
Springer Nature Customer Service Center GmbH
Europaplatz 3, 69115 Heidelberg, Germany

Printed by Libri Plureos GmbH
in Hamburg, Germany